CHICKEN SOUP
FOR THE
FISHERMAN'S
SOUL

Chicken Soup for the Fisherman's Soul
Fish Tales to Hook Your Spirit and Snag Your Funny Bone
Jack Canfield, Mark Victor Hansen, Ken McKowen, Dahlynn McKowen

Published by Backlist, LLC,
a unit of Chicken Soup for the Soul Publishing, LLC. www.chickensoup.com

Front cover design by Larissa Hise Henoch
Originally published in 2004 by Health Communications, Inc

Back cover and spine redesign by Pneuma Books, LLC

Distributed to the booktrade by Simon & Schuster. SAN: 200-2442

Publisher's Cataloging-in-Publication Data
(Prepared by The Donohue Group)

Chicken soup for the fisherman's soul : fish tales to hook your spirit and snag your funny bone / [compiled by] Jack Canfield ... [et al.].

p. : ill. ; cm.

Originally published: Deerfield Beach, FL : Health Communications, c2004.
ISBN: 978-1-62361-016-6

1. Fishing--Anecdotes. 2. Fishers--Anecdotes. 3. Anecdotes. I. Canfield, Jack, 1944-

SH441 .C43 2012
799.1   2012944053

CHICKEN SOUP FOR THE FISHERMAN'S SOUL

Fish Tales to Hook Your Spirit and Snag Your Funny Bone

Jack Canfield
Mark Victor Hansen
Ken & Dahlynn McKowen

**Backlist, LLC, a unit of
Chicken Soup for the Soul Publishing, LLC
Cos Cob, CT**
www.chickensoup.com

Contents

3. SMALL FRIES

4. TICKLE MY FUNNY BONE

5. FAMILY TIES

6. REEL MEN

7. REEL WOMEN

8. FISHING LESSONS

Introduction

Being a true fisherman is more than tossing crank baits, tying flies or bottom-fishing smelly baits. It is an ancient and time-honored ritual. It is the bestowing of fishing secrets collected over the decades and passed from parent to child. It is sharing with others the fish tales of a lifetime, often embellished, always heartfelt.

Fishing is challenging, inspirational, spiritual—it embraces the essence of life. Fishing nurtures relationships and defines roles. It consoles, and it heals. Fishing is a reflection of what we are and of who we want to be. It teaches patience, provides reachable goals and rewards those who educate themselves in the ways of nature—or who simply get lucky. Few other activities possess the power to help mold young lives while adding untold pleasures to our own.

And perhaps most notable: Fishing is fun!

This was our goal for *Chicken Soup for the Fisherman's Soul*—to share the best and most memorable fishing stories with you. The role of storyteller is inherent in almost all fishermen. From the millions of fishing stories that we knew were out there waiting to be visited, to the thousands that so many people kindly shared with us, we have selected those that best reflect the essence of life-challenges, inspiration, spirit and humor.

We hope you enjoy these stories, that you learn from them and that you share them with others, just as we and our authors have done with you.

1

THE JOY OF FISHING

*H*appiness isn't something you experience;
it's something you remember.

Oscar Levant

Fear of Flying

In any sport, the anticipation of what might happen is almost as important as what actually happens.

Bob Costas

We strolled down to the bank of the river and stood beside a sign. "Attention Anglers," it read. "Bow River, Highway 22X to Carsland Weir, no bait. Trout catch and release." In a field to our left, a scout troop was on litter patrol, picking up discarded papers and bottles. I noticed some of them staring at us.

"I get that all the time," Bud said, and I laughed because I thought he was pulling my leg. "No, I'm serious. It's because I bear an uncanny resemblance to Roger Clinton." I looked at Bud carefully. It was true. He was about the same height, had similar features, was a few pounds lighter and a few years younger than former President Clinton's brother, but other than that, a spitting image. I guess I'd never noticed because I'd known Bud so long; in fact, if you ask me, Roger Clinton looked like Bud.

Bud and I walked a little farther upriver. We reached a

sharp bend where an elderly woman had waded well out into the current. She leaned into the rushing water to maintain her balance and cast almost to the other shore. As she reeled in, her rod arched, slacked, then arched again. "Don't get excited," she called to her husband, who was sitting on shore in a lawn chair, methodically peeling an orange. "I think I'm just snagged." As she twisted her rod to free the line, a guide boat rounded the corner and floated past her, not fifteen feet away.

"Some people buy waders so they can walk out and fish the middle of the river," Bud said. "The rest buy boats so they can fish close to the shore. That doesn't quite make sense, does it?"

We found what Bud assured me was a "good spot" on the river and got set up. Bud had brought a box of Tim Horton's doughnuts and a giant thermos of coffee—the bare essentials, he explained, for a day of fishing. As we hunched over his fly box, trying to make our minds up between the orange stimulator and the crystal blue-winged olive, we heard a rustling in the tall grass directly behind us. Slowly, a large brown snout appeared. It mooed.

"Quiet," Bud asked, politely. "You'll scare the fish."

The cow took a step forward and mooed again. Bud shrugged. He figured the cow must have wandered into the park through a break in the fence.

Bud and I finally settled on the orange stimulators, an all-purpose, rather formless fly that looked as if it could have been plucked from a child's woolly slipper. With Flossie watching, Bud entered the river. With only one rod between the two of us, we'd have to take turns. But I didn't mind letting Bud fish before me; since it was my first time fly-fishing, I was content to watch and learn.

Bud wasted no time. Before he had even reached his spot in the river, he'd begun to work his rod, shooting line forward at an ever-increasing length. By the time he planted his feet, he was making his first cast. His line arched through the air and landed almost without a splash six feet from the steep bank on the other side of the river. Bud reeled in and cast again. I watched his every nuance.

Suddenly, Bud's rod began to dip madly. A second later a fish sprang from the water and flopped back down on its side. Bud's line zigzagged as the trout tried to break free from the hook. It jumped again, and by now it was twenty-five feet downstream from us. Bud pulled the rod sharply to set the hook and began to reel in his catch.

Two minutes later, he had the fish in his net, a foot-long rainbow trout. Gently, he held the fish by the head, and removed the hook with a pair of pliers.

"I use a barbless hook, so it doesn't do as much damage," he explained. With a twist of his wrist, Bud pulled the hook from the trout's cheek. He bent down and held the fish in the current for a moment before letting it go. He handed the rod to me.

"Now it's your turn."

I held the rod for a moment, then gingerly walked into the river. It was time to put my dry-land training to work. It took a moment to get used to my borrowed hip waders; I felt like I was adrift inside a giant rubber boot. My plan was to wade out fifteen feet or so, to the edge of the fast water, then cast to the other side where a sharp bend in the river formed a deep pool. I moved into the current, braced myself, and lifted my rod. It didn't take me long to figure out that casting in a parking lot with a hookless line was one thing; standing in the river trying to keep my balance, and trying at the same time not to impale myself with the sharp part of an orange stimulator, was another. I tried to remember my teacher's advice—relax your wrist and roll from the arm, or vice versa?—and get a rhythm going. My first cast was relatively successful, and Bud said, after removing the hook from his hat, that my form was coming along nicely. My second cast was nearly perfect, sailing almost forty feet in a relatively straight line. Had it actually gone forward, it would have been even better.

Just as I was turning around to find where my fly had landed, my rod arched backwards, then jerked out of my hands. It skirted across the water, hit the shore running, then disappeared into tall grass, preceded by the distinct sound of a cow mooing.

I ran to the shore just in time to hear a Boy Scout yell to Bud, "Hey, Mr. Clinton! I think that cow's got your line!"

Bud shook his head. "It's not my line," he said, then pointed my way. "It's his."

I don't know if you've ever run through rangeland in a pair of hip waders trying to catch a distraught cow that's dragging three hundred dollars worth of fly-fishing tackle behind her, but it's not as easy as it sounds. After forty-five minutes I managed to corner her in the parking lot with the help of the scout troop. While a ten-year-old boy fed the cow sweet grass and muttered some soothing words into her ear, I worked the hook out of her bum.

"I always use a barbless hook," I mumbled under my breath, then handed the rod back to Bud, tackle intact.

Bud stood quietly for a moment, sipping coffee from the thermos cup, deep in thought. Finally, he spoke.

"Next time," he suggested, "keep the tip up. And let the cow run a little more before you try to reel her in. Otherwise, I'd say you're doing just fine."

Christopher Gudgeon

One for the Books

We must not seek to fashion events, but let them happen out of their own accord.

Napoleon III

July 1972 promised to be a special time for my family. My husband Hank and I had recently moved to Maine and bought a home, and that summer we rented a cabin on a prime fishing lake. Best of all, my parents were flying up from Georgia to visit us.

We could hardly wait to take Dad fishing. He didn't believe me when I told him over the phone, "The fish up here just about jump in the boat and beg, 'Fry me!'"

Hank and I met Mama and Dad at the airport on one of those perfect Maine summer days. Dad and I talked about fishing all the way back. Mentally, we had our hooks baited by the time we reached the cabin. We had planned a big fish fry for that evening.

Suitcases unloaded and gear quickly stowed in the boat, Hank, Dad and I set out for my secret fishing spot. The fish didn't disappoint. Whooping and laughing, we were pulling in silver perch like no tomorrow.

"Didn't I tell you, Dad?"

"I've been trying to scratch for ten minutes," he said. "Can't 'cause there's always a fish on my line. Itchy nose. Must be somebody coming to visit."

There was!

I looked up to see a Maine State Game and Fisheries boat easing toward us. I felt sick. I hadn't thought to buy Dad a license. When the warden reached out to pull our boat closer to his, I felt as if I'd just been nabbed for bank robbery. Hank gave me the "don't panic" look.

"Sorry, Hank, but I always panic when I get my dad arrested!" I said.

The warden was pleasant, but firm. "Good spot you found here. Mind if I check your licenses?"

Hank whipped his out. The warden checked it, nodded, then turned to me. I shrugged.

"No pockets in this bathing suit. Mine is back at the cabin," I explained as I felt tears starting to well up. He was going to ask for my dad's next. My dad—high school principal, pillar of his community, deacon in his church—had unwittingly committed a crime, and I was to blame.

The warden's gaze shifted.

"Sorry, but I don't have one," Dad said. "Just got in from Georgia."

"Can't fish in Maine without a license. I'll have to write you a citation." The warden glanced at me, looking sorry for disrupting our day. "Toss 'em all back in the lake, then we'll go over to the cabin and check yours, ma'am."

Our perfect day was ruined. I couldn't have felt more miserable, more guilty. Once we were on our way back across the lake, Hank told me that Dad would have to pay a small fine, but no real harm was done. I believed him and got myself under control.

My feeling of momentary ease vanished the minute the

warden said to my dad, "Your court appearance will be next Wednesday over in Bath."

On Wednesday, Dad and I arrived early at the historic courthouse. We were both nervous, but at last the time had come. Now we could get our legal problem over with and enjoy the rest of the summer—if Dad was not behind bars for the duration of his Maine vacation.

We sat through several other cases—a speeding motor-cyclist, a deadbeat dad, a shoplifter. The white-haired judge was handing down stiff sentences. He took no guff from the offenders and seemed totally devoid of sympathy. Not a good sign. I figured the judge wouldn't see Dad's offense as simply fishing without a license. No, he would more likely brand Dad a "perch murderer."

Our game warden appeared to read the charge.

The judge said, "Mr. Lee, I want to hear what you have to say for yourself. Approach the bench." It didn't sound like a friendly invitation.

My dad was a talker. He could tell a story like no one I've ever heard. But as he stood before the judge, he remained silent. Not a word, not a whisper in his own defense.

Finally, the judge said, "Mr. Lee, I don't know how you people down in Georgia do things, but in the state of Maine fishing without a license is against the law."

Dad nodded meekly and replied, "I know that now, Your Honor."

"You didn't know it before?"

"No, Your Honor. In Georgia, senior citizens aren't required to buy a license to fish."

This seemed to interest the judge since he was a senior citizen himself. He almost smiled, I thought.

"Where exactly are you from in Georgia?"

"Brunswick, Your Honor. It's on the mainland, close to St. Simons, Jekyll, and Sea Island. You've probably heard of the place."

"Heard of it? I've been there. There's a restaurant right at the causeway to St. Simons. Best fried shrimp I ever ate."

Dad nodded and grinned. "Yes sir, I eat there often myself. Did you try their oyster stew?"

A lengthy discussion followed about the seafood restaurant, fishing techniques along Georgia's coast and the rights that all senior citizens should have. I could tell that Dad had forgotten he was in court. He had simply found in the judge a fellow fisherman.

Handing the judge one of his cards, Dad said, "The next time you're down our way, you give me a call. I'll buy you a shrimp dinner. I'll even take you out in my boat for some real fishing."

Someone came in and whispered into the judge's ear, obviously advising him to speed things along. He brought down his gavel for order, then said, "Mr. Lee, you being a senior citizen and a visitor to our fair state, I'm going to let you off with a warning and release you into the custody of that pretty daughter of yours. Now you get her to take you straight from this courtroom to buy a fishing license. And good luck on the lake this afternoon."

The crowded courtroom burst into applause. Even our game warden clapped. The judge motioned me forward to take custody of Dad.

For the rest of Dad's life, he told and retold the story of his one and only day in court. It turned out to be the highlight of his trip to Maine that long-ago summer.

As per the judge's instructions, we got that fishing license, headed for the lake and caught enough silver perch to have our fish fry that night.

Becky Lee Weyrich

In case of questioning,
Alan silently rehearses his justification.

Hooked Forever

I had just begun a new job and was working with an avid fisherman. I loved listening to Cliff's fishing tales and decided that although I hadn't taken time during the past thirty years to fish, it was time to try. I bought an inexpensive Zebco rod/reel combo and was ready.

The Elochoman River in southwest Washington is a beautiful little stream renowned among local fishermen for its fall runs of silver salmon, winter steelhead and summer cutthroat trout. Following a July graveyard shift, I decided to give it a try. I puttered along the road that escorted the meandering stream, stopping occasionally to dip my line into tempting pools. I managed to catch one nice trout and two smaller ones before heading home that day.

As I drove home, though, I watched the river more than the road and spotted another pool winking at me from the far side of a thicket. Deciding to give it one more shot, I parked and quietly worked my way through vine maples and devil's club. When I could see the sparkling water clearly, my heart started pounding! There in the shallows, just a few feet away, were three gigantic fish ranging in size from eighteen to twenty-four inches.

Nerves jangling, I shakily cast my black Rooster Tail spinner upstream and watched its silver blade rotating as the current carried it toward the fish. The largest fish ignored it; the medium one swam up to meet it, but turned away as my breath caught in my throat. In a shot, the smaller one darted forward and grabbed it. I had just hooked the largest fish of my short career!

Now what do I do? I remembered from my discussions with Cliff that I had to tire the fish before landing it. It was so big, though, I knew it would get away if I gave it a chance. Wishing I had a net, I reeled in rapidly. Not understanding the purpose of having a flexible tip on the pole, I grabbed the line and jerked the fish up onto the bank.

Of course, that was nearly the worst thing I could have done. The line snapped, the fish started flopping, and I grabbed it. In an instant, it wriggled free, used the elevation I had given it to get closer to the water, and you can guess the rest. I stood on the bank staring at a beautiful cutthroat trout that was once again swimming happily in the river, not paying the least bit of attention to the black Rooster Tail that was still dangling from the corner of its mouth.

When I returned home, it was with my first tale of "the one that got away." My wife was upset that I'd been gone so long, but so pleased with the fish I'd brought home that she agreed to go back with me the following day. When I got to work that night, I told Cliff about my ordeal. He chuckled, explained a couple of points he felt I needed to know, and then suggested I buy a net.

The following morning was so lovely I couldn't take time to sleep, so I shopped instead. I bought some more spinners and found a net that was large enough to hold the twenty-four-inch trout, yet small enough to fit into the back of my new fishing vest. I was pumped!

When I got home, my wife had a picnic lunch packed, and the kids were ready to go swimming. We loaded into the car and an hour later found ourselves parked near a spot where the kids could play in the water, and more importantly for me, within one hundred yards of where I'd lost the fish the previous day. Once the family was settled into their play routine, I grabbed my gear and headed downstream.

It took me three or four tries before I got the currents worked out and learned where to cast so that the spinner would go where I wanted. On the first cast to the right spot, the lure drifted into the pool and the river virtually exploded as the fish struck. I grinned from ear to ear, but kept quiet because I planned on landing this baby. Suddenly the line went limp and my heart sank, but remembering what I'd been told that night, I started reeling rapidly, and was rewarded. The fish had run towards me in an effort to get slack in the line, but the fast little reel caught up with it just as it swam into the pool in front of me. I swear my heart must have stopped, because it was NOT the twenty-four-inch fish. It was a silvery thirty-inch steelhead, with pale rainbow stripes on its sides. I had never seen such a beautiful fish in my life.

My heart began to race as I mentally reviewed Cliff's instructions. *Let it run, let the drag do the work of tiring it, and dip your pole tip if it jumps.* I kept up the routine for several minutes, and gradually the fish tired. I pulled the net out of my pouch and stared at it in dismay. The steelie would never fit into my net, but it was all I had.

The rocks were treacherously slick, and of course, I hadn't yet learned the trick of gluing felt onto the soles of my boots. I waded into the pool, slipping and sliding with each step. Lowering the net behind the fish and taking a deep breath, I scooped. Surprise! The worn out trout wasn't as tired as it had pretended, and a frenzied ten pounds of solid muscle began thrashing furiously! I dropped the pole, grabbed the net with both hands, lost my footing and landed on my rump in cold river water. The fish thanked me and swam away.

I'm not sure that the water running down my cheeks was entirely from the river. I picked up myself, my empty net and my pole and sloshed to shore, forming my second "one that got away" tale. But as I reached the dry rocks, my pole jerked. The line hadn't broken and the fish was still hooked!

The next few minutes were joyful. I played the fish out, and this time, when I was sure it was tired, I scooped it into the net *head* first, carried it ashore and let out a whoop of elation that was heard all the way upstream to where my family was playing. In fact, my wife thought I'd broken my leg and was calling for help. In reality, I was announcing to the world that I'd not only caught my first steelhead, but that I'd just been hooked for life on a wonderful sport.

Chuck "C.L." Bray

Becoming True Fishermen

If a child is to keep alive his inborn sense of wonder . . . he needs the companionship of at least one adult who can share it, rediscovering with him the joy, excitement and mystery of the world we live in.

Rachel Carson

Most summers, my extremely busy retirement schedule permitting, I travel to the beautiful Rocky Mountain town of Telluride, Colorado. The Sheridan Arts Foundation has an ongoing effort there, helped by a willing contingent of well-known celebrities, to restore the historic Sheridan Opera House and support its theatrical training program. Another part of the Foundation's program is its annual Wild West Fest.

Each summer the Sheridan Arts Foundation, in partnership with the Boys and Girls Clubs of America, brings a large number of inner-city and underprivileged children to Telluride for a magnificent week of Wild West activities. As part of the program, which includes mentorships in theater, horsemanship, art, music and Indian hoop dancing, they offer the kids an opportunity to learn how to fly-fish. I have been very fortunate to be involved with that program, helping these great kids learn some of the secrets of my favorite pastime.

One of my fondest memories occurred a couple of summers ago when I was teaching a young inner-city boy from Atlanta how to fly-fish. At one point, I was so taken with our beautiful Western Colorado surroundings that I asked, "Have you ever seen mountains prettier than these?"

He looked at me and said, "Sir, I have never seen any mountains."

It suddenly made me realize how blessed are we who have enjoyed the sport of fly-fishing in beautiful, natural surroundings.

Later on that day I was conducting a mentorship discussion with the kids, and I publicly asked my young fishing partner how many fish he had caught. He proudly stood up among his peers and announced he had caught four fish. That immediately caused several other kids to jump to their feet claiming five, six, seven and so on. Needless to say, when I asked how big, claims were made of every size from minnows to tiger sharks and everything in between.

It was at that moment I proudly realized these kids had become true fishermen.

General H. Norman Schwarzkopf

Old Grumpa

Yet fish there be, that neither hook nor line nor snare, nor net, nor engine can make thine.

John Bunyan, *Pilgrim's Progress*

Nearly every child who is introduced to the joy of fishing at an early age has a place they remember fondly as their most favorite spot: a particular pool in a river, a secluded lake far in the mountains or something as simple as a man-made pier jutting into a bay—all are equal "favorite spots." All are special to the individual, never to be forgotten.

For me, that place is Moonrock Lake. Surrounded by boggy marshes, the lake can hardly be labeled as one of the most scenic spots in Northern California. But what it lacks in beauty, it makes up for in productivity. Moonrock Lake is full of nice fish. I can remember hauling out vast stringers of fat and feisty perch, crappie and bass in my early days. A few memorable times we even managed to latch onto one of the enormous catfish that lived in the lake's murky recesses.

One particular catfish made its appearance almost regularly for those who fished the lake. "Old Grumpa" was rumored to weigh far more than the existing state record of thirty-six pounds, though no one knew for sure, because no one had ever been able to put a scale to him. Old Grumpa had been hooked and lost so many times that he had attained legendary fame, being the talk of the lake for as long as I could remember. Every fisherman's dream was to get Old Grumpa into a net. I shared that dream.

There were times when nothing would be heard of him for weeks. The local fishermen waited anxiously and nervously for some word, silently praying that Old Grumpa had not succumbed to old age, or been caught by one of the out-of-state anglers who frequently raided our lake. But about the time that everyone would get worried, Old Grumpa would reappear, and someone would see him wolf down the three-pound bass they were reeling in, or feel him jerk their rod so violently that the rod would snap from the pressure.

Old Grumpa became something of a ghost fish with supernatural powers, and I think a lot of the stories credited to the fish were simply hogwash. But for what it's worth, Old Grumpa was real. The catfish had been hooked and seen enough to prove his existence, and no one doubted it. Some even profited—the local tackle shops made a lot of extra money when Old Grumpa was in a biting mood!

When I was in my midteens, I left the vicinity of Moonrock Lake, thinking I would probably never return. But a dozen years later, I found myself driving down a familiar dusty road that led to Moonrock Lake's crude boat launch. With me was my six-year-old son, Brian. It was his birthday, and how better to spend a birthday than fishing with your dad? The day was warm and the lake calm as I rowed out to the places I fished when I was a boy. The fishing was slower than it used to be, and I looked sadly at the little perch Brian was catching. But one look at my son's face changed my perspective—he was having a ball. It didn't matter to him that these fish were half the size of the ones I used to catch out here. And if it didn't matter to him, it didn't matter to me either.

After a few hours, Brian suggested we move to another spot. He pointed to a nearby lily pad bed, and I began rowing toward it.

"That looks like a good spot. Maybe we'll find Old Grumpa there!" Brian's eyes gleamed hopefully.

I laughed, thinking the old catfish could not possibly still be alive after all these years, but there was no point in dashing Brian's hopes. I had told him countless stories of Old Grumpa, and this was Brian's first time fishing Moonrock Lake. I remembered how I used to always hope that I would be the one to catch him, so why not let Brian have that hope, too? He caught a few crappies right away, and I settled back into the routine of unhooking the prickly fish and offering advice. I enjoyed watching the little red bobber go under as much as Brian did, and I found myself wishing I had brought a pole for myself. Brian hooked a good-sized perch about then, and seeing that we might actually have a fish big enough to eat, I held the net ready. Brian guided it towards the net skillfully, but before I could scoop the fish, an enormous shadow came up from under the boat and engulfed the perch!

"It's him! It's him!" Brian screamed, as the line on his reel began to spin from the spool. The monster catfish was heading for deeper water, slowly, but steadily.

"Old Grumpa!" I whispered hoarsely, finally snapping out of my trance.

"I got him, Dad! I got him!" my son yelled, moving to the front of the boat, his rod bent nearly in half.

I rowed to keep up with the swimming fish, allowing Brian to gain some of the line Old Grumpa had taken, all the while telling him to keep the line tight, but not to pull too hard. The giant catfish finally slowed, and Brian gently coaxed him upward. I looked at the little panfish net and instantly knew that it would not do for this great fish. I would have to grab the fish's lower jaw and hold on as best I could. This was by far the biggest catfish I had ever seen, and when we finally got a good look at him, we could see an incredible array of lures and hooks attached to his face and head. Line was crisscrossed every which way, and some of the monofilament was cutting into its skin. This was an old veteran of many battles. There was no question this was Old Grumpa. But the leviathan stopped struggling after Brian brought him up. He didn't thrash or make a last-minute run, and he didn't even try to bite as I slipped my hand into his mouth. I can only guess that he was old and tired and had given up. As soon as I got three fingers inside his mouth, I closed my hand and heaved the fish into the boat.

"We got him, son!" I cried, unable to believe that we had managed to catch Old Grumpa. "Let's get him to shore and weigh him!" I picked up the oars and began frantically rowing towards the boat ramp on the other side of the lake. I never took my eyes off the huge catfish, ready to pounce on Old Grumpa if he should pull a last-minute trick and try to flop out of the boat.

"I want to let him go, Dad."

I stopped rowing and looked at Brian in disbelief. "What? Let him go?"

"Look at him, Dad. He's been here for so long. Look how many times he's been hooked and got away. He lives here."

Together we cut off the offending line, hooks and lures that covered Old Grumpa, and we agreed that he looked much better. The fish never so much as flopped during this lengthy process. Brian held his tail as I lifted Old

Grumpa's head, and we lowered him to the water's edge. The catfish gratefully gulped the lake water as we watched him pump water through his gills. With one powerful motion, Old Grumpa turned his head downward and thrashed his heavy tail, covering both Brian and me with water. When I was able to wipe the water out of my eyes, Brian was laughing. And whenever the name of Old Grumpa was mentioned after that, Brian would just grin and look at me, "We got him, didn't we, Dad!"

Mike Duby

A Fish Story

Human pride is not worthwhile; there is always something lying in wait to take the wind out of it.

Mark Twain

During my first three years in Gulf Breeze, Florida, I was a regular at the fishing pier—once an old two-lane bridge—overlooking Santa Rosa Sound.

One afternoon, during spring break, I noticed a young couple loaded down with fishing gear coming onto the old bridge. Instantly I knew three things about them. First, they were not Floridians, because of their pale skin and their lack of that local "y'all" twang. Second, this was probably their first time fishing, judging by their fishing rods with Zebco fishing reels vacuum-packed to the cardboard with price tags still attached. Third, they were newlyweds, because the young man was carrying two beach chairs, an ice chest, an oversized tackle box, a six-pack of Pepsi and a bait bucket, while the woman carried only her small purse slung over her shoulder and a bag of snacks. Occasionally he would coo to his young bride, "It's okay, sweetheart, I'm doing just fine," while she complained that he was lagging behind.

One of the bridge bums, the professed curmudgeon among our group, wearing a weather-beaten Atlanta Braves baseball cap and faded National League Championship T-shirt and sporting three days of beard, growled, "If that was my wife complainin' there, I'd tell her to shut up or I'd throw her carcass over the railin' and feed it to the sharks."

The other fellows on the pier nodded their heads in agreement.

After the couple had moved onto the bridge, the young man set everything down. As the young man worked, his bride kept grousing at him.

"It smells like old dead things out here. It's too hot. It's too windy. The chairs are too low; I can't see over the railing. I have to go to the bathroom, but I'm not using that smelly Porta-Potty." She ended her tirade by saying, "I want to go, *now!*"

The young man kept his peace as he worked, trying to assemble the tackle on his rod and reel. But, when she voiced that she wanted to leave, he responded with, "Sweetheart, you asked me to take you fishing, remember?"

"Yes, but the brochure at the motel said that we'd see dolphins and sea turtles and sailfish."

That brought a few snickers and suppressed chuckles from bystanders, trying to look as if they were truly fishing. I, too, found the young woman's remark amusing and pitied the young man. Rarely were dolphins or sea turtles seen here, and sailfish have never been seen, except in the Gulf of Mexico, hundreds of miles from shore.

A seasoned veteran nearest the couple evidently felt a little pity, too, because he volunteered, "Ahhh, young man, you need any help there?"

From his squat position, the groom looked up at the volunteer with the pleading look of a drowning man and asked, "Would you show me how to tie the string to the reel? It keeps slipping off."

"Ah shore nuf will."

I watched the helper with delight. Decades of fishing experience saw the line spooled onto the reel, strung through the eyelets, tackle attached properly and the hooks baited, all within seconds. The volunteer handed the pole back to the young man. "Do you know how to cast this thing?"

"Ahh, no, sir, I don't. We've never been fishing before."

That was all that needed to be said. Many of the bridge bums, the exception being the grouchy old Braves fan, suddenly moved into action, and inside of five minutes had the young couple set up, ready to fish. One threw a handful of his live shrimp into their bait bucket, tied a rope to it, secured the rope to the railing, then heaved the bucket over the side and into the water to keep the bait alive. Another put some of his ice into the couple's ice chest and put the warm sodas inside. A third helped by cleaning up the cardboard and plastic trash. The fourth volunteer showed the young woman how to rig her pole and then said, "Watch carefully now. Here's how you put a live shrimp on your hook."

He then explained how to make a perfect cast and handed the pole to her. The woman stepped to the railing and gave the rod a mighty sling. Instead of the line sailing out fifty or sixty yards in a slow, lazy arc down to the water, it shot out twenty feet, then slammed straight down into the water right under the bridge, the baited hook and sinker barely breaking below the surface.

The reel backlashed.

The woman grumbled, "Oh, I can't do this," and tried to hand the pole back to her benefactor.

Too late.

Something hit the line so hard the flimsy pole bent almost double, causing the woman to scream out, "What's happening? Oh my God, what's happening?"

The cantankerous Braves fan, the one who had made a point of not volunteering his services earlier, muttered, "Ya caught a fish, that's what."

Frantically, the woman tried to reel in her catch, but with the line fouled up on the reel she wasn't able to. The fourth volunteer reached over the railing, grabbed the line and began hand-pulling the fish up to the bridge, but before getting it all the way to the top, he handed the line to the woman, saying politely, "Here you are, Missy, you can finish bringin' it in. It's your fish, you caught it."

Quickly, she threw her pole down and grabbed the line with both hands, then began pulling it up hand over hand. A few seconds later she flung her catch over the railing; a five-and-a-half-pound Spanish mackerel. Just as the fish hit the cement bridge deck, she began jumping around, waving her arms in the air and shrieking at the top of her voice, "Oh my God! Oh my God!" while the bridge bums and I stood nearby, watching.

Finally, she grabbed the line once more and held the fish up to her husband, saying proudly, "Look, honey, I caught a fish on my very first cast, my very first time fishing!"

"It's a real nice fish, sweetheart," he beamed.

We remained silent, but looked at one another and shrugged.

Then the woman asked, "Can somebody tell me what I should do now?"

The grumpy old baseball fan piped up, "Go home lady, yer battin' a thousand."

Nelson O. Ottenhausen

Dog Days

I've had more fishing trips disrupted by dogs than by any other cause. Lassie may have been able to change the outcome of wars, bring Daddy home safely from the tavern, help frontier mothers deliver babies and save the world from martians, but Lassie on a fishing trip would be more trouble than a hungry junkyard dog in a meat market.

Rufus, our family collie, once chewed the end off a fishing rod before I even got it to the lake. The rod was in a clip holder in the back of my station wagon, and the dog became mesmerized by its bouncing.

At some point, the dog devil whispered to Rufus that the last six inches of a fishing rod taste like a steak bone. I ignored the faint crunching sounds, figuring they came from a disintegrating differential, whatever that is. Well, I may not know much about cars, but I know a destroyed fishing rod when I see one.

And it's thanks to Rufus that I know a canine can run line off a reel faster than a Florida bonefish. The dog was contemplating life behind me one day when I nailed him on the backcast with a Jitterbug, right in his fluffy drawers. Two seconds later, he was one hundred yards away, gathering speed, and my thumb had a groove a quarter of an inch deep. Forget trophy muskellunge; for a memorable fight, give me a seventy-pound collie anytime.

The same dog reinvented the rumba in a canoe. I forgot why I was canoeing on New Year's Day, but it was bitterly cold and the river was mostly slushy ice.

Rufus had never been in a canoe before and didn't like the unsteadiness. He faced me, braced his feet, and began to shift his weight to counterbalance the rocking of the canoe.

The more he adjusted, the more the canoe rocked, until we were wallowing back and forth, and I was gripping the gunwales and praying for God to strike the dog dead, or at least unconscious. Instead, Rufus looked over the side and, thinking that slush was as good as solid land, leaped overboard. I then had the problem of trying to reboard seventy pounds of icewater-soaked collie.

Perhaps the most traumatic fishing trip I had ever taken with a dog was when Chubby, my Brittany, ate a cheeseball. I'd been fishing for trout with cheeseballs molded around tiny treble hooks. (I can see dry-fly purists fainting dead away, but I was there to catch fish, not tease them.) I decided to switch lures and put the cheeseball on the boat seat. When I looked down, it was gone, and Chubby, my sweet little French Brittany, was wriggling and smiling at me. "Oh Chubby!" I exclaimed, amid visions of those needle-tipped hooks ripping her insides to shreds.

I ended what had been a fine fishing trip and raced to a phone to call the vet one hundred miles away. "Feed him as much food as possible," the vet advised. "Surround that hook with food." I think I heard a muffled aside to his assistance: "Book the Caribbean cruise."

Chubby wolfed down my lunch while my stomach growled and I salivated. I stopped at every Hardee's on the way home to stoke him with cheeseburgers. I was too worried to eat, but he gratefully gulped everything, looking at me with adoring eyes.

The vet peered at the hook with his X-ray machine, while he fondled brochures promising soft tropical nights and shipboard romance. After three days, he reported that the hook had gone right on through. We were both happy—me that the dog was all right, the vet because once again the Vances had brightened his leisure hours with a shower of money.

When I put Chubby back in the kennel and pointed to the bucket of dog food, he looked at me as if I'd just whipped him. Dogs *do* have facial expressions, and his read, "Where's my cheeseburger?"

Joel Vance

Gone Fishin'

Each person is born to one possession which outvalues all his others—his last breath.

Mark Twain

The friendship between Gene and my Grandpa Merle went back long before I was born. It seemed that Gene had always been around. Although not related to us, he was still a very important part of our family, for Gene was Grandpa's fishing buddy.

Early in the morning, Gene would drive over to my grandparents' house. My grandpa would be watching out the window for the old Chevy's headlights to flash as they turned into the driveway. Grandpa was already dressed and ready to leave, his fishing gear standing outside the door. As he shuffled through the house, Grandma's dog Shorty bailed off the bed and snapped at his heels. Grandpa laughed loud enough to wake all of us. Even a nippy little dog couldn't squelch his excitement. Grandpa was going fishing.

With nothing but a thermos of hot coffee and some cinnamon rolls from the cafe, Grandpa and Gene fished until they grew hungry enough to call it quits for the day. In the early afternoon they drove back to the house. We could hear them laughing and talking before they ever got out of the pickup. After they unhitched Grandpa's boat, they came to the house carrying the catch of the day.

We loved to eat the crappie and catfish they caught out on the lake. Grandpa would add a little hot sauce to the oil as it was heating, then drop the fish filets in when it was hot enough. Grandma would make cornbread and set out a plate of green onions. She'd add fried potatoes on the side to make it a royal feast.

Gene worked as a pipe liner. Often his job would take him away from home for a month or more at a time. Grandpa had other friends he fished with in Gene's absence, but somehow it wasn't the same. As soon as his old friend called to say he was back in town, they made plans to take the boat out to the lake.

As the years passed, we noticed that Grandpa was getting around a little slower; the cool weather bothered his rheumatoid arthritis more. A few times he called Gene and canceled their trip for the next morning, citing such excuses as the fish hadn't been biting as well lately, or the wind might be picking up too much to take the boat out on the water. When Grandpa could no longer climb into the boat by himself, Gene would gently lift his friend up and set him over the edge, steadying him until he got his balance.

Gene's wife scolded her husband for continuing to go fishing with his old buddy. She said, "What would happen if you had an accident on the water? What would you do if you were both thrown overboard?"

Gene pondered this question for a moment, then said, "Well, I guess he'd have to sink or swim." Gene and Grandpa had a good laugh over his answer, though Gene's wife frowned at their sense of humor. Grandpa laughed even harder because of it.

When Gene returned from one of his work-related trips, he was shocked at the change in his friend. Grandpa had lost weight. He seemed to be in a lot of pain, more than just the arthritis. A trip to the family doctor confirmed our worst fears.

Cancer. Inoperable.

In our grief and confusion, we tried to think of ways to beat this disease. We talked about surgery, chemotherapy, radiation and the miracles of modern medicine. We cried and we prayed. We made plans to seek a second opinion.

Grandpa, however, made plans of his own. He and Gene went fishing.

A few short months later, I sat in the funeral home listening to the preacher talk about my grandfather. My mind began to stray. I was miserable with grief. I missed Grandpa's hugs and jokes. Most of all, I missed his laughter and sense of humor.

The front of the room was awash with beautiful flowers of all colors. There were so many wreaths and sprays, green plants and arrangements that, at first, I missed seeing the yellow flowers, a bright ring of golden blooms. A yellow ribbon was draped across the front. Printed in large sparkling letters were the simple words, *"Gone Fishin'."*

I looked around the room until my eyes met his, brimming with tears. I knew without a doubt who had sent those yellow flowers. I was also sure about something else.

Grandpa would have loved it.

Pamela Jenkins

Reprinted by permission of Christian Snyder.

To Honor, Cherish and Collect Bait

Lacey is wife number three. I hate the sound of that, but we've been happily married ten years now. When the vows were read, I was reasonably confident she and I would grow old together. Any reservations I had disappeared on a wet lawn the night we celebrated our one-month anniversary.

It was Friday evening, and we were going walleye fishing the next day. As always, Lacey was excited about the trip, and I was excited about showing her a spot I had frequented as a youth. We probably should have gone to bed at a decent hour, but instead we headed into town and broke our budget at a nice restaurant. "After all, we don't have to get up early if we don't want," I said. "And you can only have a one-month anniversary two or three times in your life." Thank goodness she laughed.

Shortly after midnight, we were back home. It was sticky-hot late summer, the moon was trying to do something romantic, and Lacy was luscious in white satin slippers and a silky blue dinner dress. On the way across the lawn, she stopped, leaned against me and with a breathy whisper uttered the words a man always hopes to hear when he has just dropped a couple bills on a night out with a good-looking woman: "Let's snatch crawlers," she said.

"Say what?"

"I want to snatch crawlers," Lacey repeated.

I was incredulous. "You know about night crawlers?" I asked.

"Since I was eight," she giggled. "I used to earn my mad money snatching crawlers." She put her hand on my shoulder and kicked off her white satin slippers. "Come on," she whispered, "they've got to be all the way out of the ground by now."

She pulled a little penlight out of her evening bag and directed the anemic beam onto the wet lawn. A night crawler of nearly nine inches was stretched out vulnerably, perhaps voluptuously, hoping, no doubt, for a mate to wiggle by. Lacey went into a crouch and began the stalk.

Now, I had always been of the opinion that people who bought night crawlers in those little white foam cartons instead of plucking them from their own yards were wasting money and missing out on a good time. In my other life, however, my prefishing night crawler safaris had been solitary, late-night ventures that guaranteed hisses of disapproval. "It's okay for a kid," I was told once, "but what will the neighbors think?"

I had never mentioned night crawlers to Lacey, and now here she was on her knees in the middle of a dew-soaked lawn with a wriggling nine-incher in each hand and a penlight in her mouth.

"Come on, darling." The small light bobbed up and down in her mouth as she spoke. "We're going fishing in the morning, you know."

By the time we finally squished up the back steps to our house with enough walleye bait to last several fishing trips, our laughter and exhortations had given way to tired snorts and chortles. Lacey was wet, grass-stained and streaked with mud. She had never been lovelier.

I knew this one was a keeper.

Alan Liere

The Empty Hook

Hold fast to the best of the past and move fast to the best of the future.

John F. Kennedy

My parents shared a love of the outdoors, especially fishing. We lived in New York City, and opportunities to pursue these passions were few. When I was ten years old, my father decided we would spend part of our summer on the eastern end of Long Island. I was overjoyed at the thought of being out of the hot city and spending quality time with my beloved parents. Dad rented a small cottage on the bay that included the use of a rowboat. Each morning we would push off and row to an inlet where we fished from the shore. My dad also had a hand-made crab trap, and mother dug for clams in the sand with her toes.

Directly across the way was a vast estate, and tied to its dock was an enormous yacht. My mother referred to it as the *"Miniature Queen Mary."* Every day a very well-dressed older man was helped out to the end of the dock by a servant who set up a chair for him and handed him his fishing pole. We could tell by the thick dark glasses he wore and the way he was guided out onto the dock that he was blind.

I watched the man with great interest. He sat for hours, never reeling in his fishing line to see if he had caught anything. My parents agreed if we owned such a magnificent yacht, we would be out on it, fishing every day. The man was quite a mystery to me, and I hoped to get his attention by calling out to him every day as we left for home. "Bye mister, see you tomorrow!" I would yell. He never answered.

My curiosity grew with each passing day, and when I couldn't take it anymore, I set out on a mission. I was allowed to ride my bike after dinner one warm evening. I rode out toward the inlet, which didn't appear to be that far away; however, it took nearly an hour of riding before I sighted the old man's house. I stopped on the side of the road when I heard a car pull up behind me and watched as the driver got out and opened the back door for the passenger. It was the older man whom I had watched fishing every day.

He told me I was trespassing on private property. I apologized, but continued by saying, "Sir, I came out here to say hello to you in person. I watch you fish every day from the other side of the inlet and you never catch a thing. I thought I could help you." The man cut me off with his laughter.

"How old are you, child?" he asked.

"I'm ten years old and my name is Anne and I love to fish and my parents love to fish and we live in the city and. . . ." Once again I was stopped by his very hearty laugh.

"Young lady, you're quite a chatterbox. It's getting very late. I think we'd better get you home to your parents before they start to worry about you."

My bike was loaded into the trunk and I arrived home that evening in a shiny black limousine. My parents, both in shock, but grateful for my return, invited the gentleman in for coffee and dessert, and he accepted. He sat in our small kitchen eating my mother's homemade crumb cake and told us the story of his life.

He had been blinded in a terrible accident that years ago had taken the life of his wife and his only child, a son. Although a man of wealth, nothing mattered to him after the accident. He sold his business, shunned the rest of his family and friends, and became a recluse. He said that he had bought the yacht for his son who loved to fish, and added that when his son died, he vowed never to take the boat out, and never go fishing again.

I had been listening quietly, but at this point I couldn't help myself and blurted out, "But mister, I see you fishing on your dock every day!"

My parents gave me the look that told me I should have remained silent.

The man said, "You're right, Anne. You do see me with a fishing pole in my hand every day, but I never put any bait on my hook. I just sit on the dock and reflect on the times when fishing meant so much to me and my family."

I thought for a moment, then said, "I bet your son is very sad when he looks down from heaven and sees you so unhappy."

This time my parents hushed me with more than a look.

After a long pause the man said, "Your daughter's right. What an old fool I've been."

A few days later, the limousine arrived for us, and we spent the day on the yacht on beautiful Long Island Sound—FISHING. It was a day not to be forgotten. That night I thought about the smile on the man's face when I thanked him.

"No," he said, "I must thank you, as today was my happiest

day in years." I gave him a big hug and he hugged me back.

Years have come and gone since that day. Life has many pleasures for me today. I don't get to go fishing very often, but I have a very full schedule. I have a wonderful husband, children and grandchildren, and I reside on Long Island. I hold fast to a lesson that I learned when I was just ten years old. Life is what you make of it. I treasure a picture that sits on my desk, faded with age, but a joy to behold. It shows a man smiling and holding a very large fish that he had just caught. The words written under the photo make me smile even after all these years. It simply says, "To Anne—Life will never be an empty hook again. THANK YOU!"

Anne Carter

The Fisherman and His Femme Fatale

I saw her across the room, sparkling with sequins. She flipped her eyes up at me under a heavy fringe of false eyelashes and my knees turned to water. Patting her bouffant hairdo, she wiggled her way upstream, through the crowded party, toward me. She looked like an enchanting mermaid in that silvery dress, and as she neared I felt for the first time in my life like a piece of bait.

It was Halloween 1964. I was wearing hip waders and a fishing vest because my passion in life was fishing, and I indulged my passion every opportunity I got. As she neared, gazing at me hypnotically with her sea-green eyes, she told me she was born under the sign of the fish. I laughed, not knowing whether to believe her or not. One thing I knew, I was in trouble. She told me I was tall, dark and handsome. I told her she was bewitching. By the end of the evening she had me hooked, and by the end of the following summer, she had me landed in a small courtroom, slipping a gold ring on her dainty finger.

On our honeymoon I took her from the lights of the city to a remote valley nestled deep in the heart of grizzly bear country. For one week, we pitched our tent by an

emerald-flowing river and fished to our hearts' content.
But wait. She liked to fish too, didn't she? I asked somewhat belatedly as we rumbled down the dirt road in a battered pickup truck. Her answer? She batted her magical
eyes and just smiled.

Every day of our honeymoon, I fished. Every day, she
also fished; precisely at noon, she donned a fishnet bikini,
toss her gleaming black hair down her back and walk
barefoot to the river. I, too, was in that river, chest deep,
casting my line far downstream. She always managed to
lure me to shore. Well, almost always. Sometimes a line
would tighten, or a reel would spin crazily, a conquered
fish leaping to the surface. At those times I'd see her shrug
her shoulders and head back to the tent.

I took her canoeing and she managed to look impressed
at the salmon I threw at her pretty painted toes, telling me
I looked like a Greek god throwing tribute at her feet. One
day we rounded the corner, heading back to camp and
saw the savage evidence of a grizzly bear foray. Our
belongings were strewn everywhere as if they had been
chewed up and spit out. Upon investigation, I noted claw
marks imbedded deeply in the lid of our food chest. Giant
paw prints in the soil left no doubt whatsoever as to
whom the predator had been. She broke down in tears
and started to pack.

I prepared an airtight plea bargain that got me three
extra days on the river. That evening she dabbed on her
favorite perfume and I smiled as I hung my chest waders
in the log cabin I rented for her.

The day of our departure arrived, and I didn't share
her feelings of elation at going back to the city. As I
closed the truck door, I tried not to appear morose.
Looking longingly at the crashing waterfalls that
tumbled over the majestic mountains, the deep secret

forest and the shining river that I loved, I asked what she thought of the valley.

"Very beautiful," she replied absently, checking her makeup in the windshield mirror. I thought *she* was beautiful as I saw the eagerness on her face.

I made up my mind then and there, kissed her soundly and told her bluntly, "I'm glad, because this is where we're going to live."

A look of horror crossed her features as I realized my blunder. That eager look of hers had been to high-tail it out of the wilderness, not live in the wilderness. Desperately, I began to play my line. I was a new stepfather to her five children—I had to think of the welfare of my new family, didn't I? In the valley there was no danger, except for bears, and I had a rifle. There were gardens, and game to hunt in the fall. I always hunted with a fishing rod in one hand and a rifle in the other, because I never knew when I might run into a stream. There would always be plenty to eat for the children. And—I told her dramatically, saving the pièce de résistance for last—I would build her a dream house.

That did it. She agreed. But somehow I suspected she knew the real reason for my wanting to move the family twelve hundred miles—for the fishing. I hadn't mentioned that little fact, but if she had asked, I would have confessed. I knew I had married a wise woman when she didn't ask.

Happy with her dream home—a beautiful custom-made log cabin—we moved the entire family to paradise. On our first Christmas, I bought her a fishing rod. Now she could fish with me! Our girls took me to task, and on her birthday I bought her perfume with the money from the sale of the rod. But, to her chagrin, I also bought her a canner to can the steady supply of coho and spring salmon I regularly brought in from my daily forays to the river.

She always wondered where I got the feathers to tie my flies. One day she pulled her hatbox from beneath the bed, lifted the lid and gazed into it, stupefied. Like naked chicks, embarrassed for lack of feathers, laid her hats. One by one she picked them up, not knowing whether to laugh or cry. A lone feather floated to the bottom. I had forgotten one. She picked it up and stuck it in my wallet beside my credit card. That year she had the best vacation ever.

Time passed. The children left home. She packed away her false eyelashes and got rid of the bouffant hairdo. I packed away my rifle, but there was no way I was going to get rid of my fishing rod. As much as my declining health allowed, I still fished.

On our thirty-fifth anniversary, outside a log cabin not far from where we had once pitched our honeymoon tent, I unwrapped a framed collage of photographs. Stormy rivers bleak with snow, rain swollen or hotly sun dappled, fishing through the years, casting, reeling, angling, in the glory of it all, I stood. Wiping a tear from the corner of my eye with an arthritic finger, I told my femme fatale that *she* was the best thing I had ever caught. Then I kissed her and together we walked into our log cabin and closed the door, forgetting my fishing rod outside.

Graham Hall
As told to Janet Hall Wigler

Graham and his femme fatale wife, Angela,
pose for a fish picture outside of their log cabin.

A Special Place

Wheresoever you go, go with your heart.

Confucius

His name was Beauford. I met him in the summer of 1978 when I was guiding in Alaska.

I liked him from the start, and in his eyes I could see a genuine love for the wilderness around us. As we introduced ourselves and shook hands, I thought I may have seen a faint tear fall quickly down his aged face. What that meant, I did not know, but it was time to go fishing and I quickly dismissed it.

Savage, two-foot-long rainbow trout were hitting mouse imitations with a vengeance on the Toagnak River. I suggested we go there, just as all the other guides were doing.

But Beauford grabbed my arm gently and looked at me with all seriousness. "I want to go to the Ninilchik, in particular, the place where Quartz Creek runs into it."

I knew the place, having fished the Ninilchik a few times earlier in the season. The trout were smaller there, and not very numerous. I started to again suggest the

Toagnak, but caught myself at the last moment. We would go where he wanted to go.

So we fished the Ninilchik at the deep, gentle-flowing pool created by tiny Quartz Creek. I rigged a red and green streamer fly for Beauford to try and could not help but marvel at the incredible beauty of the place. I took a few pictures of Beauford fishing, wondering how the man had known about this particular spot.

Beauford let out a shout of joy about then, and I could see the rod dipping heavily with the strain of a fish. My guest praised the fish for every leap it made. Every strong surge was accompanied by words of encouragement from its captor. It was almost as if Beauford wanted the fish to fight itself free. Finally, I gently lifted the rainbow from the water, quickly shook the hook free and held the fish up for Beauford to admire.

"Isn't that the finest trout you have ever seen?" Beauford said breathlessly.

I nodded dumbly. In truth, the Toagnak held rainbows that would eat this one for breakfast and look for more. But I could not ruin this moment for my elated guest, so I pointed out the intricate spots and incredibly diverse coloring of the native trout.

We released him and Beauford just stood there with this grand smile on his face for a long time. He was staring at a large flat rock across the river.

"Do you see that rock over there?" Beauford asked.

I nodded. Often I had thought to cross the river and fish from it, for it would make a fine platform for casting.

"Anything in particular about it you've noticed?" he queried.

I shrugged, mentioning it was probably the best seat on the river since there was always a shadow lying across half of it.

Beauford just smiled.

We fished the same spot on the Ninilchik for all five days of Beauford's stay. We caught fewer fish than any of the other parties, but Beauford didn't seem to mind at all.

On the last day he told me he was going to wade across the river and sit on the big flat rock he had admired every day. I got up to go with him, knowing the slippery rocks could be treacherous.

But Beauford stopped me. "I would like to be alone for an hour or so." In his eyes I could see that same firmness and intensity that had been there when he first told me we would fish the Ninilchik.

I should not have done it, a guide should never leave a client alone in the Alaskan wilds. There are bears, slippery rocks, strong currents—a hundred ways to get in trouble. But I let him go, promising him I would come for him in an hour.

Beauford came to fish with me every year after that first trip, sometimes twice a year. Each time, we would fish the same place on the Ninilchik River, each time Beauford showed that same excitement when he would catch a trout, and each time he would want to be alone for a while, sitting on the rock he had come to so dearly love.

I asked him about it a few times over the years, but Beauford would only smile. "Someday you will see it as I see it, Mike, and then you will understand."

Finally the year arrived when Beauford was not on our list, and I discovered that he would not be coming up this year. I sent him a letter, worried that something might be wrong.

A few weeks later, I received a reply:

Dear Mike,

The years have finally caught up with me, as they do to all men eventually. My days grow shorter and shorter and it gets harder to wake up each morning. I am not sorry, I have lived long enough in this world and I am ready to go on. My only regret is that I will not be able to go fishing with you anymore. Those were good times, Mike, and I want you to know that I will always be thankful for those days on the river.

Before I go, there is something else I want to tell you. I have never spoken of this before, but the time has come for you to know.

I lost my wife two years before I first came up to fish with you, Mike. There was a car accident late one night and the Lord took her from me. But we had a few moments together before her life faded, and she said she would always be at our special place on the Ninilchik River. We used to go there when we were younger, Mike, and she would sit on the flat rock and watch me fish.

Remember that shadow you said you saw on that rock? Next time you're there, try to find out what makes that shadow. You won't find a source. That is my Rachel, and she still sits there, waiting for me.

Now you know why I have such a love for that place.

Goodbye my friend,

Beauford

Beauford passed away before I received his letter.

I made a trip to the Ninilchik soon after. I pictured my friend effortlessly casting into the swirling waters, his thrilled laugh when he hooked a trout and the way he looked at the flat rock on the other side of the river.

I looked myself, remembering what he had told me in his letter. This time I could make out the image of a young woman sitting there on the rock, and I knew it was her, Beauford's Rachel.

I would never again see that silhouette on the rock as just a shadow.

Now there were two.

Mike Duby

2

FIRST CAST

*Only the curious will learn and only the
resolute overcome the obstacles to learning.*

Eugene S. Wilson

"You certainly had a nice cast going there, young man."

A Simple Plan

I found my great love for fishing while growing up on the San Carlos Apache reservation in Arizona. Whenever my uncles or neighbors went fishing, I grabbed my tackle box and fishing pole and jumped in the back of their pickup truck. My dad never understood why I enjoyed fishing so much, but because he knew his three sons liked to fish, he bought us fishing rods and tackle. He even helped us look for worms, but never showed any interest in the sport.

One day my two younger brothers—ten-year-old Carl and nine-year-old Boy—and I somehow talked our dad into taking us to nearby San Carlos Lake. As we began to cast out, Dad remained in the truck, reading his paper.

All of a sudden I had an idea! *What if I talked Dad into fishing just this once? What if he somehow caught the biggest fish today? Then he'd have to fall in love with fishing, too! Then he'd want to take us fishing ALL the time.* What a great plan!

I shared my amazing plan with my younger brothers. We coaxed Dad out of the truck, and to our surprise, he walked down and joined us at the shoreline. But he ignored the fishing poles and simply opened his lawn chair and continued reading his paper. My brothers and I looked at one another, dumbfounded. *Now what do we do?*

Then, a possible answer—a large fish jumped not far from us. Quickly I put on the biggest worm in our can, cranked back as far as a twelve-year-old could, then let the line fly. I hit the spot almost dead-on where the big fish had jumped.

Propping my rod next to Dad and his newspaper, I walked over to my brothers and pretended to untangle their lines. Every now and then I would glance at the bobber on my line. After what seemed hours, the bobber moved! Then it moved again!

"Dad! Grab my line! I can't get over there," I yelled. "Carl's line is all tangled up!"

"You boys come pull it in before it eats your worm," he countered.

All four of us watched the bobber dance on the water. Then Dad scooted to the edge of his chair and dropped his newspaper on the ground. Suddenly, the bobber disappeared.

In unison, my brothers and I yelled, "Pull the line, pull the line!"

Dad jumped up, grabbed the rod and pulled the line tight. "Something big's on here, boys!" he shouted. "Get over here and help me!"

We ran over and stood by him as the line moved slowly through the water.

"Don't lose him, Dad!" I yelled.

"Don't give him any slack," my brother yelled.

"Start turning the handle; reel him in!" screamed my other brother as we watched a grown man holding tight to a fishing rod, straining as it bent from the weight of something big.

"Turn the handle now, Dad, pull that fish in, Dad. You got him, Dad!" I yelled again. It was funny to see three little boys, jumping up and down and yelling orders at their dad as he tried to land his first fish.

Finally Dad, all excited about the fish he was about to catch, braced himself.

"Okay, Dad, we'll get him when you drag him out," my brothers and I said. One last pull and out came the . . .

"It's a turtle, a big turtle!" we yelled.

"Turtle!" Dad gasped as he instantly jumped back. "See? See? You boys know turtles are not to be touched by Apaches—they are taboo!" he said, as the turtle wiggled on its back. "This is why I never wanted to fish!" He dropped my pole and stormed back to the truck.

My brothers and I stared down at the turtle wiggling at our feet.

"You take it off!" my brothers said.

"No, you take it off!" I answered.

"No, no, it was your idea," they reminded me.

Many years later, I can still hear my brothers' words, and I smile, remembering that day long ago when we tried to get our dad to fall in love with fishing. I really don't recall who took the hook out of the turtle that afternoon. But one thing I do remember. Although Dad never did develop an interest in fishing, he did help us dig for worms many more times, and he still took us on many more fishing trips during our childhood—and he did it simply because he was our dad.

Kenny Duncan Sr.

Hezekiah

"Hezekiah is the biggest and most ornery muskie to ever make his home in Edinboro Lake," explained Grandpa Braley as he rowed us out onto the lake. "I hooked him once, maybe two years ago—back in 1949. Got him up to the boat, but my net was too small. When I tried to grab him by the gills, he jumped, shook loose and snapped the line. On his way back into the water, he somehow managed to put this scar on the back of my hand. Guess he didn't appreciate my effort to invite him to dinner as the guest of honor. Well, Robbie, this looks like a good spot. Let's drop anchor and start some serious fishing."

Grandpa's words filled my six-year-old mind with excitement about catching a fish that big, and also with fear about catching a fish that *bites*. "Why do you call him Hezekiah? And if I catch him, will he bite me?" I asked.

Grandpa, being an ordained Methodist minister, explained, "The biblical Hezekiah was a king who was dying, and God gave him another fifteen years to live. That muskie also had new life given to him the day he escaped my hook. That's why I named him after the former king of Judah. The way I figure it, old Hezekiah, king of the lake, was teaching me patience. Someday, if I keep trying, we will meet again. Hope it doesn't take fifteen years, though."

Grandpa went on to assure me that he wouldn't let any fish bite me. Armed with a tin can full of night crawlers and a bright red-and-white cork bobber, I threw my line into the smooth, blue-green water. As instructed, my eyes intently watched the bobber for any sign of movement. At first, my heart was beating with excitement, but after about the first half hour, I grew weary of the bobber's stillness in the water.

"Where are all the fish?" I whined.

"Patience, Robbie, patience," reassured Grandpa. "I'll pull up the anchor and we'll drift for a while. Let's see if that changes our luck."

This was how the rest of the day went. No matter how much we drifted or moved to different parts of the lake, no fish were biting. I was extremely discouraged and had thoughts of never fishing again. Finally, by late afternoon, Grandpa started rowing us back to the dock.

On the way back, he explained to me that even the greatest of fisherman have bad days. He told me the biblical story of a fisherman named Peter, who was having several bad days in a row. Being a man of little patience, Peter became angry and headed back to shore. His thoughts were to sell his boat and give up fishing forever. As the boat approached the shoreline, Peter noticed a stranger standing on shore, watching him. The stranger saw Peter's frustration and yelled out to him, "Throw your net out one more time."

Peter yelled back to the stranger, "No way, there's no fish this close to shore."

The stranger, undaunted, insisted. "Trust me, go ahead and cast your net."

Peter thought to himself, *This guy is crazy, I'll just have to show him there are no fish here.* He then begrudgingly cast his net one more time. When he brought it back up, he could not believe his eyes. The net was jammed full of fish. "Thank you!" Peter shouted to the stranger. "You taught me a lesson in patience." The stranger turned out to be a man named Jesus.

Grandpa finished the story of Peter just as we pulled up to the dock. "Tell you what, Robbie, after I tie up, go to the back of the boat and throw your line in one more time just as Peter did," he instructed. "I need to get something and should be back in about ten minutes. There may be some pan fish hanging around the dock, so be patient."

I did as he said and resumed my vigil over the red and white bobber. It might have been only ten minutes, but it seemed like an hour before he returned. I never really paid much attention to what he was doing as he set his old camera on a tripod. While engrossed in my boredom and concentration on the bobber, he snapped a picture.

Just as Grandpa finished packing his camera, I saw the bobber move slightly. I awoke suddenly from my boredom. It moved a second time and then a third. I felt the tug on the line as the bobber disappeared below the water's surface. My eyes lit up and my body reacted with a quick jerk on the pole. I felt the weight of the great fish on the other end of the line. It felt huge, and I screamed with excitement, "Grandpa, it's Hezekiah! Come quick!"

Grandpa stepped into the boat and instructed me on the proper way to land a fish. As I pulled the mighty fish to the surface, Grandpa looked at me with a straight face and said in all seriousness, "Robbie, that is the biggest sunfish I've ever seen."

I was as proud as I could be of that sunfish, showing it off to Mom, Dad and everyone else back at the cottage. Grandpa taught me how to clean it and Grandma fried it up special for my supper. After eating, Grandpa told everyone of our adventures and how I hooked "Little Hezekiah" using my newfound fisherman's skills.

Robert Bruce Riefstahl

After returning from the trip, Grandpa Braley sent Robert this picture that he calls "Patience."

The Catcher of Rainbows

If you want your dreams to come true, don't sleep.

Yiddish Proverb

You cannot expect fish to jump into your boat when you go fishing. The fact is, you should not expect it to happen at all. But then, you don't know my friend Fred.

Fred was a widowed gentleman who had retired and moved to our area so he could fish. He had always dreamed of catching rainbows somewhere, sometime, but had not taken the time to do so. He had never even learned to fish. Fred was one of those folks who never seemed to win at recreational things, not even when he was the only one in the contest. I would watch him drift by me on the river, thrashing about, cursing his tackle, letting his boat get away from him and just generally having a terrible time.

He was a very likeable fellow. Fred found humor in almost anyone and even in his frustrating efforts to catch that big one—or any fish for that matter. When I invited him to come along in my boat, he refused, saying, "There is no way you will catch fish if I am in the boat." He thought he was cursed.

I finally coaxed him into joining me. However, after a few outings with Fred, I was beginning to believe him. Fish would suck worms from his hook without getting hooked. His float would insist on sinking. Tree limbs and underwater snags would claim his lures. The snarls he could create with his reel were legend. Yet his humor didn't waver in all his misfortunes. I became determined to do my best to remove the "fishing curse" from Fred's mind. I was sure the aura of bad vibes he brought with him each trip tended to cast a spell on the both of us. I even found myself snarling my reel now and then.

Soon Fred was reluctant to go out in my boat. He wanted me to catch fish. Only after I promised him some of my home brew if he *didn't* catch a fish did he brighten up and get into the boat. For him, the home brew was a sure thing!

We were drifting along in the slow current about fifty feet from shore. Fred had his tackle box open trying to decide which lure he should lose first. I had cast my line toward shore and it found its way over an overhanging limb and dropped into the current. Frantically, I began to reel in, trying to flip the lure back over the limb as we drifted past.

WHAMMO! A nice-sized rainbow took charge!

I attempted a mighty heave to get my lure and the hooked rainbow over the limb. It worked! Over the limb they came. The rainbow shook itself free from the lure, sailed smartly to the boat, struck Fred in the chest and fell directly into Fred's open tackle box. Realizing the tackle box was no place for him, Mr. Rainbow thrashed madly about until he was hooked on nearly every lure in the box.

I managed to retrieve my line and lure without Fred noticing.

Fred was ecstatic. He stood up in the boat, whooped and hollered and danced about. I thought I might have to hit him with an oar to restore order and keep the boat right side up.

Well, for awhile we had a super fisherman on our hands. Fred was proud to show off his tackle box and announce he had caught a rainbow trout with every lure in the box! He was equally proud to announce he did so without even tying a lure to his line! He bragged that his lures were so attractive the fish "just flat jumped into the boat to get at them!"

It turned out Fred did not see me hoist that rainbow over the limb. He actually believed the fish did jump into the boat. His attitude toward fishing changed overnight. We had many a wonderful drift together down the river after that day.

Fred is gone now. I do miss him. I am sure, up there where he is, he is bending the ear of all who will listen, extolling his prowess as the catcher of rainbows.

Pat MacIver

Beyond the Breakers

We are made to persist. That is how we find out who we are.

Tobias Wolff

On my desk there is a faded picture in an old wooden frame. It is my most cherished memento of my father. He's dressed in a pair of waders pulled down past his knees, a light wool jacket, and a faded cap cocked at a jaunty angle upon his head. He's young and robust, and in each hand he holds a striped bass weighing close to thirty pounds.

Gazing at that picture is like traveling back in time to when I was four or five, watching my father strap on a heavy canvas knapsack, grab a mammoth surf rod, and finally look down, asking, "You want to come along?"

I'd look up into his cheerful face with his infectious grin and my heart would leap in anticipation of spending a day with my hero—my father. He'd take me by the hand, and we'd walk the several blocks to the beach.

When I was nine, Dad gave me a rod and reel of my own. My chest swelled with pride. My initiation to fishing had begun.

"Try to get your line past the second breaker, Gary.

That's where the fish will be." I always thought they were waves, but Dad explained the waves were farther out. As the wave speeds inland it swells, then breaks over itself heading toward shore. I tried to mimic my father's cast, but my sinker would land in about a foot of water several feet away. I would never be able to reach that far! Then I'd watch his cast and how the bait arched high in the air, slowly reaching its apex to curve and land with a barely discernible splash well past that second breaker. Oh, how I wanted to cast like that, but I was just a little kid. There was no way I could do it.

After many frustrating attempts I'd quit and sit down dejected and watch as he made cast after cast. But on the days I kept trying and didn't give up he'd make the cast for me. Then we'd place our rods in the sand spikes and open our thermoses. Coffee for him, hot chocolate for me.

He heaped praise on me when I got past the first breaker, but it took nearly two years until, finally, I succeeded. Then within several months I became nearly as proficient as he. And nearly every time I cast out he'd remind me saying, "The second breaker, son. Cast beyond the second breaker."

After high school, I spent a few years in the navy. When I came home on leave, Dad and I would head for the surf. We'd make our casts, then sit back in the sand and talk, catching up on each other's lives while sipping the hot coffee that was so welcome on those cold foggy days. I don't think we cared if we caught anything. We were simply a father and son reminiscing over past fishing trips and catching up on our separate lives.

It was on one of these outings that I asked, "Dad, why did you make me struggle so much by insisting that I do the casting myself? We could have caught more fish if you'd have done it for me."

He looked at me and smiled. "I guess you were a little put off, son. But it wasn't all about catching fish. You'll understand when you have a son of your own," he said, with a knowing grin.

"Wasn't about catching fish? What are you talking about?"

"It was all about doing for yourself."

I reeled in my line, checked my bait and cast it out once more. Dad nodded toward the spot where my line disappeared into the water.

"You learned that on your own, didn't you? All I taught you were the basics. In this world, Gary, nothing worthwhile comes easy."

The years passed swiftly. I married my childhood sweetheart, and before we knew it, our family grew to two girls and a boy. Unfortunately, due to my work, most of our time was spent abroad.

Dad retired to a small house in southern Oregon. It was a little over an hour's drive to the coast, and he could go fishing anytime he wanted.

One night the phone rang. It was Dad, telling us he had been diagnosed with leukemia. We were devastated. He was okay for the time being, but eventually, as the leukemia progressed, we thought it best that I take an early retirement and return home to offer what assistance we could.

Even as the disease began to sap his strength, he still wanted to surf fish. So Dad, my ten-year-old son and I went fishing as often as possible. As my son struggled with his fishing rod, Dad smiled and said, "Don't worry, he'll catch on. You did!"

Dad seemed to grow weaker each day. On our last trip together he couldn't quite make the cast beyond the second breaker and after several tries he reeled in his line, looked wistfully out to sea and shook his head in disgust. I took the rod from him, and with moist eyes, made his cast. He nodded in satisfaction and smiled at me with that infectious grin I remembered from my youth. Dad and I had come full circle in our lives together. I guess he sensed this, for he put a hand on my shoulder and said, "It's okay, son."

Six months later, he died.

To this day I have tears in my eyes at the loss of him—of his wisdom, his patience and his love.

Recently my son's family came to southern Oregon for a visit. My grandson is almost ten years old and the spitting image of my father.

One day the three of us packed up the fishing gear and headed for the ocean. Dad's old surf rod felt comfortable in my hands as I made my cast, and I have to admit I was flushed with pride and my eyes became just a little teary when I heard my boy tell his boy, "The second breaker, son, cast beyond the second breaker."

Gary B. Luerding

Gary's father, "Red" Luerding,
with his catch of the day (c. 1928).

Reprinted by permission of Gary Luerding.

Tadpole's Triumph

The walls inside Johnny Mercer's Pier, located on Wrightsville Beach in North Carolina, were tiled with dusty black frames. Some held clippings and pictures of the pier after various natural disasters. Most were yellowed photographs of huge fish and smiling fishermen. All the memories reflected in the old photos intrigued me; at the age of ten, I, too, wanted to have my photo on the pier's wall.

Catching a king mackerel is the Mt. Everest of the "Johnny's fishing experience," as we called it, and I wanted to catch one so bad it hurt. But part of the problem was all the best spots for king fishing were at the end of the pier and jealously guarded by the regulars. Fortunately, Mr. Henry, a pier favorite, always made room for a kid or two. He never could remember our names, so we all fell under the blanket label of "Tadpole." Halfway up the pier, I recognized him by the old Panama hat covering his wispy gray hair. He looked up from his battered red thermos cup and waved when I called out. He had a spot open for me next to him at the left corner.

It was a typical Carolina scorcher, ninety-eight degrees and a zillion percent humidity. Fishermen lounged around, keeping an eye on the baits while the old-timers reminisced about the huge kings they'd caught before them "damn Yankees" came down and messed up the fishing. As usual, most of them were drinking beer. I sat in the sparse shade of a trash can, sucking on a Coke and cleaning the junk out of my tackle box.

The box used to be my dad's, back when he took time to fish, but now it was mine, along with all the other gear he'd collected before life got too complicated to enjoy. Under a layer of tangled leaders and empty hook cards, I discovered a large lure. It was about a foot long, looked like a blue fish, and weighed nearly a pound. The underside bristled with two enormous treble hooks, dwarfed by an even bigger one dangling from its tail. I cut it loose and held the lure up for inspection. All conversation around me stopped.

"You ain't plannin' on usin' that thing, are ya, kid?" slurred one of the regulars. "If ya are, could be time to get outta the sun. I think yer cheese done slid off yer cracker."

"Uh . . . well," I sputtered, startled by the attention, "I kinda figured I'd see how it moved in the water."

"How it moves? Ha! Did y'all hear that?" he crowed to his inebriated cronies.

"I'll tell ya what, pup," piped his buddy, another red-nosed wonder. "After it smacks the water like a rock throwed off the M-pire State Building . . ." He lost his balance and sat down heavily on a large cooler, but didn't miss a beat, ". . . It's gonna sink like a harpooned balloon!"

The rowdies laughed, spit and slapped white hand-prints on each other's backs as I tied on "Big Blue." I had an audience by the time I was ready to cast. Moving down to a neutral area, I reared back and heaved with all my strength.

I'd never cast anything so heavy, but Big Blue flew like a rocket. An impressive splash marked the spot Blue crashed into the water. Whoops and hollers erupted.

"Don't pay any mind to them fools," Mr. Henry yelled over the din. "Most of them don't have the common sense God gave a mosquito."

I stepped up onto the first board and leaned out. With quick snaps I jerked the rod tip down to the right and left as I reeled in. The plug dove and dodged from side to side, wiggling its tail seductively. Then a tremendous FLASH backlit the lure. A king rushed up to slash at Big Blue. It missed, but another leapt from ambush below. The fish bit down on empty water as Blue managed to elude its toothy mouth.

An astonished crowd packed the railing now, cheering me on, holding their collective breath, and moaning in unison with each strike and miss. By the time the lure had traveled halfway back, four kings were diving and twisting in hot pursuit.

Bullets of advice shot past my ears. "Slow it down. . . . Speed it up. . . . Don't jerk it. . . . Let the danged fish have it, boy!"

Mr. Henry appeared at my side, "Give the boy some room!" he bellowed. Blue, having apparently grown a mind of its own, continued evading the feeding frenzy.

"Okay, Tadpole, all you need to do is snap it a couple more times like you have been," he said gently. "Then hold the rod tip down and reel like the devil. If you're ready, on three, reel for all you're worth."

I nodded my head and snapped the rod down two more times as he counted in my ear. "One . . . two . . . reel boy! Reel!" The crank handle threatened to slip from my sweaty fingers. Six crank revolutions later a king caught Blue from behind.

A cheer punched the air as the hook slammed home. The king became a lightning bolt, ripping a jagged silver path away from the pier. Yards per second screamed off the reel. I held the bent rod high, stumbling down the rail with the fish. "Fish on!" Mr. Henry yelled excitedly. "Clear a path!"

The king cleared the water with a crowd-pleasing leap as line continued to peel off, and the rod butt punched a new belly button in my gut. My skinny arms quivered.

Mr. Henry stood behind me, gripping my belt as I braced against the fish's pull. He told me when to pump and retrieve line and when to let the king run. As I moved with it, Mr. Henry stayed with me. We did a little four-legged shuffle dance as he gave me advice and encouragement.

Young muscles were no match for the power of the fish. My strength evaporated. The rod slipped out of one sweaty hand as my knees buckled. I barely managed to recapture the rod. "This is your fish, Tadpole!" Mr. Henry said, hauling me back up. "It's up to you! Do you want to catch it or let it go?"

My shoulders and back screamed. A big raw spot marked where the rubber rod butt met my stomach. "I want to catch it!" I squeaked, unsure how much more I could take.

"That-a-boy! You can do it! You're almost there, Tadpole; his runs are getting shorter. It won't be long now . . . just tough it out. Anybody got some cold water?"

An obliging man stepped forward and dumped the entire contents of his cooler over my head, soaking Mr. Henry's arms and filling the back of my pants with slush.

Air temporarily deserted my body. "I'm cool! I'm cool!" I gasped when the cold finally released its grip on my lungs. A racking shiver ran up my spine as the ice worked down my pant legs, but the pain was forgotten.

Under Mr. Henry's guidance I horsed in line, bringing the king up to the pier. The battle was won, but the war wasn't over. It was time for the wire basket, which slowly descended, entering the water without a splash. I guided the king over it. A collective intake of breath underlined the silence as the fish approached the basket. It's a wonder the entire railing didn't collapse as everyone leaned over. A touchdown roar rewarded the men who trapped him in the basket and hoisted it and the fish quickly up onto the pier.

The king looked enormous as I collapsed next to the basket. The big fish couldn't have spit out the hook; Blue's hooks were firmly embedded in both sides of its toothy mouth. My arms were numb, so I just sat there, hands in my lap, looking at the fish as people crowded around, slapping me on the back and mussing my hair.

Mr. Henry came over and sat down next to me. "You know, Tadpole, in the sixty or so years I've been fishing off this pier, I've caught a passel of fish. Some bigger, most of them smaller than that monster you've got there. But I think that's the most fun I've ever had."

Years have passed and Mr. Henry is long gone, along with the pier and most of the men who crowded around me that day. I understand now what Mr. Henry was trying to say that day on the pier. I've passed his gift on to a multitude of people over the years—it's the joy of helping someone achieve something they didn't know they could do. I think about Mr. Henry and smile as I share their personal moments of accomplishment. Mr. Henry was right. This is more fun.

I wonder what ever happened to the picture they took of me, Mr. Henry and the king I had caught that day, the one I signed, "To Johnny's: you're the best!"

Banjo Bandolas

Taking Turns

Give what you have. To someone, it may be better than you dare to think.

Henry Wadsworth Longfellow

Neither my eleven-year-old daughter, Maya, nor I were big on fishing, even though we lived near Lake Pend Oreille in Idaho. I preferred kayaking on the lake, and Maya loved horseback riding, spending hours each week on her horse. But one year some friends from Pennsylvania changed our minds about fishing.

Paula and Jake came for a visit right after school let out for the season. Twelve-year-old Jake had saved for months in order to hire a charter fishing boat during their stay in the Sandpoint area. Jake lived for fishing. When Maya taught him to drive our Honda ATV, they stopped down by the creek and cut an alder bough. From his pocket, Jake pulled out some line, showed Maya how to rig it with a hook, and next thing she knew, my daughter was fishing for the first time. Her opportunities were limited in tiny Dunn Creek, but Jake coaxed her to try the real thing. He and his mother had scheduled their fishing trip to leave from Bayview Marina the following morning.

"Come with us," Jake said.

"Sure, why not?" Paula seconded the invitation. "It won't cost any more. The kids will have fun together."

The next day we boarded the boat and headed for deep water. The sky was overcast, and a cold wind kept us huddled against the fiberglass wall of the cabin. The kids chattered over huge rods set into heavy clips at the stern of the charter boat. Jake explained each piece of equipment to Maya, and she nodded solemnly. The boat trolled four rods, and small kokanee salmon hit the line over and over during our first hour on the water. The two young people agreed to take turns reeling in the strikes. The kids tossed them back in; keepers had to top twenty inches.

When the big one hit, our charter boat captain yelled, "Whose turn?"

Maya swung her head toward Jake. It was her turn. She stared at her friend. Though she didn't speak, it seemed she was offering him a chance to snag the action.

"Her turn!" Jake yelled. One corner of his mouth twitched up in a lopsided grin. Maya returned the smile and lunged for the pole.

Paula and I exchanged a look. I was sure our thoughts matched: *This was Jake's trip, and he had paid for it. He ought to be the one reeling in any big catches. Besides, what did Maya know about landing a giant fish?*

I cleared my throat. "Maybe you should let Jake do this one," I said to my daughter.

Maya swung her head and stared at me. Her eyebrows drew together and the freckles on her face stood out against suddenly white skin. She opened her mouth to speak, but Jake cut in.

"No!" he yelled. "Fair's fair. It's her turn. Let her reel it in." His voice cracked, and he shook his head.

Paula shrugged her shoulders. Maya seized the pole as the captain pulled it from its sturdy clip. Jake was everywhere: reeling in lines from the other poles, stowing gear, grabbing a net, leaning over the side of the boat.

"C'mon, Maya! Put some muscle into it!" Jake said.

Maya fought the fish. The sky grew darker and rain spit against the deck. Paula and I kept quiet while the kids ran the show. Thirty minutes dragged by. My daughter's thin arms shook with fatigue. When the captain offered to help, she shook her head.

"I can do it," she said.

"She can do it," Jake agreed. "Just let her do it."

Jake talked Maya through ten more minutes of muscle-numbing work, and then we caught a glimpse of the fish a few yards out. It was burly! Our captain hung over the side, brandishing the net, but all at once the fish dove under the boat.

"Don't let it snap your line!" Jake yelled, leaning so far his feet dangled above the deck. Maya drew a deep breath, and I could see her knuckles were blanched white. Five minutes later, she bullied the fish out from under the boat and our captain swooped in with the net, then dumped a twenty-one-pound rainbow trout onto the deck.

"Whoa!" Jake yelled. The fish flopped while its smooth, speckled skin glistened in the fading rays of evening sun. We all stared in awe at the monster.

"How'd I do?" Maya asked.

"You did great!" Jake said. "Good job!"

My daughter wrapped her shaking arms around Jake, and they hugged each other. Then Maya and Jake stood together holding the fish between them, each gripping the metal hook with one hand and smiling their widest, as all three adults snapped their picture. Later, the kids agreed on a way to split their treasure: Maya would get the meat, while Jake had the carcass mounted for a trophy.

The tender white meat of that trout is long gone, but every time I look at my photo of those two young people holding up their prize, I think about how Jake's generous spirit made them both winners that day.

Ann I. Clizer

Maya, the trophy fish, and Jake—the fish was so heavy that it took both of them to hold it up for the camera.

First Day Fishing

All adventures, especially into new territory, are scary.

Sally Ride, Astronaut

All summer, our six-year-old son Chris had been begging his dad to take him on his first fishing trip. Tomorrow was the big day, but now Ron had to work and the day was ruined. I could see the disappointment in our son's eyes. Choking back the tears, he turned to walk away.

"Wait a minute, Chris," I heard myself say. "Can I take you fishing?"

"Well, uh, okay, Mom," he answered as if he wasn't sure he'd heard me correctly.

"We'll get up at five o'clock in the morning. Is that all right?"

"Sure," he said with a smile quickly replacing his tears.

I should have thought it through more clearly before I had spoken; I hadn't been fishing before either.

The alarm buzzed at 5 A.M. I couldn't remember the last time I'd been up that early. After eating a quick bowl of cereal, we hoisted the ice chest into the car. It was loaded with sandwiches, lots of drinks and plenty of ice to pack all the fish we were going to catch. With a list of things we needed, we headed for the nearest bait and tackle shop to buy a pole, line, hooks and some worms. Then we were off to the lake.

It was a typical August morning with the sun already scorching. We trudged along the rocky shore carrying our gear and finally settled under a "wannabe" tree. I explained to Chris that a wannabe tree is a *want-to-be* tree, because the trees here in Arizona don't grow very big due to the extreme heat and lack of rain. He agreed that the small amount of shade was better than none at all.

I attached the line to the pole and secured the hook with a knot that would have held Moby Dick.

I was dreading the next step.

"Mom, can you put a worm on my hook for me?"

"Okay, but you'd better learn quick. This is my first *and* last time."

All right, I can do this, I thought as I scrunched my eyes shut and quickly grabbed the first worm that unwittingly wriggled between my thumb and forefinger. The next chore was putting the worm on the hook. I didn't know worms came in different sizes; this one was really skinny. Chris stood back, partly because of the look on my face and partly because it amazed him that I'd even dare touch a worm. Chris must have been reading my mind as I wondered how this worm was going to stay on the hook.

"It doesn't want to stay on the hook," he murmured as the worm kept falling off.

Suddenly, quite by accident, I stabbed the worm. There it hung mortally wounded and writhing in pain. "Quick, throw the line into the water!" I screamed. There was no way that Chris was going to be able to skewer these skinny worms onto a hook without hooking himself. The realization that I was going to have to put the rest of these wriggling, slimy little crawlers on the hook for Chris didn't thrill me, but I soon became quite the expert at "accidentally" attaching worms to the hook.

Three hours later and with three small bluegill neatly lined up in the corner of our ice chest, we decided to head for home. The fish had given up trying to make a meal from our "slim" offerings, and the glaring sun had sent them for deeper, cooler water.

Ron was still at work when we arrived home. I was relieved because I was sweaty, smelled of fish, and our meager catch didn't qualify for bragging rights.

"Mom, are we gonna cook 'em?"

"I suppose we could," I grimaced. The thought hadn't even entered my mind. The fish were so puny that we'd be lucky to get more than two small bites out of each one. Nevertheless, I popped them into the pan, and within minutes they were ready to eat. I put all three fish on Chris' plate.

"No, you get one too, Mom," he insisted.

My plan hadn't worked; I was going to have to eat one. Chris took the first bite and didn't spit it out, so I tried a bite too. It tasted just like the fishy lake water, but I forced it down. Ron walked in just as I was taking my last bite.

"Well, how was your trip?" he asked.

Chris began talking before I could swallow my last mouthful.

"It was great, Dad! The water was so clear and smooth, and the sky was really blue. There were no boats when we first got there so it was real quiet. We could hear the birds singing. Mom and I sat on a rock and watched a duck swim and make a trail in the water. It was really fun and Mom was the best!" He then told Ron all about wannabe trees. When he had finished talking, Chris turned and hugged me.

Was the sky that blue? What singing birds? And I hadn't even seen the duck. I had been too engrossed putting the worms on the hook to appreciate the beauty, but Chris had taken it all in.

"Thanks, Mom. Let's go back to our wannabe spot again real soon," he said, his eyes sparkling.

How could I refuse his irresistible offer?

"Yes, we'll go again soon."

Tanya Breed

The Fish That Got Away

*I never caught a little fish—Yes, I am free to say.
It always was the biggest fish I caught that got
away.*

Eugene Field

In 1957, at age six, I caught the first of the only two fish I have ever landed. The Buchanan YMCA in San Francisco's Fillmore District provided a summer day camp that served the neighborhood's inner-city kids. Every week we were introduced to a new outdoor experience. This particular week, two dozen of us visited Muni Pier for a day of fishing.

We loaded onto the Muni bus with our counselor in the lead. She had successfully guided me through several other outdoor adventures, including camping on nearby Mt. Tamalpais, so I was open to letting her teach me what fishing was all about. My entire knowledge of fishing came from having viewed extensive cartoons. I knew that when you caught a fish, the pole would bend, and if you weren't strong enough the fish would pull you in.

We exited the bus at Aquatic Park and paraded down to the pier, which to us was just a long road without cars.

Concrete benches lined the sides, and fishermen had already settled onto each one. They casually gazed out over the San Francisco skyline to the east or at the Golden Gate Bridge to the west.

The chaos began as we found an open spot along the pier. Instead of fishing poles, our counselor pulled out a bag of "drop lines." The drop lines consisted of fishing line wrapped around small square frames with small hooks and weights attached. It was only moments after she distributed the drop lines that the first scream broke the relative stillness of life on the pier. One of the girls had a hook in her finger. It was bleeding profusely, and she was hysterical. Soon, several more of my cohorts came crying to the counselor, all with hooks in their fingers. This was going to be a tough day for all of us.

As I watched our counselor remove the hooks from my friends' fingers, and becoming more and more concerned about this particular outdoor experience, a friendly fisherman sitting nearby pulled me aside. He showed me how to safely put a shrimp on my hook and throw the line into the water. He suggested I keep a finger on the line and said that when I felt several tugs, I should check the line because I might have a fish. As our counselor finally got everyone to settle down, I started thinking we might have some fun after all.

One of the boys caught the first fish of the day. Naturally, we all ran over to witness the excitement and, in the process, allowed several lines to fall into the bay, while others became entangled. We saw the strangest fish ever. It was brown and had a large head and tiny body.

"Oh, that's a bullhead!" our counselor announced.

Even though the fish had no body that could be eaten, the boy kept it anyway.

I went back to my spot on the pier, picked up my line and kept my finger on it, hoping to catch something, too.

Soon, more kids were pulling bullheads out of the bay. I couldn't help but wonder if our equipment prevented us from catching real fish.

All of a sudden, I felt a pull on my line. It was one small tug after another, just like the fisherman had described. I screamed with excitement. Friends and onlookers surrounded me as I began to pull the line in. As it came up, I could see a shiny fish on the hook. I had caught a *real* fish, not one of those bullheads!

My fisherman friend helped me bring it up and over the pier's concrete rail. I grabbed the little fish, which was about the size of my six-year-old hand, and was surprised by its slimy texture and its strength. The fisherman removed the hook and commented that it was a nice shiner perch. I studied one of its eyes, wondering if it was looking back at me. I watched it gasp as I proudly showed it to my friends. When the group's interest had faded, I carefully placed my catch in the pocket of the red-hooded coat I was wearing. Periodically, I would check my pocket to make sure it was still there, each time reliving the excitement of its catch.

The San Francisco fog and westerly winds began to kick up, and soon I sought refuge on a concrete bench along with the other bored and whiny day-campers. The excitement of fishing had passed, and we were all ready to go home.

We retraced our path and left the pier to catch the bus for our return trip. We transferred to the Geary bus, loaded with commuters heading home for the day. The bus riders seemed tolerant of us. A lady smiled at me, the way people tend to do with young children. I smiled back and dipped my hand into my pocket wanting to share with her the excitement of my little shiner perch. As I lifted it up for her to view, rather than the proud look I expected, she gave a look of simultaneous surprise, fear and anger, and knocked the fish out of my hand. It dropped behind a seat and became wedged between the seat and the wall of the bus.

I didn't have time to be angry with her because I was immediately focused on the need to dislodge and retrieve my fish. I was tossed and rocked as the bus made its stops through the city. *I wanted my fish back.* My arm was small enough to fit behind the seat, but it wasn't quite long enough. I stretched with everything I had. I could just feel the tail with my fingertips, but it was too slippery to latch onto.

We arrived at our destination, and after reluctantly extracting my arm from behind the seat, I stepped off the bus with my friends and our counselor, but without my trophy fish. As I dismally watched the bus roar away in a cloud of diesel fumes, my shiner perch lodged behind the seat, I silently made a wish that someone else would rescue my lost fish and enjoy it as much as I had. Who knows . . . wishes sometimes do come true.

Carol Nelson

Monster on a Pink Jig

The last weekend of August, my partner Dave and I had invited our friends John and Nora to join us on a fishing trip on a lake bordering the United States and Canada. Nora was celebrating her fortieth birthday, and it had always been her dream to catch a trophy muskie. As a professional guide, Dave said he would try to help her catch her dream.

After jigging over several reefs, we had a few walleye and perch in the live well. Jigs have a tendency to plant themselves between the cracks and crevices of the rocks below, and often require some skill and luck to free them—or a hard pull to break the line. Nora's jig was fuchsia-colored, her traditional favorite ever since the first time she fished with her husband.

Nora and I both announced that we had caught the bottom again. While I was struggling to free my jig, Nora said, "Oh my God, I've got something! It took off!"

All our eyes followed the direction her rod and line were being pulled—straight toward the rocky, tree-shaded shore. Suddenly, her catch broke out of the water and jumped into the air, spraying showers of water, its rainbow of colors flashing. It was huge!

We all gasped at once, "It's a muskie! Wow! Did you see it?"

"OhmyGodwhatshouldIdo?" Nora said in one word as the monster fish dove deep and fought with all it had. I suddenly felt like I was in slow motion as I continued trying to free my snagged jig from the rocks below, then tried to break the line, finally getting it free and out of the way of the battle that had just begun.

We all gave advice steadily. For nearly fifteen minutes Nora fought the muskie, wore it down and finally led it up next to the boat where the guys (it took both of them) scooped the net around it and hoisted it into the boat. They got it into the live well quickly, after I had taken just one hurried photo of Nora stroking the fish's back, staring at it in total amazement.

The huge fish filled the live well, the few little walleye and perch flipped around near its head and tail as we all stared, trying to steady our shaking hands and slow our racing hearts. We stowed rods and gear to make room in the boat for picture taking, then the guys carefully lifted the muskie and helped Nora hold it while we took more pictures.

They set the fish out flat on the side of the boat where Dave had a thirty-six-inch measuring tape—it was way longer than the tape. It was fifty inches long! The feat that Nora had accomplished was even more amazing considering the fact that she was fishing with a little Berkley rod, a Zebco 220 reel and eight-pound test line. While we weren't able to weigh the fish, some muskie pros estimated it to be between thirty-five and forty pounds. Many people spend a lifetime, and many thousands of dollars on gear and tackle, yet never catch a trophy muskie like this one.

There was a short discussion after the picture taking as to whether Nora should keep the fish and have it mounted. But Nora decided the awesome creature should be returned to the lake, to swim free and maybe give some other fisherman the thrill of a lifetime, or maybe even us, since we knew where it liked to hang out.

Releasing the muskie gave us more time to marvel at its size and beauty. Dave put it in the water, holding its tail gently to prevent the worn-out fish from rolling on its side and dying. After several minutes, it began to recover from the trauma and slowly swam away, waving its red tail at us as it headed home.

Carla Mistic

Nora admires her fortieth birthday present as husband John holds her prized catch.

Reprinted by permission of Carla Mistic, John Mattei and Nora Mattei.

3

SMALL FRIES

*Pretty much all the honest truth-telling there
is in the world is done by children.*

Oliver Wendell Holmes

Counting My Blessings

*I love to fish because it is totally relaxing. I love
the water. I can concentrate and forget all my
worries. I count my blessings while fishing.*
                                             George H. W. Bush

You asked me about fishing. Well, okay, here goes.

I love it. I love fishing for striped bass, bonefish, permit
or char, salmon or blues. I'm no fly-fishing expert, but I'm
getting there. Put me down as a true enthusiast, though—
my favorite is fly-fishing in salt water or in the rushing
Atlantic salmon rivers of Canada. Or maybe it's bass fishing with my sons for striped bass, largemouth bass—why,
any old bass will do.

While I really love going after all these fighting fish, let
me tell you about fishing for the little tinker mackerel here
in the bay by our house in Kennebunkport, Maine. The
mackerel was the first fish I ever went out for, right here,
around 1930, with my granddad. Using a silver jig tied to
the end of a handheld hunk of green cord line, we'd put a
piece of white cloth on the jig and then troll behind the
Tomboy, my granddad's thirty-three-foot boat that looked

just like the Maine lobster boats of today. What memories I have of those days.

The reason I like mackerel fishing is because it's easy. When the fish are running, you can't miss. You can get five at once on a mackerel jig. They hit hard. People on the ranches of Wyoming or Montana would kill to catch trout the size of our larger mackerel. But no one talks about mackerel back at the Links Club. It's always rainbows or browns or cutthroats.

Eating them is another matter—Barbara likes them, but I don't. They're too oily for me. But they are beautiful fish. Caught on a fly, they're really pretty good fighters.

The best mackerel fishing, by far, is when I take a couple of the grandkids out in my new, very fast, thirty-one-foot center-console Fountain fishing boat named *Fidelity II*. I gave the old *Fidelity*, a twenty-eight-foot Cigarette, to my library. It was exactly twenty-five years old. A lot of fascinating calls were made from that great boat, some on secure voice during Desert Storm. The press accused me of "vacationing." No, no—I was laboring away out on *Fidelity*. Okay, so I did take a few fish at the same time!

Anyway, the new Fountain flies and handles big Maine seas with ease. My grandkids love it when we speed to our fishing waters. "C'mon Gampy, let's go fast!" They need to learn the joy of just being out on the sea, watching the gulls, seeing the waves crash against the rocks, waiting for fish to break the water. They need to grow up, but, like any grandparent, I don't want them to do that.

It is heaven to me when my grandson Walker pulls in four squirming mackerel and starts yelling, "I got four! Look at what I caught, Gampy!" When this happens, I remember exactly how I felt when I was his age. I remember it so clearly. I can even see the smile on my grandfather's face.

I'm so much older now, but I don't feel old. I meditate a lot when I am out fishing. I wonder how many more years I will have to fish with my sons, my grandkids.

I count my blessings. I want to keep on fishing.

I want to teach Gigi, my young granddaughter, how to fish. When the fish aren't biting I want to listen to her tell me what makes her happy and what makes her cry.

I won't tell her I was president. I'll just try to tell her about the wonders of life and have her understand that our family is what matters. Out on the boat she is captive. She can squirm, but she can't hide.

I will tell her I love her. And when she asks, "Are you crying?" I'll say, "Yes, but these are tears of joy. Older guys do that, Gigi."

You can do that kind of thing when you go mackerel fishing.

George H. W. Bush

"Come on, Grandpa.
There's still some good ol' days left."

Father Knows Best

I am not young enough to know everything.

Oscar Wilde

Tepid days and cool nights are the greeting cards of summer in the lower Sierra Nevada mountains. What better place to escape the stifling summer heat of the Sacramento Valley? My eight-year-old son Logan, his Uncle Neal and I did just that, traveling to the cooler high country of the Feather River region for some camping and fishing fun.

After setting up, Neal headed upriver to fly-fish the pools and riffles, while Logan and I fished a little closer to camp. It wasn't long before Logan hooked a nice-sized rainbow trout and landed the brilliantly colored prize by himself. His excitement about catching the fish puzzled me.

"Logan, why are you so excited?" I asked.

He looked at me and said with a prideful grin, "Because this is the first fish I ever caught."

"No it isn't. You've caught fish before, even bigger than that one," I reminded him.

"No, Dad," he patiently, but excitedly, explained. "This

is the first fish that *I've* ever caught. You always hooked it and then handed me the pole."

Logan was right—this was the first fish he'd ever caught by himself. But this was just the beginning of the ensuing dilemma.

"So, Logan," I asked, "are you going to throw your fish back so it can live, or are you going to eat that sucker for dinner tonight?"

Logan was perplexed by my question, not knowing how to respond. Very much an animal lover, this was a big decision for him. To help ease his mind, I finally put the fish in an old bucket filled with river water while he pondered his answer.

Over the next half hour, Logan continually talked to the fish, so much so that he and the fish were becoming fast friends. Much to my chagrin of missing a wonderful fish-fry dinner, I figured the fish was going back into the river. But that was okay—it was Logan's fish and Logan's decision.

"Dad, do you think I should throw him back or keep him?" he asked, glancing at the bucket and his new fish friend. It was obvious that Logan didn't want to make the final decision and was hoping I'd do it for him. After a few fatherly moments trying to figure out the best way to help my son with this impasse, I came up with an idea.

"Tell you what, Logan," I said. "If Uncle Neal comes back with a creel full of fish, then we'll keep him. If he doesn't, then we'll throw him back because even though he's a big fish, there's not enough of him to feed all three of us. How does that sound?"

"Oh, that sounds great, Dad!" Logan thanked me and turned to the bucket to share the decision with his friend.

Soon after, a small figure could be seen in the distance— it was Neal slowly working his way downstream. Logan spotted him and took off running. Did Neal have a creel-full or did he get skunked? I looked at Logan's land-locked friend waiting patiently to learn its fate. In a way, I felt sorry for the fish. I was also worried about Logan if his uncle was successful in his outing; would he honor the decision?

When the two were within earshot, Logan was talking excitedly to Neal, telling him all about his catch. Suddenly, Logan darted past me and flashed a grin. *Okay,* I thought, *his friend's going to be saved, returned to its mountain stream for another day and another fisherman.*

As Logan raced by, I looked at a beaming Neal. He opened his creel, showing off a basket full of sparkling rainbow trout, which totally threw me off. I quickly turned to Logan, ready to offer fatherly advice to my dev-astated son.

Logan was on his haunches and staring in the bucket. Knowing his intense love for animals, I waited for Logan to apologize to the fish.

With all the courage he could muster, Logan had only six words for his friend.

"I'm going to eat you, sucker!"

Jeff Wise
As told to Dahlynn McKowen

A Lesson on Faith

Children are likely to live up to what you believe of them.

Lady Bird Johnson

One day last summer my five-year-old son Parker and I decided to go fishing. We picked the perfect day for it. The wind howled at forty miles per hour out of the south, the red dirt blew past, rubbing our skin raw for the eager UV rays, and clouds of mosquitoes parked on our lee side.

Parker had fished before, but hadn't yet developed the same passion for it I had. We'd go to a farm pond, hook on a dab of earthworm, throw Parker's line into the water, and in about three seconds the bobber would go under and Parker would tree-top a three-inch bluegill.

Parker considered all that a great and exciting adventure. Then he was off, throwing rocks in the water, looking for frogs, picking flowers for his mom and generally ignoring this whole process of fishing.

So on this particular day, I resolved to teach Parker a lesson. I wasn't taking him to just any farm pond, but a fisherman's haven—a place by the name of Dewayne's

Pond. What's more, we were leaving the earthworms behind. I brought along a minnow bucket and on the way out of town we stopped at the bait shop and ordered two dozen shiners.

Bass bait.

And that meant bass fishing.

Yes, I had decided that Parker needed to graduate to *real* fishing. I knew there were enough bass in Dewayne's Pond to keep us stepping lively, and I figured Parker might even catch a couple in between me hauling several out on my plastic-worm rig.

I figured wrong. I managed to catch a couple in between all Parker hauled out. And of the twenty or so bass Parker caught that day, two weighed more than two pounds.

"Creel-worthy," I said and put them both on the stringer.

"Wow!" Parker said, "I bet Mom won't believe I caught both of those and you didn't catch any."

"She might," I ventured. "Now hush and try to catch another one."

Parker tried, but he couldn't keep his mind off the two monsters already on the stringer. I could tell, though, that something was beginning to bother him.

"Dad," he said, prodding one of the bass with the end of his fishing pole. "We're taking these home to show Mom, right?"

"Certainly," I said. Parker concentrated on his bobber for a moment.

"How are they going to stay alive?" he asked.

I anticipated his question and congratulated myself for having a ready answer.

"Well," I began, trying to be as gentle as possible, "they aren't. I mean, we're going to clean them when we get home so we can eat them, and they'll have to die then, right?"

"I guess so," Parker replied. He remained silent while he caught a couple more small ones that we threw back.

"Dad," Parker finally said in a small voice, "we'll see these fish again in heaven, won't we?"

This question blindsided me. I didn't know what to say. It wasn't the theological ramifications that stymied me, it was my young son's total faith. I had planned on teaching Parker a fishing lesson, and he turned the tables on me.

"Gee," I said, sheepishly. "I don't know what we'll see in heaven, son."

"I've got an idea," Parker announced.

"Tell it."

"Let's put them back in the pond."

"I'm with you," I said, unsnapping the stringer and letting the two fish slide free. We stood together and watched them swim lazily back into the green depths of the water.

A couple of lessons came my way that day. First, I hope that in my zeal for the outdoors, I never do anything that would diminish Parker's respect for God's creation. And second, I pray I can learn to hold my faith as dear as does my young child.

Keith Long

The Purple Plastic Worm

Watch. Wait. Time will unfold and fulfill its purpose.

Marianne Williamson

Summer of 1973 was the peak of my tomboy years. My family was camping at a nearby state park, enjoying a long, relaxing weekend, far removed from the everyday stresses associated with home and work. I, however, was about to embark on a serious mission. I was determined to earn the respect of my father and younger brother, both avid fishermen, by catching a trophy bass. I also wanted to capture a coveted invitation to participate in their exclusive fishing expeditions.

Throughout that long weekend, I followed my younger brother like an overeager puppy dog. Wherever he and his Zebco went, I trailed behind, determined to be an ideal fishing companion. I refused to complain about biting mosquitoes and pesky gnats, and I kept talking to a minimum so as not to frighten away any fish. I always asked for his sage advice on bait as well as the proper depth at which to fish. And, despite my aversion to night crawlers and crickets, I diligently baited my own hook.

One bright morning, I trotted doggedly behind my brother to a lake near the campground's serene outdoor chapel. I observed my brother tying on a purple plastic worm and immediately followed his lead. He cast expertly into the still water with barely a ripple disturbing the surface. I replicated his every move and breathed a sigh of relief when the line sailed smoothly through the air and landed in the water without incident.

We had been silently casting without so much as a nibble for some time when two older men entered the cove in a well-equipped bass boat. The voices of the fishermen broke our reverie.

"You kids catchin' anything?" one called out.

"No sir," answered my brother, "not a bite."

"Whatch'all usin' for bait?" another asked.

"Purple plastic worms," I responded enthusiastically.

Their guffaws echoed across the peaceful waters. "Well, at least you'll be able to spot them things when you get 'em snagged!"

My brother squared his seven-year-old shoulders and proudly cast his line. At the same moment, I felt a tug on my line. My initial thought was that my purple plastic worm had selected the most inopportune moment to become snagged on an underwater obstacle.

"Hey," I whispered, "I think I'm hung up!"

He groaned. "Geez!" he whispered back. "Just keep reeling and see if you can pull it off. Otherwise, you'll have to break the line." He turned away, ignoring my predicament.

I began reeling desperately, expecting the line to snap at any moment. I felt utterly defeated. There went my opportunity to impress my brother.

"Hey! That ain't no snag," called my brother, who had been secretly watching. "That's a dawggone lunker bass!

Keep reeling!" he commanded excitedly.

Of course, we had once again attracted the attention of our comrades in the boat. They watched in disbelief as my rod bent double with the weight of the fish. I felt a surge of energy as my adrenaline kicked in. I reeled and pulled as I had often seen my brother and father do, silently praying that I had managed to set the hook well, and thankful, too, that we were in such a sacred location near the chapel.

As I got the fish closer to shore, a mighty leap by the finned monster revealed that the plastic worm was precariously close to coming out. I gazed longingly at the slick, silvery body glistening in the early morning sun. Though in reality, the fish was a mere two pounds or so, it was the trophy I sought, and I was going to lose it before I could wrestle it ashore.

Then, without regard for life or limb, my little brother tossed aside his own rod and braved the muddy, murky waters to save not only my fish, but our pride as well. He splashed in the lake and pounced on the bass as I continued reeling.

Moments later, with the fish cradled in his arms, he turned to the fishermen whose mouths remained agape. "Y'all might want to try some of these purple plastic worms."

I smiled proudly at my brother and gathered our tackle. We marched back toward the campsite, my brother refusing to relinquish possession of the fish. As we approached our little pop-up tent, he offered me a dollar to say that he had single-handedly caught the bass. I considered his offer briefly, but then came up with a better deal. He could keep the dollar if he promised that I could go on the next fishing trip with the boys. When we shook on the deal, I had accomplished my goal.

These days, I often join my own son and daughter on

fishing trips with their father. I still recommend purple plastic worms and prayer as the best bait.

Terri Duncan

"Ray? No! Believe it or not, Jason caught it using a toy fishing pole and a piece of Play-Doh as bait!"

The Fishing Lesson

If I'd known grandchildren were going to be so much fun, I'd have had them first.

Bill Laurin

Fishing with my dad was a big event for me, but this trip was going to be extra special, because my grandfather was joining us. Dad and I were in our old Ford truck heading over to pick up Grandpa on our way to the lake. I was so excited to be included in this trip.

"Dad, does Grandpa know how to fish?" I asked.

Dad looked at me and smiled. "Your grandpa taught me how to fish," he said. "And you should know this—Grandpa doesn't like horsing around in the boat."

"Okay," I said. *Wow,* I thought, *Dad catches most of the fish when we go fishing together, and Grandpa taught him how to fish. Grandpa must be the best fishermen ever!*

It was a little crowded in the pickup, but I felt pretty important sitting there between the two of them. They talked most of the way, and I didn't mind much because it was fun listening to them talk about work, and even about Mom and Grandma.

As we pulled up along the lake, Grandpa nudged me and asked, "Who's going to catch the biggest fish today?"

"Me!" I answered.

"Well, we will just have to see about that," Grandpa replied.

While Dad and Grandpa had talked most of the way in the truck, they were very quiet in the boat. Grandpa hooked the first fish, then Dad bested him by two. Me? Not even a nibble.

"Grandpa," I began chattering. "Do you think something is wrong with my bait? I'm not even getting any bites. Maybe I need to do something different. Grandpa, I think I need a new worm. Grandpa, can . . .?"

Grandpa interrupted me. "Raymond, the reason you're not catching fish is because you aren't holding your mouth right." His comment was perplexing to me.

Grandpa ended the day with five fish on the stringer and Dad had four. Dad told Grandpa that it was a tie because one of his had dropped off the hook and bounced inside the boat, but ended up back in the water, so it still counted. Grandpa argued that it's what you end up with that counts, and you can't count fish you can't eat.

Well, needless to say, I had an empty stringer again, and according to our fishing rules the one who catches the least cleans all the fish. It was a chore I didn't mind, but I would have enjoyed it more if just one of the fish had been mine.

Later that evening after supper, while Dad was cleaning out the boat, I went over to him. "Dad, what does holding your mouth right have to do with catching fish?"

Dad stopped hosing out the boat and looked at me, seeming rather surprised I had asked the question.

"Raymond, I will let you in on a little secret that I had to learn the hard way from Grandpa. But don't tell him I told you, okay?" he said.

We sat down and he explained that when he was about my age and wasn't catching fish, Grandpa told him he wasn't holding his mouth right. So one day while fishing, Dad began making all kinds of faces. After a few minutes of silence, Grandpa turned to see why my dad had become so quiet and saw him making all those silly faces.

"Charles," he asked my dad, "what in the name of God is wrong with your face?"

Dad explained that he was trying to find which way to hold his mouth so he could catch fish. Grandpa started laughing so hard he nearly tipped the boat over.

My dad finally explained it to me: "Raymond, what your grandpa meant was that I was talking too much. When you're fishing, the way to hold your mouth is *closed*.

"Why?" I asked.

He explained that when I talk too much, the noise moves my fishing pole, making the line vibrate and scaring the fish. At least that was Grandpa's theory.

"But don't tell Grandpa I told you so," Dad warned me again.

"How long was it before Grandpa told you?" I asked.

Dad chuckled again. "Well," he said, "I can tell you I got pretty good at cleaning fish, just like you."

All that winter I thought about what Dad had told me, and it felt pretty cool that I knew the secret. When spring came, all three of us once again went fishing. Dad and Grandpa were quietly talking in the back of the boat and I was in the front when I felt a fish strike, so I gave my line a little tug. They never even noticed. I knew I had one hooked, but I didn't call out to them just yet.

It was then I started making all the weird faces I could muster. Finally, they both stopped talking and looked at me.

"Look at your son's face," Grandpa said. "What in the

world is he doing?" They both started laughing.

At that moment, I jerked back on my pole and yelled out, "I GOT ONE!" They both stopped laughing.

I was even in for a little surprise. That fish jumped clean up out of the water and skipped across the top of the lake, then my reel screamed as it took out more line. I fought that fish back and forth for what seemed forever. When I finally got the fish in the boat, Grandpa and Dad were both speechless.

"Yep, guess you just got to hold your mouth right!" I said.

Grandpa cleaned fish that night, including my five-and-a-half-pound rainbow trout. Dad said later that it was bigger than anything either he or Grandpa had ever caught.

Raymond Morehead

A Sacred Part of Fatherhood

Keep your fears to yourself, but share your courage with others.

Robert Louis Stevenson

No one ever told me that when I became a father I would have to touch fish.

"Hurry, Dad, it's gonna get away," my eight-year-old son complained.

We'd gotten up way too early for being on vacation, but Brandon wanted to catch his first fish. He'd been talking about it nonstop for weeks. My head was foggy, and I had a sharp pain in my sternum. We'd been hunched over the railing of the local pier for two hours, and the top rail had etched a permanent mark in my chest. The smell from the sardine scales on my hands, coupled with the sight of the seagull droppings all over the pier, was making me a little nauseated.

I've already touched the sardines, isn't that enough! I screamed inside.

Imagine my surprise when the weather-beaten old man who ran the pier sold me the bait. "Those are dead fish!" I protested.

"They're sardines," he instructed. "Best darn thing for catching mackerel." After receiving a complete lesson in how to cut up the sardines and bait the hook, I was sent off to the chopping station.

I had been anxious all morning over what I was going to do if we caught a fish. How was I going to get it off the hook? Ever since I was a boy, I'd been afraid of fish. The first fish I ever caught was a sunny, and when I tried to take it off the hook I got spined. I had never gotten over the fear.

I must have baited our hooks more than thirty times. If we stood on the bottom rail and leaned out far enough we could see the fish nibbling at our bait. Suddenly one latched on. I reeled in the fish, and we both stood frozen, staring at it.

"Hurry, Dad, it's gonna get away. Get it off!"

I just stood there, frozen, holding the fishing pole. I looked like one of those posed suits of armor in a museum, except that I had a flailing mackerel on the end of my lance. People were beginning to stare.

In the softest, most soothing voice I could muster, I said, "Okay Brandon, I want you to grab the fish around its middle, and then carefully take the hook out of its mouth."

He took a step back. "I can't. I'm afraid."

I was stunned. It was as if I was looking at myself thirty years ago. My throat tightened. My son had thirty years of fear ahead of him. Thirty years of struggling with loving to fish, but not being able to take his catch off the hook. Thirty years of snickers over his innovative ways of removing a fish from a hook without having to actually touch it. Thirty years of shame.

The prospect of it was more than I could bare. In disbelief, I heard myself saying, "It's okay, son, there's nothing to be afraid of."

Brandon watched in awe as I firmly gripped the six-inch mackerel around its middle. He took a step closer. The mackerel's eyes bulged slightly from the pressure, and its mouth opened wide. It was as if the fish were helping me. It felt natural. I removed the hook from the fish's lip with ease and rested the pole against the rail.

"Dad, can I hold it?"

It was tricky, but I handed off the prize to my eager son. When he was through admiring his first catch, Brandon agreed that we should throw it back. We leaned over the rail and watched it swim away.

As we packed up our gear, Brandon asked, "Dad? When you were my age, were you afraid of fish?"

"A little. But I got over it, just like you."

Peter Balsino

The Midnight Fish

*F*riendships that have stood the test of time and change are surely the best.

Joseph Parry

I was eleven years old when we moved to the large, long house next to the sea. Our new house seemed to have draped itself over the grassy dunes that slid onto the beach, and to us children it felt as though the house had always stood there—airy, cool and homey. Its wooden floors were stained dark by a decade of saltwater-wet feet, and when we were bored we would make a game of imagining the people who had left their mahogany shadow imprints on the wheat-gold floors.

One of our new neighbors was a tanned blond boy, whom I met when I fell into an elephant trap he had built. I was scuffing along the beach when the warm sand disappeared from under my feet, and I fell into a damp, sandy pit. I landed hard, and while I was trying to collect my scattered wits, a head of white-blond hair appeared over the edge of the hole.

"A girl," announced the blond head, obviously disappointed with this worthless catch. The head paused, deep in thought, and then added, "You're new—who are you?"

"We've just moved into the house on the end there," I answered, with as much dignity as I could muster under the circumstances.

The head studied me for a minute, then stated, as though I was being granted a favor, "I'll pull you out."

So began a relationship that many saw as highly unsuitable; a wild tomboy (me), mixing with the town's spoiled bad boy. We drove our respective parents to despair.

One morning Andy (the elephant-trap builder and my new bosom buddy) suggested we go and fish out in the bay. Andy had received the enviable present of a small rowboat for Christmas, and he was longing to try out the newly named *Armada* on a more daring challenge than the lagoon (as dictated by our parents). I was dutifully enthusiastic about fishing in the bay, and suggested we do it after dark, seeing as we had both been threatened with a fate worse than death if we took the *Armada* out of the safety of the lagoon.

That afternoon we dragged the *Armada* up the beach and hid her in the bushes next to the lifeguards' hut. Andy and I parted at six, each with our tasks firmly established. I was to prepare the refreshments for the trip, while Andy had to smuggle the rods and fishing box out of the house. I was secretly more than a little worried about the dangers of the open sea, especially at night, and terrifying visions of sharks kept me awake for nearly an hour before I could sleep.

With a hollow stomach, I met Andy just before half-past eleven, and after a whispered greeting and an appraisal of my choice of snacks, we launched the brave boat. Andy took the oars and began to row us out of the lagoon mouth into the dark waters of the bay. It was very spooky—no human sounds except Andy's breathy grunts as he strained against the oars, while the cicadas buzzed in the thick bush around the beach.

After a while, Andy stopped rowing and let the boat drift lazily in the current. The moon had come up, and in the silver and black shadows we ate the frankfurters and biscuits that I had brought. Feeling refreshed, we prepared our rods, baited our hooks and cast off into the dark water. We sat there for a while like two silent statues, neither of us speaking, when, with a jolt, all hell was let loose.

Andy's line gave a sudden buck in his hands, and his reel began spinning violently. We saw the flicker of a small, glittering fish, about as long as my father's hand, leaping on the end of his line. Then something happened that I have never seen again, and which today I can only wonder about. As Andy reeled in the fish, we saw a silver flash streak up through the water and make a grab at the smaller fish. The water turned dark with blood, and then Andy was straining against a different fish than the one he had first caught; a larger, bulkier fish, with snapping jaws and a thrashing sickle of a tail. I could see Andy was having trouble keeping hold of his precious rod, and the *Armada* was rocking precariously.

"Let go of the rod, Andy, let go!" I shouted, clutching the sides of the boat.

"Are you crazy?" snarled Andy through clenched teeth. "This rod cost me a small fortune, and I want that fish!"

"Andy, the boat's going to overturn. This is no time to haggle about the price of a rod!" I screeched. At that moment, Andy's rod ran out of line and the tug-of-war became a battle of muscle alone.

Soon Andy's feet were bleeding from raw blisters as he tried to gain a grip against the wooden sides of the boat. He continued to ignore my frantic pleas that he drop his rod, forget the fish and just get us home to safety. All his efforts were directed at landing the fish. It was only after I had been clutching the heaving sides of the boat for what seemed hours that I realized we were no longer tossing in the gentle waters of the bay. We were out on the open sea, where the waves were slower but much, much bigger, and where there was no comforting green shoreline on three sides of the boat. After a particularly rough session, when Andy and the fish jerked each other backwards and forwards, nearly overturning the *Armada* in the process, the movement stopped abruptly, and the whisper of the quiet roared in my ears.

"Where's it gone, Andy?" I whispered.

"I don't know," he replied, "but it's still there. My line's still tight."

As he finished his sentence, there was a loud splash to the right of the boat. The fish leapt high out of the water and threw its full weight backwards in a dive that left us both soaking. With a sharp crack, Andy's line snapped in two and whistled into the waves after the silver shape. We sat there, stunned into silence, before Andy spoke in a hoarse voice.

"Guess we'd better be getting back."

I felt strangely embarrassed at being there to witness his loss and humiliation, and I just nodded dumbly.

When he looked around us, Andy couldn't believe how far we'd been dragged by the fish, and because his hands were bleeding and stiff, I changed seats with him to sit next to the oars and row us home. It seemed like hours later, when, having taken turns to row through the rolling waves, we were able to glide into the shelter of the lagoon and wade out onto the sand, dragging the boat behind us. We unpacked our fishing tackle in silence.

As we drudged up the sandy path, I could see that my family's curtains were drawn back. They were awake and surely knew that I was gone. Andy and I parted outside my house, wishing each other good luck in facing the inevitable music.

There was a strained hush as I entered the kitchen, rod in hand. Stern eyes turned to survey the tattered individual that stood there. Mother's eyes flicked from my blistered feet to my raw hands and hot, dirty face, and then looked meaningfully at my father, who had opened his mouth to speak.

"Where on earth have you been?" he asked in his deepest, slowest, most dreaded tone.

"Fishing with Andy. We got dragged out to sea by this huge fish and we couldn't get back," I gabbled.

My father looked at my exhausted face and tried to suppress his smile. "What will you and that Johnson boy get up to next?" he sighed. I shrugged and shuffled away upstairs, thanking an unknown God for my parents, who remembered what it was like to be children.

Gaynor E. Lawson

Biblical Interpretations

Shortly after our daughter Nicole was born, father-daughter fishing trips became a regular occurrence. We would most often fish from my little aluminum boat at a small, shallow lake near our house. By age three, Nicole had an uncanny ability to sit in our boat for long periods, certain that a fish would bite at any moment.

Our family has also always been actively involved with our local church. One Sunday when we went to pick up our daughter from her Sunday school class, the teacher asked if we could meet with her for a moment afterwards.

Every parent knows that instant of dread associated with wondering what your three-year-old may have said or done to someone. We mustered up our courage and waited.

Finally, alone with her teacher, the truth came out. The week's memory verse was James 1:19. *Be slow to anger.* When the teacher asked the children if anyone could explain what that passage meant, Nicole's hand shot up:

"It means that when you go fishing," our daughter explained, "you crawl to the front of the boat and put the front *anger* down very slowly." Nicole continued, "Then you crawl to the back of the boat and put the back *anger* down very slowly. That way, you don't make a splash and scare the fish away."

Dan DeVries

"I don't want to go in the water—
That man said the fish are really biting today!"

Reprinted by permission of Patrick Hardin.

Wallet Whopper

Reminders about the little things in life are important to me. For instance, each time I open my billfold, which happens often, I smile upon photographs of my two towheaded granddaughters, Emily and Sarah, beaming in their frilly dresses and coifed Shirley Temple ringlets. The two always elicit "How adorable!" and "You must be a proud grandfather" from those who chance to see their photos. Little do they know that another young child's photograph is also in this senior's wallet, that of a ten-year-old boy proudly holding a prized rainbow trout.

That skinny kid, hair slicked back, wearing a striped T-shirt and Cheshire cat grin, is me. Faded and dog-eared after forty or so years, the photo delightfully casts my memories back to that fateful day when a skinny kid from Sacramento ascended one step closer to becoming a man.

In the 1950s, life was carefree and innocent—summer vacation from school and work fit the bill for children and parents alike. My family favored picturesque Lake Tahoe for our summer ventures, staying in a cabin on the north side of the popular Sierra Nevada tourist destination.

Lake Tahoe was the ideal vacation retreat, especially for myself, my younger brother Bob and the many fast friends we made each year during our weeklong stays. Biking, exploring, boating, fishing, hiking, and just getting into good, clean mischief were rules of the week, rules that we preteen guys reveled in and lived by.

At the midpoint of our annual summer vacation, Bob and I had attempted, and fairly accomplished, all the "cool-guy-things" to do at Lake Tahoe. Our adolescent boredom began filling the cabin. Our folks had reached their vacation midpoint, and their breaking point of parental patience. They shooed us both out the door, fishing gear in hand. We reluctantly headed to the dock, formulating what trouble we could brew.

At the dock, we haphazardly threw our lines into the crystal blue water and continued our planning. While we'd been known to catch an occasional trout or groupie from the shore over our many summers there as we fledging fishermen grew, the fingerlings we once excitedly landed were now embarrassing to be seen reeling in. Our egos only catered to big fish, and this trip was not any different. Catches thus far were nothing spectacular, and we decided the lack of "big ones" was attributable to the moon or something like that and certainly not to our fishing expertise.

As the two of us put the finishing touches on a brilliant scheme to cause some pre-teenage ruckus at the nearby bait store, my pole suddenly jumped right out of my hands and onto the dock, snagging itself on the railing. We both jumped, first from sheer surprise and then from sheer excitement. As Bob grabbed the net, I quickly retrieved my pole and attempted to set the hook, a fishing tactic my father could do effortlessly, but for a ten-year-old boy, it was an attempt in futility. Having no luck, but still feeling the fish tugging on my line, I let it run with the line, trying to wear it out while giving me time to think, which was hard to do since Bob was yelling and jumping about, quickly attracting a crowd around us. All eyes were on me—from fellow fishermen and curious tourists—ready to judge my fishing prowess and the wiggling prize on the other end of my line.

Determined not to let this one get away, I planted my feet firmly onto the dock, reeled in the slack and then gave a quick snap of the pole to make sure the hook had dug itself deep into the mouth of my adversary. After what seemed like an eternity, the fish arced out of the clear water, its brilliant rainbow body reflecting in the summer sun. I had finally set the hook! The fish returned to its aquatic realm with a great crescendo, only to reappear even more magnificently on its next attempt to gain freedom. I worked the pole and the fish quite flawlessly, to the wonder and enjoyment of the growing crowd.

Nearly fifteen minutes had passed since the fish first struck, and by now my shoulders and arms were nearing exhaustion—but if the fighter on the other end of my line wasn't going to give up, then neither was I. Bob pleaded to have a go-around with the "lake monster," as the crowd was now calling it, and several adults offered to help land the fish. There was no way I was going to give up this prize, no way. This monster was mine.

Suddenly, as if for no other reason than our mutual exhaustion, the line suddenly went limp and the horror of the "big one that got away" leapt into my stomach. *How could this happen! I did everything right,* or so I had thought. As the disappointed crowd started to fade, Bob shouted with glee! There, on the end of my line the trout had surfaced and surrendered itself to my fisherman's will. I had won!

I reeled the weakened fish into Bob's waiting net, then pulled the four-pound prize out by its gills for all to see and admire. The waning crowd quickly reassembled, delivered their congratulations and took numerous photos. I was the hero-of-the-hour, having landed the largest fish off that dock all season. I was proud of my accomplishment and could hardly wait to share the feat with my parents.

So, whenever I open my billfold, I reminisce about that wonderful day when a bored adolescent, in an attempt to quell the summertime blues, received a little reminder from Mother Nature herself—enjoy your youth and its special moments, for they may never come along again.

Gaylord Moulds

Gaylord with the "wallet whopper"
that cured his summertime blues (c. 1952).

Reprinted by permission of Gaylord Moulds.

Boys' Day Out

After the greatest clouds, the sun.
Alan of Lille

"Man Crippled in Fishing Accident, Nowhere Near Water." The headline flashed across my mind as I reached for the practice lure. The orb hung there, just beyond my grasp, like a defiant Day-Glo orange Christmas ornament. I heard a creaking sound. Whether it was the limb I was standing on or my knees, I couldn't be sure. But I knew my nearly forty-something, two-hundred-pound body had no business being there. I shot a quick glance through the branches below. Graham and Anders, my five-year-old twins, stood there shoulder-to-shoulder, squinting up at me in awe and with more than a little amusement.

"Maybe we should come up, too?" Anders asked hopefully.

"No, I think I've almost got it," I lied.

The cast that sent me up a tree occurred minutes into the boys' first fishing lesson.

"Watch this," Graham said, whipping the rod forward and releasing the button on his tiny new reel. We watched the lure arc from his rod tip, rise and disappear into the foliage. *Should have bought more lures,* I thought. At the same time, I couldn't help but admire the distance.

So there I was, thirty feet off the ground, perched on a magnolia limb no thicker than my wrist. Stretching to the brink of shoulder dislocation, I was finally able to grab the lure and snap the line. I stuffed it into my pocket and climbed back down, trying to make it look easy.

Other than climbing trees to untangle a few dozen monofilament bird nests, the practice session went well. I knew of a small stretch of trout stream about an hour away that would be just right for our first *real* fishing trip. I promised to take them the following weekend.

The big day began at 5:30 A.M. I put coffee on and crept upstairs to confront the first obstacle I'd face with my new fishing buddies; the boys aren't what you'd call morning people. By the time I'd dressed their somniferous little bodies and strapped them in their booster seats, we were an hour behind schedule. The boys finally woke as I parked on the shoulder of the dirt road that meandered alongside the creek.

I assembled their gear beside the car while they munched bananas and Pop-Tarts. The next order of business was to teach them how to bait live night crawlers. We live in the city, so their experience at handling wild animals of any sort was, shall we say, limited. I assured them that worms were "friendly," but they had absolutely no interest in holding onto the slippery little guys. And the idea of stabbing their new friends to death with a hook was even less appealing, especially over breakfast. I switched them to the default bait, canned yellow corn. We gathered our stuff and headed down the path toward the creek. We'd covered less than twenty yards when I heard a scream behind me.

"Daddeeeeee!"

I whirled and saw Anders, wide-eyed, frozen in place. He was pointing, like a miniature grim reaper, at a fallen tree beside the path.

"Don't move," I said.

As calmly as I could, I walked back to him, fully expecting a water moccasin or a swarm of hornets. I followed Anders's stare down the log until my eyes finally rested on the object of his terror; a millipede was inching its way along the tree trunk. To a child who'd never encountered anything more menacing than a cockroach, it must have looked like some horrible interplanetary creature waiting to pounce with all thousand legs on the next small boy who wandered by.

"It's just a millipede," I said. "It won't bite."

I leaned down and touched its back to show him, then turned to tell Graham to come over and look. He was already on his way, brandishing a large stone. For some reason, the compassion he felt for earthworms was totally lost on invertebrates with legs.

"Let's kill it," he said.

"Leave it be," I said. "Let's go catch some trout."

Unfortunately, while searching for his antimillipede missile, Graham had left his rod and reel in the woods. I had the boys stay on the path while I kicked through piles of leaves and brambles. In the few minutes it took to locate and extract the rod from a bed of poison ivy, the sky darkened considerably. Then it started to rain. Hard. And with that, our planned assault on the trout population of the creek turned into a full-scale amphibious retreat back to the car.

We piled, soaking, into our seats. "Aren't we going fishing?" they asked in almost perfect unison. Two small chins started to tremble.

"Tell you what," I said. "Let's go for a ride and see if this lets up." For the next two hours, we cruised through the downpour and a maze of gravel U.S. Forest Service roads, taking careful aim at every puddle. As the boys discussed the morning's events and needled each other about mis- placed tackle and multilegged beasts, their moods light- ened considerably. The rain finally stopped, but I knew the creek would be too high and muddy for fishing.

Just as I was about to point our car back toward the highway and break the news, I saw a sign: "Stocked Pond—Rainbow Trout by the Pound." I pulled in. For the avid fisherman, the "stocked pond" isn't exactly sporting. The pond was about the size of your average backyard pool, and with all of the rippling, flashing and finning, it looked like you could walk straight across it on the backs of all those trout without getting wet. We grabbed our gear and baited up. It took less than ten minutes for each of the boys to hook and land a monster rainbow.

While one brother (with a little help) wrestled his prize into the net, the other slipped and slid on the wet bank, shouting at the top of his lungs, "Reel him faster! Don't let go! You got him!"

The pond's owner weighed and cleaned the trout, then put the pink slabs on ice for us. We loaded up and headed for home. By the time we reached the highway, the twins were asleep, each with an arm draped across the cooler that rested between them.

Not the day I'd planned, but I couldn't have scripted a better ending. A few small adventures, a slight case of poison ivy (mine) and two trophy-sized rainbow trout— much larger than anything I'd ever caught in a stream. The bill was a whopper too, about five times what we'd pay for trout at the market.

Best money I ever spent.

Robby Russell

4

TICKLE MY FUNNY BONE

*You can't deny laughter; when it comes,
it plops down in your favorite chair and
stays as long as it wants.*

Stephen King

Kiss 'n' Tell

If you watch my TV shows, you'll see me kiss the bass I catch before I release them. That's become something of a Jimmy Houston trademark, and folks are always asking me how I came up with the idea.

I've got to say I honestly can't remember. It just happened spontaneously one day, and when I saw what it looked like on film, I decided the gesture really does convey my gratitude to whatever bass are nice enough to jump on my line.

By the way, that's how I tell the sex of a fish. If it's a female, she'll pucker up *before* I kiss her. If he's a male, he'll pucker *after* I kiss him.

Folks also ask what my wife thinks about me coming home with my breath smelling of fish. Chris says that considering the possible alternatives, it had better be fish I smell of!

Jimmy Houston and Steven D. Price

Jimmy Houston puckering up
to one of his TV show guests.

Reprinted by permission of Ken Conlee. ©2000 Ken Conlee.

Hooking Greenbacks

Nature provides exceptions to every rule.

Margaret Fuller

In 1988, I took my twelve-year-old son Jason on one of our annual father-son summer vacations to Yellowstone National Park. It was an exceptionally hot summer, the same year the great fires swept through.

Jason and I had already been fishing inside the national park, where there were lots of rules protecting the fisheries. With few exceptions, only lures and flies could be used. Dead or live bait was taboo. We'd fished the Madison, Gibbon and Yellowstone Rivers, and Jason tried to blame his lack of success on his fishing pole. I had to admit his old spinning rod had seen better days.

One morning we left the park and drove about twenty miles out to Hebgen Lake. The idea was to rent a boat and try some trolling. As it turned out, a strong wind kicked up by the time we arrived, and the lake was much too choppy for fishing. Jason and I tried fishing from the dock in the marina's sheltered waters. A short while later I headed up to the marina's combination bar, restaurant and tackle store to meet an old friend and enjoy a cold brew.

My friend asked about Jason.

"Yeah, he's down on the dock, catching some strange-looking fish," I said, "and he's still complaining about that old fishing pole of his."

Someone else piped up, suggesting I buy the kid a new one.

"Oh, I will, but I was holding off until his birthday next month," I answered.

About fifteen minutes had passed when we heard someone running up the wooden ramp to the side screen door that led to where we were sitting.

"Dad! Dad!" Jason yelled as he burst through the door. He was carrying his old fishing pole with something dangling from his hook. "Look what I caught!" he exclaimed. He was grinning from ear to ear.

Several of the bar regulars and I did double-takes at his prize catch. There—green, dripping wet, but the real thing—was a twenty-dollar bill attached to his hook.

I must say, the sight of that greenback immediately grabbed our attention. I surmised that Jason must have spotted the bill in the clear water while standing on the dock and used his lure to drag the bill across the lake bottom to shore. He then stuck it on his hook for a more dramatic presentation, and it worked! Jason turned and quickly headed back outside, obviously still excited. He said something about catching enough money so he could buy that new fishing pole. I remember quite a few chuckles at the bar.

Ten minutes hadn't passed when Jason returned with another dripping wet twenty-dollar bill attached to his hook. We made him show us the first one to be sure he wasn't pulling some kind of practical joke. The chuckles turned to laughter, with more than one of the regulars looking out the window toward the dock.

Jason quickly unhooked the second soggy twenty-dollar bill, stuffed it into his pocket with the first and ran back out the door and down the ramp with his fishing pole in hand. When he returned ten minutes later with a wet ten-dollar bill attached to the same hook, a couple of the bar regulars quickly downed their beers and cleared out, we assumed to get their own fishing poles. But by that time Jason had snagged all the greenbacks out of the old marina fishing hole, and there was nothing left but those strange fish.

Someone took a Polaroid picture of Jason proudly posing with his fishing pole and greenbacks and added it to the bulletin board that displayed other lucky Hebgen Lake anglers proudly showing off their catches.

I took Jason back to West Yellowstone where he bought that new fishing pole, and we returned to Yellowstone National Park so he could break it in on the real thing. The good news was that Jason's luck changed. Although he didn't spot any more greenbacks, he did out-fish me during the remainder of our father-son vacation. I still grin every time I remember that picture on the marina bulletin board of Jason holding his greenbacks alongside photos of other fishermen holding their trophy fish. You have to wonder who had been the most excited.

I returned to Hebgen Lake and the same marina about twelve years later and the photo was still there. Today, I have it as a souvenir from that most memorable trip.

Ken McKowen

Jason shows everyone the money.

The Boss Who Hated Fishing

Conform and be dull.

Frank Dobie

We were on a small party boat fishing for salmon off the Oregon coast. Fishing was slow, but my father and I, two of a party of six, had each caught one. The others were still trying for theirs when the captain suddenly emerged from the cabin with a question.

"Is there someone aboard named Pierpoint?" he asked.

When I answered that there were two fishermen aboard by that name, he said the Coast Guard had called with a message. Dread hit both of us with our wives still ashore in the port of Gold Beach. Had something happened to them? Then the captain explained that the Coast Guard had requested that Mr. Pierpoint call his boss in Washington, D.C., as soon as he hit shore. As a White House correspondent for CBS News, that had to be me. I was relieved.

My naïve assumption was that something had happened at the White House that required my expertise. But that was not the boss's message. No, he said that Dan

Rather's grandmother had died, and Rather had to go to the funeral in Texas. Rather also covered the White House, and the boss said this meant I was to cancel my long-planned fishing vacation and return immediately, which I did. I got the impression that the boss didn't care for fishing vacations.

This lesson was reinforced on my next fishing vacation to northwest Montana with my wife to fish for trout on the Swan River. Our guide was a local veteran fisherman with the improbable name of Muggs Huff. After the second day on the river we returned to our small hotel in Big Fork to find a message from Washington. "Please call the boss, immediately." I knew what that meant, and this time I was not about to cut short our much-anticipated vacation. So the three of us held a caucus and decided to revolt.

I asked the lady running the hotel to please deny that we ever got the message from Washington. Muggs knew a pilot who would fly a small plane into a grassy landing strip in the Bob Marshall Wilderness, and he also knew a local from the Kalispell who ran a camp near the airstrip. Muggs arranged the whole thing, and the next morning at dawn we were headed over the mountains. The pilot had to chase a moose off the airstrip before we could land, but we made it. The camp owner, who had been alerted by radio, met us and transported our gear a half-mile or so to one of his tents. There we spent a wonderful week—fishing, riding horseback and hearing no phones ring.

When we returned to the hotel the manager said that, after a couple of phone calls, my boss had given up trying to locate us. It all worked so well that I decided to write a story for an outdoor magazine on how to get away from a boss who doesn't like fishing vacations. I submitted the piece, complete with names and details, to *Field and Stream* magazine, and a short time later the publication sent me a sizable check. For the next several months I kept buying copies of *Field and Stream,* hoping to see my story. It never appeared.

Finally, in frustration, I put in a personal call to the editor. When he came on the line he said, rather gruffly, "Pierpoint, didn't you know *Field and Stream* is owned by CBS!"

I didn't know. Furthermore, I didn't ask why he had paid for the piece if he was not going to print it. That I did not want to know. Anyway, the check had already been cashed.

Robert Pierpoint

A Day to Remember

As a fishing guide in the icy cold waters of southeast Alaska, I can remember a great many wonderful memories that all are worthy of telling. What stands out most of all is a day of fishing in 1996, when Mother Nature did everything in her power to keep us from taking her fish.

From the start, I should have gotten an idea of what was to come. We had finally hooked up to one of the prized king salmon that anglers from all over the country come to Alaska to catch. I stood on the swim step of my boat, net at the ready as the rod pressure brought the fish closer and closer. *Almost there, almost . . .*

Suddenly, a huge brown streak raced by from the side, directly at both me and the king salmon I was about to net! I recoiled crazily, and, of course, fell backward into the boat and into my surprised guests. Don, a guest I had fished with for many years, caught me just in time to prevent a nasty fall.

In the meantime, the determined gal with the fishing rod was not about to give up her fish—even to the huge denizen of the deep that was so obviously coming for it. She pulled mightily this way and that, trying to drag the salmon away from the monster that was chasing it.

Finally, I recovered from my own ordeal, regained my composure and assessed the situation. The sea lion (not Jaws, as I had first thought) finally caught up with the unfortunate salmon and promptly bit it in half.

"Reel! Reel quick!" I shouted, hoping to salvage at least half of the fish.

But it was not to be. After eating the tail half of the salmon, the beast returned for the head half just as I was reaching out with the net again. Not at all about to test the daggerlike teeth of the creature, I retreated into the boat, this time much more gracefully. We watched as it carefully chewed around the head, eyeing us balefully the entire time. When it was finished, we reeled in a very squashed and sorry-looking salmon head.

The sea lion followed us for a few minutes, hoping we would hook another fish, but it would get nothing more from us! I pulled in the gear and headed for another area. If only I had known what was to come, I might have taken my chances with the sea lion.

We hooked fish immediately after setting lines at the new location, and after boating a few small silver and king salmon, we took another strike. This fish took out a good deal of line, and I could tell by the way the fish was pulling that it was a good-sized pink salmon. The man who was up was an elderly gentleman who had caught a good many salmon with us in the past. His method was to concentrate solely on the rod tip, and when a fish was on, he was all seriousness.

As was my custom, I looked back to see the fish and what it was doing, and as I did, I noticed one of the many bald eagles glide off a tall treetop and soar our way.

"Do eagles ever take your fish?" Don asked me, for he too had seen the eagle.

"No, they . . . ," I started to say, but never finished as the eagle went into an amazing dive *right at our fish!* I couldn't believe it as the eagle hit the water with an incredible splash, hooked its talons into the six-pound salmon and pushed upwards with its powerful wings.

Never before had I seen such a sight. The flasher was lifted free of the water behind the hooked salmon, flashing and spinning in the air behind the ascending eagle!

Now the elderly gentleman had no idea what was going on, despite our shouts, as he was concentrating on the rod tip no matter what distractions might come his way. I will never forget the look on his face as the line began pulling his rod tip *upward* instead of down. Stunned eyes followed the line higher and higher, his mouth forming a huge "O." The expression of confusion and disbelief tripled when he finally got a look at his fish being carried away by the bald eagle. Somehow, the eagle managed to break the twenty-pound test line and carried its prize safely back to its nest.

We resumed fishing, deciding that the sight of such an occurrence was more than worth the loss of another fish. But nature wasn't done with us yet! Despite the obstacles we were encountering, the fish were biting well, and we soon had nearly a dozen salmon in the cooler. Stopping at a well-known spot, we added several nice halibut as well.

Our nice, sunny, calm day suddenly shifted when a cold north wind pushed us farther out to sea. Fighting heavy seas back toward the lodge, I looked back when I heard a strange thump behind me.

In disbelief, I saw that one of the halibuts had miraculously flipped open the cooler lid with its powerful tail, and as we rode the waves up and down, the salmon were sloshing out of the cooler and back into the ocean in a steady stream!

I shut the boat down and ran out to tie the cooler lid shut just as the halibut made a tremendous effort and propelled itself upward and out, landing with a loud splash in the freedom of the sea! I groaned when I beheld the cooler, now totally devoid of fish. Mother Nature had indeed taken her fish back. We didn't have a single fish, despite an entire day of effort.

I still smile whenever I see a sea lion head our way or an eagle perched high in a tree above us. The memories will always be there—and they always give me something to talk about with my guests.

Mike Duby

Gimme a Call!

Never let the fear of striking out get in your way.

Babe Ruth

A few years back I was working as a physician's assistant at a rural New York health clinic. A doctor who was relatively new to the area was taking a tour of our facility when I met him in the hall. He wore a baseball cap with the word "TROUT" sewn across the front of it. After we were introduced, I said, "I assume you fish?"

"Yes, I do," he replied.

"Would you be interested in going fishing with me sometime?" I asked. "I just got into fishing recently, and I'd like to go with someone who knows what they're doing."

"Sure," he said. "Give me a call sometime and we'll go!"

On my way home from work that night, I thought about all the times I'd made tentative plans to get together with someone and never followed up on them. *This time I'm going to do it,* I thought. So as soon as I got home, I looked up his name in the phone book and called him. When he answered the phone I said: "Hi, this is

Mark. I was thinking we should make plans to go fishing instead of just talking about it. How about tomorrow morning?"

The phone connection wasn't very good, but I heard him respond, "Good idea. Where do you want to go?"

"We could take my canoe up the Susquehanna River," I suggested.

"Well, do you have hip waders?" he asked.

"No, but I have some knee-high boots."

"Okay," he said. "But how about meeting at my house and we could go trout fishing in the creek nearby instead of hassling with your canoe?" I liked his suggestion better. He then gave me directions to his house and told me to be there by 6 A.M.

The next morning, I followed his directions and found myself driving my pickup down the driveway of a beautiful estate. Usually new doctors are weighed down with a couple hundred thousand dollars worth of school loans, so I was surprised by these surroundings. As I pulled up next to the house, he came out to meet me. In the twilight of dawn and without his cap, he looked different than he had the day before. I was startled to see that he had gray hair.

"Hello," he said. "Why don't we take my van? It has all my fishing gear in it."

"Okay," I agreed.

"I'll be back in a minute; I have to get something." He disappeared into the house and returned a few minutes later with a pair of hip waders. "What size shoe do you wear?"

"Nine-and-a-half."

"Well, these are a ten. I came across them at a yard sale the other day. They must have been meant for you!"

I thanked him and we both got into the van. It was then we looked at each other close-up for the first time that morning. The mystified look on his face must have mirrored my own.

"I don't know you!" I exclaimed.

"And I certainly don't know you!" he replied.

"So I didn't meet you at the clinic yesterday?" I asked.

"No. I thought you were the guy I sat next to at a fly tying class I took a couple of years ago. I couldn't remember his name, but he had said we should go fishing sometime."

It turned out I had dialed the wrong number by one digit and connected with another fisherman who lived about five miles from the doctor I had originally met. The mistakenly identified fisherman and I went fishing anyway. It turned out that we had a lot in common, so we had a great time.

I learned a lot about fishing from him, gained a pair of old hip waders and made a new friend.

Mark VanLaeys
As told to Emily VanLaeys

Fish Tacos

*Just as in cooking there's no such thing as a
little garlic, in fishing there's no such thing as
a little drag.*

H. G. Tapply

Oh, how my dad loved to fish! He fished when it was
hot enough to fry eggs on the road beside his favorite hole
along the Yellowstone River. He fished when the ice flows
were challenging the accuracy of his fly casting.

For my dad's birthday one year, instead of a gift, I gave
him myself for two hours as designated rower of his boat
on any river of his choosing.

He opened up his present and laughed. "I have just the
place for that trip. We can float and talk and watch the fall
colors together on the Yellowstone River, and it's only a
two-hour trip, no more." This suited me fine, since I didn't
care for the sport.

Our chosen day was beautiful, the air cool but not cold.
The sky was the blue that only a clear, cloudless day in
Montana can offer. As we launched the boat I looked at
my watch and sighed to myself. It was ten o'clock in the

morning. If everything worked out I'd be pulling this boat out of the Yellowstone River around noon. My old man was happier than a dog with a new bone. Wearing his new vest from my mom and his new hat from my sister, he looked great standing there wedged into his casting station.

"Here's my offer," I said. "You get me off this river by noon and I'll buy the tacos. Later than noon and you're buying. Deal?"

"Deal," Dad said.

With a devilish grin, he asked if I wanted to fish while he rowed. Just for that I gave one of the oars a good pull and almost tipped him into the river. We both laughed. I watched as my dad cast his line out. His casts were that of a master. Quickly he started pulling in fish. He loved the excitement of the fish hitting his flies and didn't care if the fish stayed on the line or not. Fishing had been a lifelong project for him; he first learned how to fly-fish as a young boy in Minnesota, and sixty years later he was still fly-fishing.

Dad knew the river well, and he knew each hole with intimate detail.

"This hole has a great fish in it. A great big one that broke my line before," he'd say. Or, "See that ripple up ahead. There's a big ol' rock behind it, and we need to steer clear of it."

The morning was great, and as we drifted downriver I watched my dad and the birds in the sky, and otherwise kept myself entertained as best I could. People who knew my father and me laughed because of the differences in speed. My father was the turtle and I was the hare.

I had made the taco bet because I wanted tacos for lunch, and I didn't mind paying if it meant spending only two hours on the river. I was positive I could get us down that river in record time. With me working the oars, my dad did the casting. I kept moving the boat along, but I didn't seem to be making the kind of progress I thought I should be making. The river was flowing really well, but the boat seemed to be moving too slowly. I was also having some trouble controlling the boat.

"Everything okay back there?" I asked my dad.

"Yup, everything's okay. You're doing great. No problems."

He cast out his line. It was obvious he was having a really good time. I wasn't having a really good time. I was struggling. I felt like I was trapped like a rat in a maze. But it was a maze of my own creation since I had volunteered for the job.

It was funny thinking about the two of us. My father was in heaven, fishing away. I was in hell rowing like a madman trying to get us off that river within two hours, watching debris float down the river faster than we were. I decided to make the best of my punishment. I turned it into time with my father on the Yellowstone River.

I bounced off a few rocks that I should have missed. "You sure we're doing okay?" I asked again.

My dad looked around us again. "Yup. We're doing great."

Cool. Old age has to be mellowing him a bit after all, I said to myself. On previous trips when I hit rocks that hard I'd get the "Dad look." Everybody alive knows it—the look that makes anyone of any age feel like they're three years old again. I looked at my watch, "Dang." We were only two-thirds of the way to the end. I looked up at my dad. "It's noon; you're buying."

"Really!" he said in disbelief. "Look again. You've got to be wrong."

"Nope," I said. "It's twelve, and I'm getting hungry."

I knew where we were, and I knew the end was near. I felt like a marathon runner. I checked my reserves of strength and recommitted my tired arms to the task of getting this stupid, broken-down, miserable boat to the end of the line. Another really frustrating and torturous half-hour, and I was able to get our boat to the bank where I could back the truck up to it.

As I cranked the winch to pull the boat onto the trailer, I noticed my dad at the back of the boat doing something.

"Dad, what are you doing back there?" I yelled to him.

"Nothing! Just keep winching her up."

I continued cranking, but the boat felt awkward. I stopped and went back to see what my father was doing.

My father, who loved fishing more than anything, was trying to hide his secret weapon—a large tin can filled with cement was hanging over the back of the boat!

"What's that?" I asked.

"Nothing!" he said.

"I can't believe it! You just made me row that dumb boat for two-and-a-half hours dragging that anchor in the water the whole time, didn't you?"

He was caught and he knew it.

"I did," he said sheepishly. "But I lost the bet, so I'm buying the tacos!"

Joseph T. Lair

Killer Catfish

My father's uncle, Ed, was a huge bear of a man with a deep rolling voice and a love for storytelling. When I was a kid, Ed and his wife Nedie would watch me while my parents were at work.

At the beginning of summer, when I was six, Ed brought home a little plastic wading pool. I loved to swim and would sit in it until my skin pruned up. Ed would sneak up behind me and pinch me on the back, "Don't let them big catfish get you," he'd say, laughing his booming laugh.

Ed's passion was fishing, and his favorite quarry was catfish. I was a little guy back then, and he was always telling me stories about him and my dad catching fish as big as I was. I laughed, knowing that he was kidding. My family fished in the river behind our house all the time, and I'd never seen anybody catch anything bigger than my arm.

Ed kept all of his fishing supplies in the detached garage, which was usually locked. One day, when Ed was preparing for a big fishing trip, he left the side door open. I had been swimming and was trying to convince Tippy, Ed's little dog, that she wanted to swim, too.

Tippy had other plans and ran off, straight into the

garage. I was sopping wet as I ran across the driveway, the soles of my feet barely registering on the points of the rough gravel beneath them. I pushed the door open and ran in, making it to the center of the garage before the door shut behind me. A row of small windows allowed a bit of light in, hardly enough to find the little fur-ball that was hiding under a worktable on the far side of the building. I ran over and picked her up, scolding her for running away when, all of a sudden, my eyes fell on a monster far uglier than any previously envisioned by my six-year-old brain. I turned toward the door, and there was another one, and another! I was surrounded by dozens of them, all with their mouths hanging open and murder in their glassy eyes. I screamed and ran. Tippy squirmed out of my hands in the confusion and ran between my legs. In my mind her wet fur was the whisker of the giant catfish, and I was crying in terror as I burst out the garage door.

Ed came out of the house to see what all of the fuss was about and discovered me lying on the ground, crying and shivering.

"What's the matter?" he asked.

"There're monsters in your garage," I said through my sobs. "You said if I kept swimming the catfish would get me, but I didn't believe you. Then I was swimming, and I wanted Tippy to swim too, but she ran away, and I went to get her, and the giant catfish attacked me."

Ed looked toward the garage, and then back at me shivering on the ground. He tried hard not to laugh, but I could see it creeping into his eyes. The longer he looked at me, the harder it was for him to keep a straight face. Finally, his laughter broke loose. I couldn't understand how he could think that this was funny.

"They almost ate me up," I wailed.

This caused Ed to shake so violently that tears spilled from the corners of his eyes. He grabbed his side and struggled to stand upright, but every time he saw the serious look on my face, he would double up again.

As Ed convulsed, I forgot about how scared I was. His laughter had that effect. He laughed so deeply and so hard that it was impossible to resist, and by the time he collected himself, I was giggling right along with him.

Ed picked me up and took me back into the garage, this time with the big overhead door open. The sun streaming in gave me a better view of the "monsters." They were the preserved and mounted heads of all his biggest catches. He took me around to look at all the fish, telling me where and when he'd caught each one. Then he took me into the backyard and put Tippy and me into the belly of his aluminum fishing boat. He grabbed hold of the anchor rope and pulled us around the yard until I had forgotten how scared I'd been.

The last time I saw Ed, we were in the visiting room of his nursing home. Alzheimer's had taken his memory, and he hadn't been able to recognize people for quite some time, but sitting there, with a spring breeze blowing in the window, he began to mumble. On and on he went, until the sounds he made took on a familiar cadence. Occasionally he would raise his head and smile or burst out laughing. As I left he was sitting in the chair, his eyes closed, grinning from ear to ear. I couldn't understand his words, but I think he was telling me stories—tales about huge catfish, scared little boys and boat rides in the backyard.

Robert Spencer

Fish Punks

Every year, my dad, affectionately called the "Fish Master," goes on a weeklong executive fishing trip to the Kenai Peninsula in Alaska. This is no ordinary fishing trip. It's an all-inclusive, cigar-smoking, hanging-with-the-guys salmon fishing trip. It usually consists of my dad, a few of his close friends and some family members.

Last year my cousin Pete and I were invited. We were instantly coined the "Fish Punks," partially because Pete hadn't fished since summer camp, and I hadn't reached "Fish Master" status yet at the ripe old age of twenty-six.

In my mind, this was going to be the best seven days of salmon fishing in the world. We started out each morning with a gourmet breakfast at 4:30 A.M., and then tour guides picked us up and drove us to the river, where we were separated into small boats to fish. Thousands of salmon were spawning; you could almost reach in and grab one. We usually caught our limits by 7:30 A.M., then it was on to bowling and the movies, ending with a dinner and a few rounds of drinks at the local night spot.

After a few days of reveling in this, we chartered a small seaplane to take us across Cook Inlet to a remote river site in search of a true wilderness experience and more of the greatest fishing on earth.

Roll call included the "Fish Master," my uncle, a judge, an attorney and us, the Fish Punks, who brought up the rear carrying all the gear. The guide and his black Lab, Buddy, met us at the airport. They lived in a tent next to the river and guided city tourists like us into unforgettable, amazing backwoods fishing holes.

One night, at about 11:30 P.M. (Alaskan dusk time), our guide asked if anyone wanted to fish at a secret hole upriver. Room was limited, so two members of our group would not be able to go. Relegated to the bottom of the fishing totem pole, Pete and I were left behind.

After a bit, Pete and I became bored and decided to fish off the banks about one hundred yards downriver from our tents. We felt confident with our fishing abilities and secure with my field training in the army.

So, on a quiet summer evening, two Fish Punks were on their own in the woods. Two trumpeter swans trumpeted overhead, two beavers beavered across the river; it was a scene out of Noah's ark. I had my line in the water trying to catch that champion king salmon and become a "Fish Master," when all of a sudden we heard some loud ruffling in the bushes across the river. Just as I yelled "Fish on!" Pete yelled, "Bear!"

I wasn't giving up a potential trophy salmon because of some bear across the river, even if it stood ten feet tall. I saw the bear look across the river at me with a fish on my line, then at Pete who was freaking out. The bear didn't seem to have any interest in the beavers, which didn't bode well for us.

Pete dropped his fishing pole and ran off, quickly returning with a chain saw he tried to start. *Rummmm ummm mm . . . spatter spatter . . . Rummmm ummmm cough, puff, ummmm rumm hmmmmmmmm.* Finally, he got it going.

The bear remained on his side of the river, just a stone's throw away; I was still yards downriver fighting my champion salmon. The swans flew overhead, the beavers hid under a fallen tree in the river. The bear calmly went about his bear business, then disappeared back in the bushes.

Pete killed the chainsaw and ran to where I was still trying to land my fish. My heart raced as I reeled it in: a midsized, nothing-spectacular fish! I started to unhook it, feeling pangs of disappointment, until I noticed a rainbow hue reflecting in the water. It was a champion-sized Dolly Vardon trout. A glimmer of hope returned. I ended up catching that fish—it was the biggest one caught in the river that season. And to think I might have forgone the opportunity to avoid an old bear.

The fellas came home with a boatload of fish. We told the guide our story about the bear, and he laughed, saying it was probably a beaver, not a bear. Even so, he suggested putting the fish in garbage bags and leaving them in the boat on the riverside to protect them from the bear or other hungry animals.

John, the attorney, decided he would stand guard all night to protect the fish from whatever might steal them—just him and his old buddy Jack Daniels. He set up a lounge chair next to the fire as the rest of us settled into our small tents for the night.

In the morning, we were awakened by Buddy's barking and our guide yelling, "Get out of here!" The ruckus was accompanied by several gunshots. I jumped up and ran out of the tent to witness a huge brown bear running away with a bag of fish over its shoulder looking like Santa scurrying off to deliver Christmas presents. In his other paw he had a six-pack of beer to wash it all down, or at least it seemed so in my state of drowsiness.

We all regrouped around the remainder of the campfire.

The fish guard was happily laid out, fast asleep, on his very comfortable beach chair. We saw the bear's footprints walking through camp: *step, step, step, step over John, step, step, step, bag of fish, turn around, step, step, dropped parts of fish, step over John, step, step, bear scrambles, step, run, running full speed from the crazy shooting man and the barking black Lab.*

John swore he hadn't fallen asleep while protecting our catch. Since we know all attorneys are true to their word, it must have been the bear that finished the bottle of J.D.

Rod Scott

Buzz Bombs

As kids growing up in the small coastal community of Powell River, British Columbia, my friend Ryan and I took all kinds of odd jobs to earn spending money. We mowed lawns, stacked firewood, washed cars and stayed on the lookout for anything else that could net us a few dollars.

But our favorite scheme, by far, was selling Buzz Bombs.

At the time, there were plenty of salmon to be caught in the Strait of Georgia, and the Buzz Bomb was the best lure for catching them. It was a simple white lure shaped like an elongated diamond, and Ryan and I had both caught some good-eating salmon using it.

Our favorite fishing spot was just off the end of a rocky point, and we often rowed there in Ryan's grandfather's old wooden rowboat to jig or troll. It was easy to lose a lure by snagging it on the rocky bottom or in the thick beds of kelp. Most fishermen lost one or two every time they fished there. One day Ryan had the idea of diving for lost lures and selling them for fifty cents—half of what the general store charged for them.

So a few times each summer, we would don swim trunks and diving masks, anchor the rowboat off the point in about ten feet of water, and dive for Buzz Bombs. I can still remember the sunlight sparkling through the clear water and dancing on the smooth rocks at the bottom, revealing waving anemones, colonies of mussels and the occasional darting school of herring. There were always plenty of lures—mostly Buzz Bombs—wedged between the rocks, along with other assorted treasures like sunglasses and cans of pop.

At the end of a successful lure-hunting expedition, we would arrange our wares on a log near the road where the fishermen parked their cars. Then we would sit behind the log, a couple of eager salesmen waiting for customers.

One Saturday afternoon when business was slow, Ryan and I wandered down the beach to build a log fort when we spotted a man dragging a ten-foot aluminum boat out of the water. We raced back to our "shop" and crossed our fingers as he set down the boat and approached us.

He was a massive, muscle-bound fellow with a bushy beard and sunburned face. I grew nervous when he demanded in a booming voice, "What have you got there?"

"Lures for just fifty cents," Ryan squeaked. "Half price and they're hardly used."

"I can see that," the man snapped gruffly. He towered above us, eyeing the lures with a disapproving scowl, and the three of us stood for a moment in awkward silence.

Among the twenty or so different lures on the log, half were white Buzz Bombs, with the exception of one I had found earlier that day. It, too, was white, but had a pink stripe down each side. Our massive customer's eyes seized on this pink-and-white Buzz Bomb, and he picked it up, turned it over wonderingly between his giant fingers, then fixed me with a startlingly ferocious glare.

"This is my lure!" he snarled. "Where did you get it?"

I cleared my throat, reeling in terror. "It was . . . it was on the bottom. . . ." I stammered, wondering what he would do to me, the boy who had taken his lure.

"We found it," Ryan piped up, nervous yet defiant, "so it's ours to sell."

"Is it really?" the big man growled with a sneer. He lowered his head until our faces were inches apart. He narrowed his dark eyes. I swallowed and prepared to die.

With a quick glance at the lure in his hand, the man whispered, "I paint the stripes on the side with a pink marker. Caught a twelve-pounder with one of these once. You better not tell anyone how I do it or there won't be any fish left."

Ryan and I stared as he dropped the pink-and-white Buzz Bomb into his pocket, then brought out two one-dollar bills and placed them on the log.

"Will that cover it?" he asked in a voice that was suddenly warm and friendly.

We nodded, speechless. With a wink, the man turned and walked back to his boat.

Curtis Foreman

Naming Worms

The great man is he who does not lose his child-like heart.

Mencius

I think my dad wanted a son. Instead, he got three daughters. Seeing as how the son he anticipated was never forthcoming, Dad decided to improvise and I, being his youngest, won the privilege of being nurtured outdoors.

Being turned into a tomboy didn't bother me in the least. I loved putting on my plaid, flannel shirt and doing things outside with Dad, especially fishing. Whether we oared across a lake in a rowboat or hiked down a cliff with nothing more than a hook and some string, I could think of no better way for a dad and his little girl to spend the day.

I would marvel at how patient and focused Dad was when he fished. He would concentrate on his line for hours at a time. If he was any more calm, he would have slipped into a coma. This used to drive me bananas. Being seven years old, I craved more excitement. I imagined a huge fish, bigger than me, gulping down my bait and flapping ferociously in the water until I heroically hauled it into the rowboat. This never happened. Instead, I would spend my time watching Dad as he stared intently at his line. He never blinked, sometimes for the whole day. How could he be so patient?

One day Dad's patience was put to the test when my fascination shifted from the fish to the bait. While waiting for a nibble on my line, I peeked into the can of worms we had in the rowboat with us. I dug my little fingers into the moist soil and pulled a resisting worm from his burrow. I let him squirm (I decided it was a "he") across my hand. It tickled. I took another worm from the can. Then another. Then another. Soon, three or four worm heads popped out of the soil to see what all the commotion was about. I was in love.

I felt as though I had made a can-full of new friends that would keep me company during these long, uneventful fishing trips. Each worm was given a name according to his personality. When you are seven years old, worms have personalities. There was something endearing about my mucous-covered companions with no faces. I promised each of them that not one would be put on a hook and fed to the fish.

Then disaster struck. Dad pulled Hamilton out of the can. I gasped in horror as he attempted to manipulate his poor, writhing body onto a hook. There was a terrified look where Hamilton's face would have been, if he had a face.

"Daddy, No! Don't put Hamilton on the hook! He's my favorite!"

Dad raised an eyebrow. "You named the worm?" he asked in disbelief.

Exhaling and shaking his head, Dad pulled out another worm. It was Wigglesworth. He was the skittish one who was particularly worried about being used as bait. I had made a special promise to him and could not possibly allow the poor little guy to be hooked, for I was a woman of my word.

"That's Wigglesworth! Don't hurt him!"

Dad's frustration grew as he pulled more worms from the can. First Winthrop, the shy worm. Then Slimey, the friendly worm. And Marvin the show-off. Finally, Dad pulled out Maxwell, Sammy, O'Reilly, Buster and Doug. Dad groaned as I pleaded for him to not hurt my friends.

"Don't tell me you named *all* of the worms in this can."

With a sheepish nod, our fishing trip was suddenly over.

The next day, Dad drove into town and picked up a bucket of crawfish. When he brought them back to the cottage, I opened the lid and peeked in. I heard a despairing yelp emerge from his throat—I turned around to see him running frantically toward me, with his arms flailing and a look of terror on his face.

"No! You have to quit making friends with the bait!"

Allison McWood

5

FAMILY TIES

The family is one of nature's masterpieces.

George Santayana

A Father's Love

Nothing is impossible for a willing heart.

John Heywood

Nearly fifty years ago, during one of my summer college vacations, my father drove me to my favorite fishing spot at Candlewood Lake in western Connecticut. The winding country road paralleled a beautiful little stream, about thirty feet wide, which flowed into the lake. As I soaked up the passing scenery, I decided to tell him about an idea I had been visualizing for several weeks, even if he thought it was outrageous.

We had taken this route many times before and had established a now-familiar routine. My father would bring me to the lake, carry my wheelchair to an easy location at the water's edge and then carry me to my wheelchair. He'd make one more trip from the car to bring me my fishing rod, spinning reel and tackle box, which also contained my snack. My mother was sure I'd get hungry.

Despite my cerebral palsy, I had found unique ways to cast my lure between fifty and one hundred feet. The biggest trick was how to hang onto the line after releasing the bail, and then let go of it at the right moment while casting. Believe me, there was a lot of trial and error in the backyard before I finally got the technique just right.

Truthfully, I never cared whether I caught any fish or not. I wanted to be out in nature by myself for awhile, just like other people. My father, another nature lover, understood perfectly well and, by mutual agreement, he would leave me at the lake for three or four hours before returning to pick me up. Only once did he have to return earlier than planned because of a sudden downpour; I was pretty wet by the time he arrived, but it really didn't matter. In fact, it was fun.

But on this particular day I asked him to pull over to the side of the road where we could easily see the gently moving stream.

"See that big rock out there in the middle?" I asked him.

"That flat one?" my father asked.

I had a hunch he knew what I was going to ask next. "Yes. Do you think you could carry me out there?"

He laughed at first, then said, "Let me take a look." I watched him walk to the edge of the stream, scouting for a way to step from rock to rock without getting wet. Then he began stepping carefully across the water until he was on my desired location. Though getting there did not look easy, he didn't get wet and it was obvious, as he looked all around, that he enjoyed the short journey. When he came back to the car, he said, "So you really want to fish out there?"

"Yes, I'd love to. I've always envied guys who fish standing in the water up to their knees or higher in the middle of a fast-moving stream. Several weeks ago, when we drove by here, I noticed that rock and thought it looked perfect for me, if you can just get me out there."

"Well, I'm game if you are," he said. So we began our routine, but in a different location this time. I watched him set up my wheelchair in the middle of the rock, making sure to put the brakes on, a very necessary precaution, especially in this case. Then he came back for me. Truly, I was a little scared as we went from one small rock to another because he could not use his arms for balancing as needed, but we somehow made it across the water. We were both relieved when I was sitting safely in my chair. After bringing me my usual equipment, he said he would return in a couple of hours.

And then I was alone.

The sounds of the rushing water got louder and it seemed to flow faster, as if saying, *"What are you doing out here?"* But I knew it was only my imagination and some of my fear of being there all by myself. "What ifs" began popping into my consciousness: *What if Moby Dick grabs my lure and pulls me off this rock? What if the water rises? What if someone sees me out here and calls the fire or police department to rescue me?* I quickly told myself how silly I was being and started appreciating how awesome the site truly was.

I began fishing and noticed that I could let the water's current carry my lure away instead of me casting it. I liked that. Fishermen really don't want to work too hard. Reeling it back to me was easy, despite the tug of the current, and I soon felt wonderfully calm as my lure went out and back, out and back. It was a beautiful day, and time flew by.

My father came back for me a little early that afternoon, but it didn't matter. I hadn't caught a thing, except great personal satisfaction from fulfilling a small dream. I also gained an awareness of how much my father loved me. He demonstrated it many times throughout my life, willingly taking risks for me, so that I too might experience what everyone else does.

Donald Zimmermann

Summer Memories

The first duty of love is to listen.

Paul Tillich

The sun was barely peeking above the mountains when we arrived at the harbor. Once we had gathered our gear, purchased fishing licenses and paid for the rental boat, the two of us headed for the dock. I couldn't help but notice the smile on Dad's face as we climbed into the aluminum vessel. After we settled into the small boat, Dad pulled the starter cord on the outboard motor and guided us into open water. Inside, my heart was jumping for joy. This was a rare opportunity for me to spend time alone with my hero. Opting to sleep in, Mom and my sister Rochelle declined the offer of going fishing at 5:30 A.M.

It has been our family's custom since my birth to go on a weeklong summer trip every year. This year we had once again decided upon the beauty of Canada. Our fishing gear was brought along instinctively. Dad knew that his girls would want to catch some fish before the end of the week. Today was no exception, and I had been anxious to try Dad's new fishing pole since the day we arrived.

"Better hold on to your hat, Harmony. Otherwise the wind will take it away," he said, laughing above the roar of the boat.

"I'm trying!" I squealed, attempting to hang onto my hat and the edge of the boat simultaneously.

For the next twenty minutes we glided across the lake's still surface in search of a choice place to fish. I began watching my father closely as if I was staring at a new man. A big grin stretched across his now peaceful face. In his eyes, I saw a rare sparkle. *Maybe*, I thought, *this is his way of truly relaxing and winding down.*

Dad was always a man who appreciated the outdoors and took any opportunity, on trips such as these, to expose his family to the natural world. Yet, despite his enjoyment of nature, his job kept him busy and constantly out of state. At least every other month he'd leave on a business trip lasting anywhere from three days to a full week.

"When is Daddy coming home?" I often asked my mom. Every day I'd repeat my question, wishing that he would arrive soon and once again fill our house with his presence. Sometimes I would even secretly wonder if he would ever come back, but when he finally walked in the front door, the rest of that day was like Christmas for me.

"This looks like a good spot," Dad said, breaking the silence of my reflections.

Excitedly, I clamored to find a spot next to him as I watched him tie on the hooks and attach bait to them. I begged to use his new pole, and he let me try it out for a few casts.

"Dad," I asked, "when do you have to go back to work?" I watched carefully as he lifted his eyes to look at me. His carefree smile faded.

"A couple days after we get back, honey."

He suddenly looked much older.

"Why?" he inquired.

"I just wanted to know," I said, groping to find the right words. Suddenly, I felt the strongest need in my eleven years of life to be reassured by my father. I spoke the words that I had tried to say just moments before.

"Dad, do you miss us a lot when you go away?"

Concern now filled his handsome hazel eyes as he began to understand where I was headed. He shifted himself closer to me and took my hand in his as I set the fishing pole down.

"Harmony, I miss all of you very much when I have to travel," he said. "Even though you're asleep, I come into your rooms at night to kiss you and Rochelle before I leave. I call you as often as I can while I'm gone. I love you, Harmony. I want to spend more time with you, Rochelle and your mom. That's why I bring you guys on these vacations. I know I'm gone quite a bit, but you know that I would never leave you, right?" he questioned as he squeezed my hand.

"Yes, I know! I love you, Daddy," I said. Relief flooded through me as I threw my arms around him and laughed. "Thanks for bringing me out here today."

He hugged me back and squeezed tight as he gently replied, "I love you too, Harmony. Thank you for coming with me."

As my dad held me in his arms I could see the sun in the distance, rising above his shoulder and the mountains also, ever brightening the pristine sky. *Thank you God*, I said silently. *What a beautiful day, and I have the greatest dad to share it with!*

The rest of the morning we spent laughing as Dad poked fun at my inability to cast the line as gracefully as he could. I pointed out that he, as the more experienced fisherman, hadn't caught a single fish, so he was in no position to tease. When we finally decided to head back after three hours on the lake, we had only caught two pike, and both of us were thoroughly hungry. Yet that did not really matter to me as I pondered the time Dad and I had spent together, realizing suddenly that a deeper hunger had been filled. The man I loved most had shared a part of himself with me this day, and that I can never forget. Those nagging doubts that can fill a child's mind were now completely dispelled.

Now, more than six years later, that day still comes back to me as vividly as if I were still out upon the lake with him. Though Dad's busy work schedule has become more time-consuming, I am quite satisfied with the relationship we share. He still tells me he loves me, hugs me tight and is a continually supportive father and husband. We even talk about that day we spent together on the lake, recalling the things we had said and done.

"That was a good day, wasn't it, Harmony?" he says, as a glow fills his eyes again. I can't help but smile.

"It sure was, Dad. Our fishing experiences have always been good." As I near adulthood, in my heart I remember that summer day in 1996 as the best fishing memory Dad and I will ever share. No words need to be spoken for what the heart already knows.

Harmony Zieman

Grandma's Catfish

What can one do with the past? Let it enter into you in peace.

Iris Murdoch

I was living my dream, working as a state park ranger in Lake Tahoe, California. I spent my spare hours cross-country and downhill skiing during winter and fishing the nearby Sierra streams all summer and fall.

My mother lived in Sacramento, the hot valley a short two-hour drive from the high country. She called me one day and said that my grandmother's already frail health had taken a major turn for the worse. My grandfather had died years before, and now the doctors were saying they didn't expect Grandma to live past the end of the day. I headed down the mountain.

When I arrived at the nursing home, I was welcomed by several members of the staff who told me of a near miracle. When informed about the promised arrival of her first and favorite grandson, Grandma suddenly grew stronger. When I entered her room, she looked up at me, her eyes instantly brightened, and she squeezed my hand as I hugged her. Her voice grew stronger as she spoke to me, telling me how excited she was to see me. We chatted for awhile as my mind raced back over the years. She and Grandpa had taught me to fish, first on the local rivers and sloughs, then at Clear Lake where they lived following Grandpa's retirement, a two-hour drive west into the coastal mountains from Sacramento.

Her smile suddenly broke into a big grin. "Do you remember that big old catfish that broke my fishing line?" she asked.

I assured her that it was a summer morning I would always remember. She insisted that I retell the story for the benefit of the staff who had gathered around to witness her miracle recovery. I thought about that day more than twenty years earlier and launched into the tale:

Early one summer morning, Grandpa, Grandma and I loaded ourselves and our fishing gear into their small wooden boat. The air was crisp and clean as I let my hand hang over the side and splash in the cool water during the torturously slow, five-mile-per-hour ride out of the marina toward the main lake. My ten-year-old patience was really being tested. Soon enough we were speeding through the open water, finally turning up into a narrow, tule-lined slough where we coasted to a stop. Grandpa tossed the homemade anchor—a coffee can full of concrete—into the water.

We baited our hooks and cast them into the water, setting the bright red and white plastic bobbers so the chunks of old, smelly bait hung just off the bottom of the shallow greenish water—there was nothing clear about Clear Lake's water. We soon caught several channel cats, some reaching a pound or so.

Suddenly, Grandma's bobber dove underwater. A huge blue catfish had grabbed her bait and headed up the slough. Grandma got really excited having such a big fish on her line, yelling for Grandpa to grab the net. It was the biggest fish she'd caught since the five-pound bass she's landed the year before. Just as the battle got going, she moaned disappointment when her line snapped—but it broke above her big red and white plastic bobber. After it appeared that the bobber and her trophy catfish had headed for deeper water and safety, it happened! Her bobber popped back to the surface and began circling about ten feet from the side of our boat. Grandma still had her fish!

"Grab my bobber, Kenny, hurry!" Grandma frantically yelled to me. "Get him before he gets away!" She was trying to stand in the small rocking boat, pointing to the erratically darting bobber. I was stretching out as far as my short arm could reach, but the bobber was starting to move farther away, and with it any chance of me grabbing her errant fish.

"Walter, you start that motor!" she yelled at my grandfather in her excitement. "Get us closer so Kenny can grab it!"

Grandpa rolled his eyes, but after several yanks on the starting rope, fired up the boat motor.

"Hurry up, Walter, you're going to let him get away!"

Grandpa began maneuvering around closer to the fleeing bobber that periodically disappeared underwater, only to reappear farther away several seconds later. Every time the bobber reappeared, Grandma pointed in another direction and yelled at Grandpa that he was going the wrong way. Grandpa would mumble something about not being able to read Grandma's mind, let alone the fish's mind, then he'd reverse direction and head toward the bobber's last known location. Finally Grandpa got lucky: The fish turned the wrong way and headed at us.

"Kenny, grab the bobber, grab the bobber!" Grandma

yelled repeatedly. "Grab the bobber! You be careful and don't fall in, now. There it is again, get it!" She was jumping up and down in her seat and rocking the boat as she pointed at the approaching bobber. "Walter," she ordered my grandpa, "you get Kenny closer now. Don't let my fish get away."

After a couple of near catches, with Grandma continuing to yell directions to which the fish paid no attention, I managed to stretch my arm out far enough over the side of the boat and grabbed the fleeing bobber. By some miracle, the fishing line didn't slip through the bobber as I tugged and strained to pull the huge catfish to the water's surface. Grandpa netted the monster and dropped the huge, flopping, whiskered cat into the middle of the boat, adding to the water and fish slime that already covered the floor. We all yelled in celebration as we watched that monster catfish flop around, not the least bit aware that he was going to be dinner in a few hours.

The retelling of her favorite fishing story had worked its magic, putting the biggest smile imaginable on Grandma's face. But it was one of her last smiles. Grandma only lived a couple of days more, but they were days the doctors had not originally given her. I still smile when I think about the joy derived from fishing with my grandparents, and especially that single summer fishing adventure. I'm sure Grandma's still smiling—and Grandpa's still mumbling something about not being able to read minds.

Ken McKowen

Little Kenny holding up the catfish they caught that day.

A Boy Named Hot

The Little Satilla River in southeast Georgia was my favorite place for fishing. We'd wade waist deep out into the river on sandbars, and fish along the undercut opposite banks on the outside of curves in the meandering stream. It was a remote and lonely site, so Daddy and I stayed fairly close together. We fished with pond worms and caught mostly large bream—redbreast, warmouth and bluegills—all of which we called "copperheads" because of the color engendered by tannin in the water. Since we were always in the stream, we kept our caught fish on stringers tied at our waists.

Late one afternoon when I was about ten, Daddy asked me to keep his fish while he walked down the river to talk to some of his friends. I tied his stringer with mine on the belt loop on my downstream side while I continued fishing, enjoying the steady pull of the current on our day's catch. It wasn't long before I watched my cork move slowly and steadily up under a snag and knew I had a big one. After a few minutes I saw the copperhead, the largest fish of the day. As I struggled with the sharply bent cane pole, I wondered how I was going to hold the fish while untying the two stringers. Then a cold chill went down my spine as I realized that the tugging of the current on the stringers was gone, as were all our fish! My belt loop had broken.

I threw my pole up on the nearest sandbar, forgot the hooked fish and began to dive madly into the river below where I had been standing. Then I heard Daddy's voice calling me:

"Hot," he said, "what's wrong?"

"I've lost the fish, Daddy."

"All of them? Mine, too?"

"Yes, sir." I began to cry, even as I continued diving, and the tears and water ran down my face together each time I came up for breath.

Daddy was rarely patient with foolishness or mistakes, but after a long silence, he said, "Let them go, Hot. There are a lot more fish in the river. We'll get them tomorrow."

I almost worshiped him.

Jimmy Carter

Stubbornness and Faith

There is always one true inner voice. Trust it.

Gloria Steinem

One Friday evening my parents, five brothers and I made the half-hour drive in our protesting old car from our Utah family farm to a favorite mountain meadow. The overnight adventure was a wonderful family respite from the constant demands of hard country living, especially during this era. The year was 1930 and the Great Depression was crippling the nation. Getting away as a family was more important than ever.

Following a wonderful dinner of cold fried chicken, potatoes and salad, we circled the smoky campfire to talk about fishing and what our opponents' tastes might be come morning—bugs, night crawlers or artificial lures. Then we sang our favorite songs, agreeing we sounded as good as any choir we could think of. And when you spend time outdoors, you welcome sleep at an early hour; thus, with our stomachs content, our vocal cords exercised and dreams of fishing fresh in our minds, we let the campfire diminish to cooling embers, rolled up in our blankets and slept soundly. The gurgling water of the nearby stream made a melody sweet and comforting to the ear.

As dawn broke, I heard Daddy making a morning fire. I knew Mother was getting breakfast ready, so I rose to help her. To get her sons up and going, she cut thick slices from a bacon slab and arranged the meat in a large frying pan, which was set over the fire. Soon, the aroma of sweet cured bacon drifted through the early morning air, stirring my brothers awake.

As in any household back then, Mother and I took care of chores inside, which included the cooking, and the boys took care of the outside chores. Nothing changed when we went camping. I was up before my brothers, slicing the homemade loaf of bread and setting our makeshift table of flat boards brought from home, suspended over tree stumps, with pie tins for plates and metal cups for milk and hot chocolate. Mother and I cooked lots of eggs, flipping bacon grease over the yolks and whites, which were added to our feast of bacon, fried potatoes and onions, and a big container of mush.

Breakfast was eaten with gusto. Then, as Mother and I cleaned up, the menfolk headed for the fishing stream, loaded down with poles and bait and harboring high hopes for what the next few hours would bring. As soon as breakfast was safely cleared away and the dishes cleaned, I quickly joined the fishermen with my can of worms and a small willow pole that sported some old household string and a hook.

At ten years of age, I was a capable fisherman, all things considered. Daddy had taught me how to thread a worm on a hook so it still wiggled just right, and the worm I threaded on this morning didn't much appreciate my expertise.

Needless to say, my time for fishing that morning had been shortened by breakfast chores, but I knew there was a fish waiting just for me. I ventured close to the small stream that bordered our camp, to a section where my brothers had fished earlier with no takers. This is where I made my stand.

The sun was up fairly high when I heard Daddy whistle, a signal to return to camp. The boys responded immediately, knowing it was time to get down the mountain and do morning chores. They returned smiling, holding the stringer of fish they had caught, comparing tales about the ones that got away. I stayed on the bank of the stream, my string and wiggling worm in the water by a large rock. It looked like a place a fish would take refuge.

The family packed and cleaned the area, left some wood neatly stacked for the next camper and piled in the car for the short trip home. Daddy came over to me and said, "Time to go, little sister."

Not wanting to upset my father, but wanting my fair share of fishing time, I shook my head "no," much to his surprise.

"Old Bossie is getting uncomfortable. She needs to be milked," he softly continued.

In my mind, I agreed with Daddy that our old cow did need to be tended to, but again I focused on that stream and that rock. I shook my head "no."

"We'll come another time—the fish will wait for you till then," he added.

With determination written on my face, I turned and looked at Daddy. *He's right,* I thought, *most fish might wait until the next trip, but not this special fish.* Again, I shook my head "no."

Realizing my stubbornness, Daddy slowly turned and walked to the car, shooed my gawking brothers and mother inside, started up the engine and pulled away. The car was on the hardtop, slowly heading to the mouth of the canyon. I watched as the car went around a curve and disappeared from sight. I was all alone.

Returning my focus to the fish, I concentrated on the worm dangling from my small willow pole. I worked the poor fellow from one swirl to another. Then I slowly pulled my string out and cast it upstream so the worm would fall slightly over the rock. Wham! The strike was decisive! I jerked the string, catching the fish in the mouth. The battle of wills was on! Finally, I eased the fish to the side of the stream, reached down, put my finger in the gill and lifted the shining beauty out of the water. I had my fish.

Scrambling over rocks and turf, I headed full-sprint for the road, pole in one hand, fish in the other, yelling at the top of my lungs, "Wait for me! Wait for me!" Reaching the hardtop and panting from the effort, I ran toward the curve in the road where our car had disappeared. To my great relief, I saw Daddy running toward me—he had heard me yelling. Seeing my accomplishment, he scooped me into his arms and proudly carried me and the fish back to the waiting car.

In the meantime, the rest of the family, first disgusted by my antics, quickly realized my triumph when we reached the car. My brothers fetched the fish tarp from the trunk and rolled it out onto the hardtop, showcasing their catch. As I gently laid my prize next to theirs, everyone was in awe. It was the biggest fish of the trip. I had made my mark.

Now that I am over eighty years old, I marvel at the wisdom shown by my parents in so many instances as our family grew up. For my stubbornness, my parents gave me leeway to experience the results of my efforts. Not all were as fulfilling as my fishing endeavors, but still, whenever the world crowds too close, I seek refuge in the wonderful outdoors, where you can be your own best friend.

DeEtta Woffinden Anderson

The Bologna Wars

My younger sister and I were dyed-in-the-wool tomboys. When our family moved from the small fenced yards of big-city living to the freedom of the country, we thought we had landed on our own little patch of heaven. We spent hours playing in the barn, walking the fields and riding our bikes down the gravel road that eventually reached a tiny town if you went the whole five miles. Near our house the road crossed a little stream that pooled on one side where a school of fish had made their home. The largest was probably only about six inches long, but to our childish eyes they all looked like twelve-pound salmon.

On occasion we would venture into the small library in town and check out books. We would lie in the grass and read and then integrate the stories into our own adventures. Once we checked out a book about the pioneers. That one really snagged our imaginations. The rolling Missouri farmland surrounding us was the ideal setting to hack out a life for ourselves with our bare hands. So with the exception of television and bathrooms, which we were sure the pioneers would have gladly used had they had them, we were determined to renounce the trappings of modern society and live off the land.

We rounded up all the fallen branches we could find and fashioned ourselves a log cabin. It was the perfect house in which to live a pioneering life, at one with nature, despite the trivial inconvenience that it had no roof. Next we addressed the food situation. Our mother kept a garden, so vegetables were no problem, but what about meat? My sister and I stared at each other, as the same thought dawned on us—*the fish!* It didn't matter that we gagged and whined every time our mother made us eat it. Our fish would taste great because they would be fresh! Fishing could become our contribution to the family welfare. We'd bring some home every night and save our parents gobs of money on groceries.

We scrounged around until we found an old badminton net pole and tied some string onto it. Then we filched one of our baby sister's diaper pins to use as a hook. Now, bait. It seemed mean and really icky to skewer a worm on that sharp pin. Instead, we bummed half a slice of bologna from the fridge. Since it was a hot afternoon, we knew the fish would be dying for a nice cool piece of meat. With our fishing pole, bait and confidence in hand, we proudly made a beeline to the pond.

Since I was the eldest and had just naturally acquired more knowledge of fishing through osmosis or whatever, I solemnly informed my sister that I would hold the pole. Fishing was tricky business, and since our family's fortunes apparently hinged upon our ability to master it, it should be handled by someone who knew what she was doing. Wide-eyed, she acquiesced. So we baited the hook, dropped it into the water and hunched on the shoulder of the road, me holding the pole and my sister sitting quietly and admiring the way I held it.

As we stared at the spot where our string disappeared into the pool, we saw a little shudder. In the heat of the moment, my sister grabbed the metal rod with both hands as the string gave a tremendous tug. We had a bite! Excitedly, we jerked the pole up and with our combined strength, we whipped the string hard enough that the diaper pin sailed over our heads and landed on the road behind us. We spun around to admire our whopper to find not only no fish, but no bologna as well. Perplexed, we looked at the hook, at the water and at the hook again. Then we gathered up our stuff and dejectedly walked home.

By the time we got there, we figured out that we must have pulled the line up way too hard. I pointed out that that's why it was best to have just one designated pole holder. My sister saw the wisdom in this and promised to work on her self-control. We had fried chicken for dinner that night. We told our parents to enjoy that chicken because by the next day, it'd be fresh fish every night.

The next afternoon, with our bologna, we marched back to the pool. We sat on the hot road, dangling our feet over the water, and waited for dinner to bite. Then my sister saw something move on the bank and we pulled our feet up, mindful of the snakes that roamed the countryside. It wasn't a snake, though; it was a frog. And he must have been one of those nuclear-radiation-mutant kinds because he was about as big and round as a saucer. While we watched, he slipped into the water, swam over to our line and dove out of sight. Suddenly, the string started dancing and I yanked it out of the water. The pin swung in little circles, naked as a jaybird. We looked at each other indignantly. That big, stupid frog had stolen our bait! We'd see about that.

We stuck more bologna on the hook, dropped the line back in the pond, then bombarded the water with gravel, hoping to stone the thieving thing as it tried again. After a minute we stopped throwing rocks and, panting and sweaty, scanned the banks to see if the slimy critter had washed up anywhere. While we were thus engaged, the pole jerked in my hand. I lifted the pin out of the water. Empty! My normally mild-mannered sister immediately began talking trash about my fishing skills and blaming me for letting the frog get the bologna. I told her she was crazy. We walked home bickering about whose fault all this was, and that night could barely bring ourselves to touch the meatloaf and mashed potatoes with homemade gravy and peas.

Like all serious pioneers, we didn't let our setbacks dampen our spirits. The next day we were ready to get at it again. We were determined to catch a fish because our mother had told us that this would be our last piece of bologna—we were apparently feeding all our dad's luncheon meat to the frog. We prudently quartered the bologna, and after checking out the shoreline and lobbing a few rocks for good measure, we dropped the pin into the water and waited.

I jiggled the line, thinking that would make the meat look more like a bug. Ten minutes into it, we regretfully decided that the fish must not be hungry and that we should save our dwindling supply of bait for another day. I drew up the line and, to our amazement, the hook was clean as a whistle. This meant war! We knew we were going to have to catch the frog or we'd get nary a minnow out of that pond. So we dangled our second piece of meat just under the surface where we could snatch it up the second that greedy frog got his mouth around our bait. We stared at that pin so intently, we saw the exact moment the frog floated up like some ugly Macy's Thanksgiving Day parade balloon and ripped the meat right off the hook. As he sank back down, he seemed to waggle the bologna at us. Man, that frog was smart! We stuffed the rest of the bologna in our mouths and walked home discussing the intricacies of building a rabbit trap.

A few weeks after this, we were driving into town with our mom. As we passed our old stomping grounds, we looked over nostalgically and, lo and behold, sitting nice as you please on the side of the road was Mr. Big Stupid Frog himself. On our turf! We screamed at our mom to stop the car, which she did, skidding on the gravel, terrified that she had hit a farmer. We eased out of the car, thinking that if we could take the old croaker prisoner, we'd finally be the queens of the pond scum. We circled the frog gingerly, step by step, effectively cutting him off from a watery escape. Still he sat there. Inching up, we nervously squatted over him. All that lunchmeat must have done him good because it seemed he had swelled to the size of a dinner plate. The two of us posed in frozen uncertainty for a minute, then my adoring little sister looked up at me expectantly. I was starting to see where this "eldest" thing could have a downside. I looked at the creepy monster. Terror must have rooted him to the spot because he hadn't moved a muscle. Well, that was good, he was more scared of us than we were of him, maybe. Holding my breath, I was stretching one finger forward to give the frog a good poke when the totally unexpected happened. He attacked, lunging straight for my face and leaving us with no other option than to scream and run away.

We dove into the back seat, slammed the door shut and sat glumly contemplating our failure during the ride into town. Once there, we went straight to the library and checked out a book on how to become space cadets. Living off the land was for the birds anyway, and dangerous to boot. No wonder all the pioneers were dead.

Tanith Nicole Tyler

Once Was Enough

Fishermen are born honest, but they get over it.

Ed Zern

The first time my father and I ever went fishing became a family legend.

We spent hours waiting for a nibble. The sun was blistering, and this was back in the days before sunscreen. We were hot, sticky and mad that the fish refused to suck up our night crawlers.

Being only seven years old, I observed that perhaps the worms were the problem. Maybe the night crawlers only wriggled at night, and now they were just lying there limp on the hook. Dad ignored my assessment of the situation.

We began to pack up to leave. As we headed back to our truck, we heard tires spinning in the distance. Getting into our truck was a grim affair. Having sat in the boiling sun for six hours, the seats were blistering. Naturally, I was wearing shorts.

I shifted from side to side in the seat so as not to cook my backside. While driving out we saw a truck with a boat trailer and boat that was stuck in the mud. That explained the sound of spinning tires we'd heard.

Being a nice guy, my dad helped pull the man from the mud. In return, this fellow gave Dad some fish for being a Good Samaritan. As Dad climbed back into our truck with a brown bag full of fish, we waved good-bye to our new-found friend.

On the drive home, we agreed to take in the fish as if we had caught them. We were sure there was no way for Mom to know the difference. It was just a little white lie.

We arrived home hot, sweaty and smelly and went to clean up while Mom prepared the fish. We made a big deal out of the fact that we had already cleaned them and put them in the bag so as not to make a mess.

After showering, Dad and I met in the hall and exchanged conspiratorial grins. Sitting down to freshly fried catfish, hush puppies and coleslaw, we dug in heartily. In the spirit of embellishment, we both went on about how good something tasted that we had actually caught ourselves. Mother looked suitably impressed.

As we got up to do the dishes, Mom cleared her throat. "I just have one question of you two great fishermen," she said. We looked at her expectantly, thinking we had another opportunity to regale her with our great fishing ability. With a tiny smile, Mom asked, "How was it again that you two managed to not only clean your fish, but also *freeze* them before you got home?"

Karri J. Watson

Get the Net!

'Tis a rule of manners to avoid exaggeration.
Ralph Waldo Emerson

During the summer of 1988, my two teenage daughters, Hylee and Shayla, my wife Scharre and I took a camping trip along the coast of California, Oregon and into the San Juan Islands of Washington.

Four days into the trip, we stopped at a campground on the coast of Oregon. After we set up camp, the girls and I took off to check out the fishing at the mouth of a nearby river that dumped into the ocean. Scharre stayed behind—she disliked the sport because the darn fish always took her bait and interrupted her from reading her romance novels.

We found a boat dock and decided to try our luck from the comfort of our lawn chairs. The dock was nearly fifty feet long; Hylee and Shayla set up at one end and I at the other, which was a wonderful arrangement since it would-n't cramp their style should any boys wander by. I left the net and some bait with them and returned to my spot for an afternoon of relaxed fishing.

A few people were fishing between the girls and me, and other campers also walked by to check out the action. After an hour of no activity, my pole started to stutter with small nibbles. Then, to my amazement, the pole almost bent in half. My immediate impression was that I had either hooked a whale or an aircraft carrier. I yelled to the girls, "Get the net. I've got a big one!"

Activity on and around the dock stopped as everyone anxiously watched the big one being landed. As my line started to clear the surface, it became slack—I feared my trophy had gotten away! By this time Hylee and Shayla were standing by with the net.

As I reeled in my line, it brought to the surface the smallest fish ever hooked outside of a goldfish bowl. It would be an exaggeration to say it was three inches long.

When the girls saw the size of my fish, they began laughing so hard they nearly fell in the river. Even the crowd that had gathered to watch the great fisherman joined in the laughter.

Embarrassed, I stared down into the river when, suddenly, a seal stuck its head out of the water, and I swear it was wearing a mischievous smile on its face. I told the girls that the seal must have had a hold of the fish until it got near the surface, causing my pole to bend as it did. They said, "Oh sure, Dad," and laughed even more.

That evening, we were sitting around the campfire fighting off mosquitoes when Shayla pointed at one and yelled, "Get the net! It's a big one!" Periodically, during the remainder of our trip, this phrase became a favorite of my wife and daughters, who would yell it, good-naturedly, with very little provocation every chance they got.

By the end of the trip, I had learned a very important lesson: It's best that the big one gets away, and nobody knows about it.

Cliff Johnson

The Worm

There was never a person who did anything worth doing that did not receive more than he gave.

Henry Ward Beecher

I couldn't put the worm on. I prided myself on being a tomboy—I hated Barbies and baths, and loved climbing trees and playing with Tonka trucks—but something about sticking a hook through a wiggling worm gave me the heebie-jeebies. Dad had somehow understood, but how could I tell old Mr. Lyons, who never had any kids? I almost hadn't gone fishing with him because of it, but Mom talked me into it. Then, the closer we got to the river, the more it worried me.

It was nice of Mr. Lyons to take me fishing. Since my dad had died the fall before, it was just my mom and us four girls, and I knew we wouldn't go fishing or camping or canoeing anymore.

I missed my dad and had taken to hanging around Mr. Lyons's yard as he worked on building his houseboat. I loved the smell of sawdust and stain—a scent that was fading from my dad's unused workshop. I think Mr. Lyons liked my company, too. He'd be hammering a nail or planing wood with his eyes squinting in concentration until his dog Brownie would announce my arrival with a bark. When he'd look up and see it was me, he'd set his tools down and scratch his gray, scruffy chin and say he was glad I came by because he needed a break.

Mr. Lyons had finished the houseboat in the spring, and he'd already taken it down to the river. He pulled the truck up next to the houseboat.

"Well, how's she look?"

"Real nice, Mr. Lyons."

"We'll just fish right off the front bow. It's nice and shady there. The fish'll be keeping cool and waiting for a worm to wiggle on by."

We got the fishing poles out of the bed of the Ford. Mine was just the bamboo pole I had dug out from the camping supplies in the basement. Dad had tried to teach me how to cast his rod and reel but I had tangled the line up something awful. Maybe now that I had turned eleven I'd have better luck.

Mr. Lyons reached back in the truck bed for the tackle box, then reached in again and handed me the Styrofoam container of worms. I followed him down the bank and onto the boat, keeping an eye that the lid stayed on.

Once on the bow, Mr. Lyons started getting everything set up. Any minute now I'd have to admit to him my aversion to worms. Then he'd probably never ask me to go fishing again. He handed me my pole, then set the container between us and fished out a worm for his pole. Then, just when I was ready to confess, Mr. Lyons confessed to me instead.

"Always hate this part," he mumbled as he held the worm in one hand and his hook in the other. "It's silly, but stickin' the poor little guy with a hook makes me feel, I dunno what you'd call it. . . ."

"Like you have the heebie-jeebies?" I offered hopefully.

"That's it exactly. The heebie-jeebies. You get 'em, too?"

"A little," I admitted, relief washing over me.

"Yeah. I guess sometimes we gotta go through the bad to get to the good. Want me to hook your worm for ya?"

There it was. My way out. All I had to say was "yes" and I'd be off the hook and my worm would be on. But I felt bad making Mr. Lyons put the worm on if he hated it as much as me. So I reached into the cool dirt and picked up a fat worm between my fingers. I tried not to think about how slimy it felt as I quickly poked the hook through its middle and wiped my hand on my jeans.

I had done it! It definitely gave me the heebie-jeebies, but I had gotten through it. I looked up at Mr. Lyons. He gave me a wink. I grinned with pride and tossed my line in the water. The bad part was over.

Today, of course, I realize my mom must have shared my problem with Mr. Lyons; I'm fairly certain he didn't have a case of the heebie-jeebies at all. But I also know that he helped me grasp, on a child's level, the principle of persevering through the bad to get to the good. My mom and sisters and I never did fish together again; the days of camping and canoeing died with my father. But we struggled through the grief and, when we got through the bad, we eventually found other good times to enjoy as a family. And I continued to fish with Mr. Lyons . . . and bait my own hook.

Julie Long

The 5th Wave

By Rich Tennant

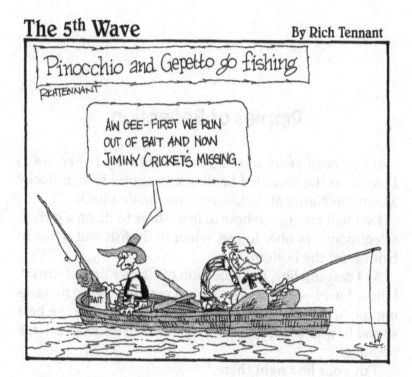

Pinocchio and Gepetto go fishing

RKTENNANT

AW GEE- FIRST WE RUN OUT OF BAIT AND NOW JIMINY CRICKET'S MISSING.

BAIT

Ripples of Reflection

It had been years since I'd fished with my father. Yet as I stood on the secluded bank of a beautiful lake in Rocky Mountain National Park, memories flooded back.

Dad had taught me how to fish—how to tie on a swivel, select which bobber to use, when to fly-fish and when to bait up for the bottom.

As I cast my line, the reflection of Glacier Basin blurred. I pulled my bobber slowly toward me, the ripples reminding me of the day Daddy taught me how to find the best spots. It was a deep, dark pool on a river, near a large boulder.

"Put your line right there."

"Why?"

"Because there's a big one waiting for your fly."

"How do you know?"

"Just try it."

My fly landed in the exact spot he had pointed to and disappeared beneath the water. I never questioned Daddy again.

While mulling this memory, I realized that he not only taught me how to fish, but how to live. In the deep, dark pool of boyfriends, he seemed to know which one would make a good husband, and he was right. With every casting lesson, he was teaching me patience and choices.

"Don't land your line over there."

"Why?"

"It's grassy under the surface. You'll lose your bait."

He could have been saying, *"Don't choose that route for your life. It's dangerous."*

With my two sons now grown and living their own lives, my husband Jim and I are enjoying our empty nest. Yet as I stood on the secluded bank of a beautiful lake in Rocky Mountain National Park, I became that little girl again.

"You're my long-legged fisherman."

"Oh, Daddy."

"I'm proud of you, daughter."

"Because I can fish?"

"Because you've grown into the woman I hoped you would."

A couple walking by asked if I'd caught anything.

"Nuthin'," I replied, with tears streaming down my cheeks.

In confusion the man said, "Don't worry, we've talked to everyone around the lake and they aren't catching anything either." They walked away quickly, most likely thinking that I was a bit too unstable to be fishing alone.

It didn't matter. If I had caught a fish that day, it would have interrupted the wonderful time I was having with my father.

Kathleen Kovach

Never Again

Shortly before Christmas in 1995, my mother was nearing the end of her battle with cancer. On her way to the hospital she had gotten money out of her dresser, which she had hidden away to buy my father a particular fishing pole he had wanted for a long time. Arriving at the hospital she slipped the money to my sister and made her promise to buy the pole for my father for Christmas. The following morning my mother passed away.

During the funeral my sister shared this story with me, and we decided we had to carry out our mother's wishes. Christmas morning arrived, and the normal Christmas cheer was quelled with sadness and reminiscences of past Christmas holidays. Later that morning we gave our father the gift and told him the story. He was sad, of course; however, he commented that even at the end Mom was thinking of other people.

Months passed and winter faded into spring, bringing the annual spring run of striped bass to the north shore of Long Island. Although time heals all wounds, a few months cannot fill a void that took forty-five years to fill. But my father realized that his late wife's gift was more than a fishing pole. It was something he could use for quiet times and reflection, and also to enjoy the sport he loves.

My father was fishing one morning with his new pole rigged up with a bunker chunk and set in a sand spike. Tragedy struck when he wandered too far off to throw out a lure with another pole. Mom's gift pole bent under the strike, then exploded out of the holder and raced to the water. My father dove into the water after his quickly disappearing pole, but it was to no avail. It was gone. He was devastated. Not only did he lose a pole, but the last gift Mom had given him. He returned home, somber, almost as if my mother's death had happened all over again.

Not wishing for our father to fall back into mourning, which had seemed to last all winter, we insisted he go out fishing with a friend. That evening he returned to the scene of his earlier misfortune. He was accompanied by an old friend who was doing his best to console my father. They were throwing out plugs and talking when it felt as though the old friend had a hit. He started to retrieve the line and turned to my father and said, "I snagged something."

When the plug reached the beach, caught on one of the treble hooks was my father's lost pole. Seeing the pole, my father ran and retrieved it. Upon picking up the pole and unsnagging it from the plug, my father felt a tug. He pulled back on the pole and sure enough there was a fish on the line. He reeled it in and discovered a thirty-seven-inch striper. It wasn't much of a fight because the fish had been dragging around a pole all day and was quite tired.

This time the fishing pole was the trophy, and what a trophy it was. My father was as happy as a small child on Christmas day. As for the fish, he set it free in appreciation for not straying too far away. And as for my father, that pole never went into a sand spike again.

Joseph Hines

". . . Mostly angel fish, and—occasionally—holy mackerel."

Letting Them Go

The best minute you spend is the one you invest in your family.

Ken Blanchard

The preparation was always exhausting, for me anyway. Of course, most of the work fell on me—and my darling wife who makes sure we don't forget anything: preparing menus, shopping for supplies, inspecting camping gear, restringing fishing reels, organizing and restocking tackle boxes, making lists and checking them twice, and making sure it all gets loaded into the van. All of this preparation was for our annual father/son canoeing and fishing adventure. We both looked forward to this trip and the time we could spend together. We were always diligent. We never embarked on our adventures unprepared. As the final preparations were concluded, an irony flashed through my mind: *All of the planning and all of the work end up with us letting them go.*

The smallmouth bass in the Ozark Mountain streams we fished were a treat to catch, for us and for many other anglers. But they were particularly susceptible to fishing pressures, so I instructed my son about catch and release. I taught him about the joy of letting them go, watching them swim away so they could come to us again another day, bigger and stronger.

This year my son was intent on exerting his independence. After a little refresher on knot tying, he successfully attached his hook to the end of his line and slipped on his bait of choice. We pushed the canoe into the river, and the adventure began. It was not long before the fish began to bite. It was time for more lessons. On each cast I offered a little advice, and help when he asked for it.

"Reel up the slack before you set the hook, son.

"Keep your rod tip up after you set the hook. Don't let any slack in the line.

"Don't reel against the drag. Let the fish take the line.

"Leave enough line so you can reach down and lip the fish, son. There you go. Now grab him quick! Don't be afraid.

"Now, leave slack in the line when you are taking the hook out. Work quickly so you don't hurt the fish.

"Here, son, let me help you with that."

As the day wore on, he needed less and less help. Eventually, I remained silent as he hooked a nice smallmouth and let him pull against the drag. He played the fish well. As the fish tired, he gently brought it to the canoe, lipped the fish out of the water, removed the hook, admired it for a moment and let it go.

As we watched the fish swim away through the crystal-clear water, my son exclaimed, "I did it, Dad! I did it all by myself! I even let it go!"

All of the preparation, all of the work, all of the instruction, just to let them go. But there was joy in letting them go, as the smile on my son's face attested.

One week later we were going canoeing with the church youth group. My son was now old enough to be a "youth," and this was his first trip with them. A lot seemed to have changed in the span of one week. My son wanted to pack his things all by himself. He didn't mind my being around, so long as I acted like I didn't know him. He even rode in a canoe with someone else. I was glad he blended in with the group so well.

As I reflected on my son's growing independence, the irony flashed through my mind again:

All of the planning, the work, the instruction, the protection and all of the love end up with us letting them go. But there is joy in letting them go.

I hope I can remember that.

Gary Usery

$\overline{6}$

REEL MEN

Many men go fishing all their lives without knowing that it is not fish they are after.

Henry David Thoreau

Primitive Man

If you obey all the rules, you miss all the fun.
Katharine Hepburn

I didn't take up fishing until after I graduated from college. After a few years of success in the sport, I realized it was time for me to make a name for myself in the fishing world. To become the envy of my friends and the pride of my family, I knew I needed to catch big trout, and lots of them.

I still lacked a major accomplishment, a trophy trout, to firmly establish my reputation as a world-class fisherman. I pored over maps and spent hours studying rivers and canyons. Then I discovered it. My secret fishing spot. My heart skipped when I asked an old-timer about the prospects of fishing in this area. "Are you kiddin'? A guy would have to be crazy to go in there" was all he said. Perfect!

The next morning, I loaded up my old Volkswagen bug and was off. When the road gave out, I was forced to hike; on foot, I crossed a steep ridge and began my long descent into the canyon. Since there was no official trail, I had to find my own way. I had been on many beautiful hikes before, but this one was stunning. The high walls, the grandeur of the canyon, the roaring river hundreds of feet below me, all combined to make me dizzy with joy and excitement. *Big fish had to live in that water.*

There wasn't a sign of another human being anywhere. At the first pool, I made a terrific cast right where I wanted to place my lure. A sixteen-inch rainbow came streaking out of the water. It ripped out my line and made several breathtaking leaps. I stared at the fish in wonder as I reeled it in, then returned it to the water. I cast again to the same spot as my first cast. Bang! The fourteen-inch sibling of the first fish took me for a wonderful ride.

After landing two more large fish, I decided to head upriver, which was not an easy task. The steepness of the canyon made it too risky to attempt climbing up the side to get around rocks and obstructions. I was forced to travel along the very edge of the canyon base and the river itself.

After an hour, I came to a shockingly large pool. I quickly pulled out many big trout, including an eighteen-inch beauty, which I released with the others. On the other side of the pool, which was fifty yards wide, was a large granite island, the perfect place to fish. But in my attempt to get to the opposite side and closer to the rock, I came to an impasse. The canyon wall I had scaled left me frozen; I was on a cliff over fifty feet above the pool with noodle legs and knees knocking. Suddenly, the solution was simple: I would just have to swim. *I was now in the trout's world,* I thought. I jumped in. The water was cold and exhilarating. I was a primitive man who, in his search for food, was forced to do what was necessary to survive. I had a family to care for. I was the provider, the *fisherman.*

I swam to the island rock, a perfect twenty-by-twenty-foot granite platform, three feet above the water at its highest point with a gradual slope into the river on all sides. Positioned perfectly for casting into the current, which was supplied by sixty-foot-high thundering falls, I took in my new surroundings. It was then I realized I was shivering in my soaking wet T-shirt, shorts and shoes. Suddenly, it occurred to me that my clothes were really not of much use anymore. *Why couldn't I fish naked?* There certainly wasn't anybody around. I'd be warmer and, after all, wasn't I a *primitive* man? That's how *he* would have fished. I stood up, and after affirming I was very much alone, stripped to nothing. "Okay, let's see how well this primitive man can fish," I said out loud as I tossed my lure toward the falls.

About halfway through my retrieve, I felt a solid hit. The fish raced toward the falls, then back in my direction. I reeled as fast as possible, but it must have spotted me, butt-naked, because it suddenly turned and made an even more savage run to the falls. Then it happened. As with all good rainbows, it decided it was time to come out of the water, and everything changed. My rainbow made a perfect crescent dive, like a porpoise, about four feet out of the water. I do believe my heart stopped for a split second. Instantly, I was no longer a cool, calm, expert fisherman; I was shaking and scared to death. *I was a primitive man with a primitive fish.* Had I really seen what I thought I had? Was it really that big? Only one thing mattered: *Do not, under any circumstances, lose that fish.* I became a man possessed. This was my trophy fish. I would be famous. I would talk about this fish for the rest of my life.

When my rainbow came crashing back into the water, I knew only one thing: it was still hooked. I was running from side to side, trying to keep the tension on the line just right. The runs had slowed, and I was gaining control. I could see it now close to the edge of the rock. The mighty fish had a lot of strength left, but it seemed like the right time to try and ease it up onto the rock in front of me. The moment of truth had arrived. I stepped back a few feet, waited for my giant to turn onto its side and be still, and then carefully eased it up onto the rock's smooth surface. It worked perfectly; the fish gracefully slid four feet onto the flat surface of the rock. It was over. I was a hero and the prize was mine.

Before I could pick up the fish to marvel at its size and weight, it suddenly lifted its head and snapped the line. It was no longer mine; it was free. One good flip toward the river and my rainbow would be lost forever. Instead of a trophy, I was looking at "the one that got away." I instinctively tossed away my last link to civilization. My fishing rod was no good to me now. We had been reduced to the basics, *naked man* versus *naked fish,* mano a mano.

The giant warrior made its move first; the major flip to freedom catapulted it back toward the water. The very split second its body left the rock, I began my charge to the water as well. I had only one desperate chance to get to the water's edge before the fish. Sliding down the rock full force into the river, I hoped my timing and luck would prevail. The monster was halfway into the river as I shot past. I made a frantic scoop-and-toss as I went by. I felt weight and resistance as I heaved the huge fish back onto the rock. Just before I went under the water's surface, I saw that my toss had been a good one. My fish had landed somewhere in the middle of the rock. I was saved. My fame had been restored.

Like a primitive creature, I climbed out of the watery depths. Near the top of the rock, yet another heart-wrenching experience awaited me. My trophy trout had plenty of life left and was now flipping its way toward the *far* side of the rock. All the emotions I had just experienced raced through me again. The scene was like in the movies where the villain is never really dead, but keeps coming back to life. Frantic, this naked, dripping man raced to the far side of the rock and repeated the exact scene. Shockingly, I pulled it off a second time.

When I scrambled back onto the rock, my rainbow was not in such a precarious position. Amazingly, the fight in that fish wasn't gone. Something still needed to be done to assure victory. In confusion, desperation and primitive man style, I dove spread-eagle on top of the fish. Holding it down with my chest and stomach, the monster continued to struggle. Finally, it was over. I rolled onto my back and lay next to my prize. After catching my breath, I leaned over and took in my gorgeous rainbow; it was absolutely beautiful and huge, twenty-four inches of magnificent fish. I had my trophy.

It's been twenty-five years since that day. Last month, I took my son-in-law on a fishing trip into *my* secret canyon. We climbed and jumped and swam and fished and had an absolutely wonderful time. But considering it's been over a quarter century since my naked foray, and this primitive man has aged just a bit, I kept my clothes on so as not to scare the fish away.

Richard Knott

Fishing for Blockheads

Finally, it was my day off. After a tough week at work, all I wanted to do was relax at one of my favorite fishing places, the San Lorenzo River near Santa Cruz, California.

When I first arrived, I thought about throwing in my line since the steelhead were running, but the river's shady banks were more inviting. So I decided to just kick back and enjoy Mother Nature instead.

As I sat there relaxing, two men appeared on the opposite bank, each carrying a short pitchfork. Intrigued, I thought, *Okay, let's throw out a line and see if there's something here to catch.* "How's it going, guys?"

They returned the greeting with a nod and kept heading my way with obvious purpose, wading across the river to a little hole about ten yards from me. They began to thrash at the limbs overhanging the deep water.

With their pitchforks poised over the water, I grew more curious. *Maybe they would take a little bait.* "Whatcha doing?"

"Oh, just fishin'." One guy sent his fork flying into the water.

"Really? They don't fish that way where I come from." *I felt a bite coming on, so I sent out a little tease.* "How do you do that?"

"Well, ya find where the fish are and scare 'em out, then stab them with the fork." *Wow, a full-on strike!* The other guy shot his fork at a movement under the surface.

I decided to set the hook. "Well, isn't that illegal?"

"SURE IS!" they said in unison, followed by another couple of stabs at the water. *They were hooked! It was time to start reeling them in.* "Gee guys, aren't you afraid of getting caught?"

Sporting huge smiles, one said, "We *never* get caught!"

Time for the net. I took my badge from my pocket and said, "*Never* is over guys. You're under arrest."

Fishing that day was great for an off-duty state park ranger. I guess there isn't much difference between fishing for steelhead and fishing for blockheads—except steelhead are a lot smarter.

Steven Treanor

RUBES ® **By Leigh Rubin**

The secret of successful steelhead fishing.

A Perfect Day

All our dreams can come true if we have the courage to pursue them.

Walt Disney

In my desk drawer, the one that accumulates things that have nowhere else to go, there's a Polaroid of two ten-year-old boys holding up a stringer loaded with bass. The ten or so fish probably weighed a total of twenty pounds, enough that I'm holding my end up with both hands. Our smiles tell the story of that day, the story of a perfect day with a best friend.

Until that summer in 1974, I had always lived in the city. Moving from a neighborhood full of kids to the isolation of the country was the last thing I wanted to do. Even though we moved only about seven miles out of town, it may as well have been a hundred.

Our new country home was located in some of the most beautiful hills and valleys in Ohio. Lonely for a friend, I soon met Duane. We quickly became best buddies.

That summer we explored every inch of the woods and fields. There were several little ponds we were allowed to fish, and we took full advantage of that welcome. But more than all the others, we wanted to fish Wilson's pond. You could see it from the road, maybe a hundred yards across an open field and down a small slope. The Wilsons lived in a big old farmhouse just down the road from the pond. They were older folks and, at least in the eyes and minds of two ten-year-old boys, scary. Knocking on their door to ask permission to fish the pond was never seriously considered.

Wilson's pond called to us because it was the only one nearby we didn't have permission to fish. For that reason alone, we just knew it held dozens of five-pounders ready and waiting to be taken.

Besides, permission from the Wilsons was the smaller of two obstacles standing between us and fishing our dream pond. The bigger problem was the bull that lived in the field between the road and the pond. Even if we had permission, we'd have to somehow get past him.

One day late in the summer, our desperate desire to fish Wilson's pond overcame our fear of the bull. I wish I could report that we came up with a brilliant strategy to distract him while we waltzed across the field, but we didn't. We simply climbed the fence and ran like crazy. From the moment we hit the ground on the bull's side of the fence until the time we reached the gate, neither of us looked back. We scaled the gate in a single, fluid move, fishing poles and tackle boxes flying. That was the longest hundred yards of my young life.

Safely on the other side, we looked back to see how close we'd come to death. Surprisingly, the bull hadn't moved a step. In fact, he was staring at us with a look of amusement. Of course, when we would later tell the story to whomever would listen, we had only narrowly escaped with our lives.

The fishing was as great as we had dreamed. We didn't

land any five-pounders that day, but just about every cast was met with a bite, and the two-pounders we did haul in fought with everything they had.

Late in the afternoon, tired and hot, but still giddy with the excitement, we looped back home through woods behind the pond. It was a much longer route, but we saw no good reason to press our luck with the bull.

Twenty-eight years later, that day remains fresh in my mind and stands out as one of the best of my childhood. Duane and I remained close throughout high school, but have since drifted apart. I went off to college, married, then to law school and haven't been fishing, or talked to Duane, more than a few times in the last twenty-five years.

Every once in a while though, I'll come across that old Polaroid of two ten-year-old boys, forever connected by a stringer loaded with bass taken from Wilson's pond, and remember what it feels like to have a perfect day with my best friend.

Brett Foster

The Secret of Success

Before getting married, my fiancé thought it would be a good idea for me to get to know her young nephew Dylan.

Wanting to make a good first impression, I selected one of my favorite sports to bond with him—fishing! I told seven-year-old Dylan that I would share my secrets to fishing success with him during the special outing. Having never fished before, he was excited, to say the least.

I prepared all of the tackle, purchased the worms, packed the snacks and headed out to pick him up just after sunrise. Having stayed out late the night before, I decided to purchase an extra large coffee for the trip. This was not a good idea. I had to urinate several times and repeatedly went downstream to do so behind a tree. To save face, I told Dylan that I was just walking up and down the creek to scout out the "hot spots" for fish.

We had a wonderful time. Dylan learned how to put on a worm, tie a knot and cast, as well as practice the rules of fishing etiquette. And besides the many laughs and silly moments we shared, we also caught lots and lots of fish!

Upon returning home, my future sister-in-law asked an excited Dylan to share his Uncle Ryan's best "fishing secret" with her. I wondered if he would tell her about the special casting or baiting techniques I taught him, or possibly the time-of-day rules, or one of my many other secrets.

To my surprise and embarrassment, Dylan replied, "That's easy. If you want to catch fish, you have to pee on them first!"

Ryan French

IN THE BLEACHERS ©*Steve Moore. Reprinted with permission of UNIVERSAL PRESS SYNDICATE. All rights reserved.*

Catch and Release

I'm a guy with a passion for the outdoors. I spend most of my free time fishing. I have waders, both hip and chest neoprenes for stream fishing, two small fishing boats, and two Honda trolling motors to go with them. Of course one can't fish during winter without the appropriate ice fishing gear—ice fishing tent, propane heater and lantern, ice auger, micro-light fishing poles, ice fishing tackle box to sit on, extreme artic cold weather gear, mittens, the works.

About ten years ago my next door neighbor invited me over for Christmas Eve dinner. He happened to mention that his single, twenty-eight-year-old niece might be there. At the appointed time I arrived at his home, was introduced to his niece and her family, and we had a pleasant chat and turkey dinner with all the trimmings.

This girl seemed very nice, and the following day I asked my neighbor for her phone number. I called her and asked if she would like to go out.

"I would love to," she replied to my offer of dinner and a movie.

Dinner was pleasant, and she was easy to talk with. She even asked what I liked to do. I replied that I was an avid outdoorsman. I suggested for our next date we visit *my* comfort zone. I invited her ice fishing.

The following Saturday arrived, and I picked her up in my old '75 Dodge Ram Charger, four-wheel drive with a pop-up camper. When we arrived at the frozen reservoir, I broke out the snow shoes and strapped them on both of us, filled the sled with all the gear, and off we went trudging through four feet of snow for probably a third of a mile.

We found an abandoned hole, so I didn't even have to drill a new one with the auger. I set up the tent, lit the lantern, set out a folding chair for her and pulled out a fat, juicy night crawler to place on the hook. I suspected she had never fished before when she grimaced as I impaled the night crawler with all three barbs on my size-14 treble hook.

From this point on events happened very fast. I flipped open the wire bail on my reel to allow the night crawler to sink to the bottom. As soon as the bait hit the bottom, my little micro-light bent at a ninety degree angle right at the rod handle, straight down the hole. I had never before had a hit like this. The fish was pulling so hard that I was sure the six-pound test would not stand the strain. "Quick, adjust the drag for me!" I pleaded.

"What's a drag?" she replied.

"That little wheel at the back of my reel," I said. "Can you turn it counterclockwise, please?" She found it very quickly, and immediately the line peeled off the reel. I thought I had a nuclear submarine by the tail. About five minutes later, I was pulling a rainbow trout through an eight-inch-diameter ice hole with less than a quarter-inch clearance. I reached down and grabbed the fish by the bottom lip and assisted it out of the hole, opened my tackle box and obtained my needle-nose pliers to remove the hook.

Just then my date became hysterical. "Don't hurt 'em! Don't hurt 'em!" she pleaded.

I watched her eyes well up with tears. She started to sob, "Let's throw him back! He's gonna die! He's gonna die!" Her reaction surprised me. In my family, everyone would have been doing the "high-five" thing, sharpening up the fillet knife, heating up the skillet or preparing brine for the smoker. That trout was a minimum of six-and-a-half pounds. His shadow probably weighed a half-pound. I couldn't wait to show all my fishing buddies this lunker.

I looked at this attractive young girl and then down at the fish, and I did what any true fisherman would do. I kept the fish and let her off the hook.

Vic Dollar

IN THE BLEACHERS   **BY STEVE MOORE**

THAT'S IT, CATHY. SCREAM. SHOUT. ROCK THE BOAT. DO EVERYTHING YOU CAN TO RUIN MY FISHING TRIP...

The Recycled Carp

Things do not happen. They are made to happen.

John F. Kennedy

The carp is the Rodney Dangerfield of the fish world; they get no respect. They're ugly and bony and will eat whatever garbage they can scoop up from the muddy bottoms of rivers and lakes. When I was a ten-year-old boy, however, that didn't mean a thing to me. All I cared about was they were BIG.

I was fishing on the dock at Suson Park, a lake in St. Louis known for its carp and catfish. For two dollars, I was allowed to catch and keep five fish. I would usually go home with five small catfish, but this time I was determined to catch a carp.

Since I was using a worm for bait, it wasn't likely to happen. The catfish were too numerous and quick to let a slow-moving carp get a hold of my bait. There was this woman on the dock, however, who was standing next to what looked like a fresh green horse plop. She would pinch off a piece and roll it in her hands, then slip the bite-sized ball onto her hook. She already had three carp in her fish cage.

"May I have some of that?" I asked.

She graciously pinched me off a piece of her "magic bait."

Casting out as far as I could cast, I set my pole down and waited. After about a half hour, I watched my line slowly moving out, becoming increasingly more taut. When I set the hook, I saw the water swirl where I had dropped my bait. I thought, *Oh, boy, here we go.* My rod bent like a bow.

I fought the fish for about twenty minutes. I was breathless with excitement but worried that if I were to reel in too quickly, my line would snap. Meanwhile, a crowd of fishermen had gathered around me, eager to see the size of the fish I was bringing in. The woman who had given me the bait was standing at my side, holding her net. As the fish came to within several feet of the dock, I could see it was the fish of my dreams. A moment later we netted the six-pound carp.

When my older brother came to pick me up, I walked to the car, hoisting the carp and breaking into the biggest smile of my life. I was so happy I burst out laughing. I had never felt so proud.

Back at home, I placed the carp in a metal tub and fetched a butcher knife. Staring down at the fish, I watched its lips move in and out. I had never cleaned a fish that big before, and the thought of trying to cut off its huge head and slice open its belly and pull out its . . . well, that seemed too gory. I just didn't have the heart, so I carried it down to the creek near our house and let it go. Even after the carp swam to the deepest part of the creek, its dorsal fin was still sticking out of the water.

The next day I visited my dad, a carpenter who was working on a house in our neighborhood. I was in the backyard when I heard someone coming up from the woods yelling. It was a local laborer who had strolled down to the creek during his lunch break. He was proudly clutching the carp I'd released the evening before.

"Look what I got!" he exclaimed. "I done caught me a carp!"

"Wow," I said. "Where did you catch him?"

"I caught him down there in that creek!" he said, putting the very heavy fish down on the ground. "I caught him with my bare hands!" He held up his hands, looking at them as if he himself couldn't believe what they had done.

"He's big," I said, watching the carp flop around on the ground. I noticed his pants were wet up to his knees and water was still dripping from his arms.

"Mmmmboy, I love carp," he said, smiling. "I'm gonna take it home and have my wife cook it up for supper! Just wait till she sees me carrying it into the house!"

I was proud and excited when I caught that carp, but he seemed even more proud and excited over catching the same fish. From the look on his face, I could tell this was one of the highlights of his life. It was also one of the highlights of mine.

The next day I visited the laborer at the construction site. He said that he and his wife ate the carp for supper, and on his lunch hour he was going down to the creek to see if he could catch another one. I wasn't about to spoil his fun by telling him how the carp had gotten there in the first place.

That fish we caught might have been nothing more than a lowly carp, what sport fishermen call a "trash fish," but it surely brought a lot of happiness.

Gregory Lamping

Black Bass

It was a few days before Thanksgiving, and my father, my brother and his family came down to North Carolina to visit for the first time. Prior to their visit, I had been catching largemouth bass quite often, and after bragging to my father and brother, they couldn't wait to wet their lines. But with our wives organizing the Thanksgiving feast and us in charge of the kids, how could we find the time to fish?

With a whole brood of kids, ranging in age from twelve to sixteen, serious fishing was definitely not on their agenda. So my brother and I came up with an excellent idea—paintball! We could kill two birds with one shot, so to speak. We would drop the kids off at the paintball field, which would leave my father, brother and me the opportunity to pursue our favorite pastime.

On the way to the paintball field, my father noticed a farm pond.

"That looks like a good place to fish," he said.

I was reluctant to fish there because it didn't seem very accessible, and said so, much to his dismay.

After getting our overly excited kids signed into the paintball center, we overly excited adults headed out to fish. My father and brother kept insisting on trying the farm pond we saw earlier. After much friendly banter, including my wanting to go to my favorite spot because I knew we would catch our fill, I finally gave in.

The small pond forced us to fish shoulder-to-shoulder. While my father and brother tried to figure out which lure to use, I selected a four-inch top water lure. After looking over the pond, I reasoned I had only a few feet of water to work with and had to flip my lure over nearby bushes in order to avoid snags.

The flipping technique worked, although my first cast was uneventful. The second cast was a different story. I retrieved it to within four feet from the bank, then proceeded to flip the lure right into my forehead. Ouch!

My dad looked at it and said one of the hooks was embedded beyond the barb. My father and brother found it quite comical.

We're African American, and my brother blurted out, "I've never seen anyone land a two-hundred-pound black bass before!"

Needless to say we were all in stitches. And, needless to say, our fishing day was ruined as we headed to the emergency room.

Several hours and several stitches later, we picked up the kids from their paintball adventure and headed home. Running into the house, the kids raved about their full day of paintball fun. When asked about our fishing luck, I removed my hat and told our story. My wife was eight months pregnant and nearly laughed herself into pre - mature labor!

Darryl Allen

Johnny

Johnny and I had only one goal that trip—to catch enough salmon to fill our freezers with fillets. It was also a great excuse to get away and have some fun. We decided to head up to nearby Ludington and catch a charter on Lake Michigan. Looking forward to some fishing R & R, we were filled with anticipation.

"You know what I'm going to do someday?" confided Johnny as we drove north. "I'm going to buy me a camper and fishing boat and just take off across the country. I'm going to find a nice spot and fish it until I don't want to fish it no more, and then I'm going to move on to another spot and fish some more. No more boss, no more lousy job, just camping and fishing." We both smiled at the thought.

"Someday you'll do it, too," I said. Johnny, my wife's uncle, was much older than me, but we had a lot in common—woodworking, hunting and fishing, which was, by far, our favorite pastime. He was my fishing buddy.

A short time later we pulled into the town of Ludington and stopped at the first bait shop we came to. We bought some tackle and headed to the pier to cast for salmon. Boats were crisscrossing the mouth of the river, which emptied into Lake Michigan.

"They must be heading inland to spawn," I mused about our intended foe. We looked at each other and just grinned at the thought of salmon stacked up like cord wood. We had heard the stories of men being able to cross the river by walking on the backs of huge salmon. Both Johnny and I could hardly wait to get out on the big lake.

We were joined at the dock by my brother-in-law Mike and father-in-law Bob. It was an absolutely beautiful day. After fishing for a bit, with absolutely no luck whatsoever, the four of us headed to the hotel to get to bed early. Our charter was launching at 4 A.M.

After a restless "fishing-eve" night, we all met up in the lobby at 3 A.M. for some welcomed coffee before heading to the marina. When we got there, the boats were lined up, rods sticking out like spines on a cactus, and the smell of diesel fuel was in the air. "Come aboard!" our captain called out to us.

"It's going to be rough," the captain cautioned us about the weather conditions as we boarded the boat. "Rough, but definitely fishable." That's all we wanted to hear.

As the boat motored the half mile down the channel, we thought the water seemed fairly calm—until we came to the lake. Then we saw what the captain was talking about. Three- to six-foot waves! The captain powered up the boat, and we began to muscle our way through some pretty thick water. Forty-five minutes later we were five miles into Lake Michigan, and the first mate was putting out lines. The sun was just coming up. It wasn't ten minutes later when he yelled "FISH ON!"

"Are we having fun yet?" Johnny said to me with a wink and a smile.

Mike got to the rod first and pulled in a beauty of a salmon. "Fish blood on the deck, captain!" hollered the first mate as he swabbed up the mess.

"That's good luck!" countered the captain.

It wasn't long before we had three nice fish on board. That's when Johnny came to me and the captain.

"I hate to spoil our trip, but we gotta go back in," he said.

"Seasick?" I asked. Several of us were queasy from the high waves.

"No, something's wrong," Johnny said, pointing to his chest.

"Do you want me to notify the Coast Guard?" asked the captain.

"You better," he replied.

That was all it took. While Mike and I helped Johnny back to the cabin, the captain put out a Mayday distress call to the Coast Guard. The others pulled in the lines and battened down for the slow and tedious attempt to slug our way back to land through what were now six- to eight-foot waves. I became seasick and quickly made my way outside to get some fresh air. A few minutes later, Mike emerged from the cabin.

"Johnny wants to talk to you," hollered Mike over the deafening roar of the swells.

I returned to the cabin and sat down next to him, trying very hard to maintain my balance. Every now and then you could hear the boat's screws come out of the water as it peaked the top of a swell and then crashed to the bottom.

"She'll take it, don't you worry," said the captain, assuring us of the vessel's seaworthiness. All the while, the captain stayed in radio contact with the Coast Guard, keeping them updated as to Johnny's condition.

"What's up, Johnny?" I said in an optimistic voice so as to not alert Johnny about my concern for him or my seasickness.

"Tell Dorothy I love her . . . tell the kids. . . ." He broke down. He was scared, and so was I.

"Don't be talking like that. You're going to be fine," I assured him. I don't think he believed me. He knew.

The captain interrupted. "Johnny, the Coast Guard needs to know your age."

Now unable to talk, Johnny held up five fingers two times, for "fifty-five."

Shortly after that the first Coast Guard vessel pulled alongside, and one of the crewmen came aboard. While the crewman was scribbling down information and taking Johnny's vital signs, Johnny's heart gave out. The crewman looked at me and asked if I knew CPR.

I nodded, and the two of us began resuscitation. After what seemed to be an eternity, pierced by swell after crashing swell, a second Coast Guard cutter finally arrived and one of its crewmen relieved me. Overwhelmed by emotion, I went up top, and grasping the railing to maintain my balance and grief, I slowly inched my way to the boat's stern where I wept uncontrollably for my friend.

At his funeral, the priest talked about the glorious way Johnny went to heaven, the way only a fisherman would want to go, doing the thing he loved with the people he loved.

Several days after the funeral, my wife, Terry, told me about a dream that had upset one of Johnny's sons the night before.

"Tim said he woke up in a cold sweat from a dream he had," said Terry. "In the dream, Tim saw his dad, but he was very young—his hair was dark and he was much thinner. He was driving a Winnebago and there was a fishing boat attached to the back. He waved at Timmy and drove off."

I just smiled and felt warm all over.

I knew someday he'd do it.

Luke Altomare

Facing Primal Fears

After many years of perfecting my skill as a fly fisher-man and learning to appreciate this most genteel of the angling sports, I recently decided to expand my horizons. I decided to take up saltwater surf-casting.

It didn't take me long to discover that I'm a terrible salt-water surf-caster—I have yet to catch a fish. I have decent equipment: a quality surf-casting rod, a good selection of lures, a handsome tackle box and a nifty hat. Still, I've had no luck.

I've bemoaned my failure to some of my more success-ful surf-casting friends and admitted my deep desire to land a striped bass from the surf.

"Live eels," they ordered.

"Ya wanna catch stripers, ya gotta use live eels, son."

"Gitcha some eels, boy."

I have a bit of a problem with this, you see. I hate snakes! And as far as I'm concerned, if it slithers on its belly, it's a snake; however, knowing as little as I did about the sport, I wasn't about to ignore sage advice from the seasoned pros. So I faced my primal fear head-on.

Armed with my twelve-foot surf-casting rod, not to mention my nifty hat, I drove the ten minutes from my home to Long Island's south shore. On the way, I stopped in at the local bait and tackle and bought two eels—no sense going overboard on my first outing.

I quietly admitted my inexperience to the rather salty-looking lady at the counter. I had no choice; she had seen me recoil and heard my little yelp at the sight of the eels. She was generous, if a bit condescending, with her advice, not the least of which was that I might find fly-fishing more to my liking. I refrained from making any snide comments about her tattoo.

I arrived at the beach just before sunset, parked and walked the short distance to the water's rocky edge. After lining up my rod and placing it in the sand spike, which I had wedged between some rocks as I had seen the real surf-casters do, I removed one of the eels from my bucket. I used a rag. I'm not crazy.

I held its squirming body and attached my hook through its mouth and out its eye as the snickering old lady at the bait shop had instructed me.

With an adeptness that belied my inexperience, I lifted my rod and brought it back, loading the tip, then snapped it forward. As if in slow motion, the line and sinker began its flight. It was magnificent, a thing of beauty. Unfortunately, the bail closed prematurely and stopped the line abruptly ten feet from the rod tip. The eel, of course, continued on, presumably to live out its life in peaceful, albeit partially blind, happiness.

I quickly glanced to my right and left, but detected no chuckling from the nearby anglers. Satisfied that no one had seen my bumbling cast, I replaced my rod in the sand spike and retrieved my last eel from the bucket.

Deftly—I was experienced at this now—I hooked the eel and prepared to cast again. This time I double-checked the bail to ensure it was opened properly. I reared back and let fly a mighty cast, sending line, sinker and eel a good fifty yards out into the bass-filled surf.

After smugly replacing the rod in the sand spike, I sat back on the rocks, mentally checking the ingredients for the feast of grilled striped bass I would proudly feed my family later that evening. I returned from my reverie. Something was terribly wrong. My eel had been sitting enticingly in the surf for a good ten minutes and hadn't lured so much as a nibble. I plucked my rod from the spike and quickly reeled in. Relief. The eel, although covered with a bit of seaweed, was still securely attached to my hook.

As I reached to remove the unwanted vegetation, the eel jerked and coiled itself around my line. I jumped a foot in the air! Once again, with narrowed eyes, I looked up and down the beach. The other anglers appeared to be too absorbed in their own activities to have taken any notice of my childishness.

As I looked back at my rod, the eel, to my horror, gave another spasm and unhooked itself. I watched in dismay as it landed among the rocks and began slithering like a snake toward the water.

My frugality overcame my fear of snakes—after all, these things cost a buck-and-a-half each—and I jumped down to the rocks to retrieve my last hope for catching a striper. My feet landed on a flat, slippery rock and slid— no, *zipped*—out from under me. I suddenly found myself in the air, parallel to the ground, wincing at the thought of the awful pain I was about to experience.

I came down with a thud and a splash, half on the rocks, half in the water. Relieved that nothing was broken, I scrambled quickly to my feet and, after some rapid in-place running usually seen only in cartoons, regained my stability.

It wasn't necessary to look up and down the beach this time. The sound of whistles and cheers filled the air.

Though I refused to give the satisfaction of a glance, I pictured placards with numbers ranging from seven to ten being held aloft, grading my Olympic ability.

After a few moments of regaining the shreds of my composure, I sighed and watched mournfully as the eel and my dignity disappeared into the surf.

Stan R. Kid

All You Ever Wanted
to Know About Live Bait

Surprisingly, many anglers are ashamed to admit they fish with live bait. You'll run into one of these so-called purists on a trout stream and ask him what he's using. He'll say, "A number thirty-two Royal coachman on a three-ounce leader." Then he'll get a bite, snap his line out of the water, and there will be a worm on his hook. "That's the problem with these tiny flies," he'll say. "You keep catching worms with them."

First off, there are only two kinds of bait: live bait and dead bait. Worms, grubs, grasshoppers, minnows and the like are live bait, unless left unattended in a hot car too long, in which case they become dead bait. I have on occasion forgotten to remove a can of worms from my car on a blistering July day, a mistake that has led to attempts to bait hooks with little balls of worm paste, not to mention the necessity of driving with all the car's windows open until approximately the middle of February. On the other hand, I've carried around salmon eggs and pickled pork rind until they showed definite signs of life.

My favorite method of preserving live bait is to store it in the refrigerator until ready for use. There are two schools of thought on the proper execution of this procedure. Some hold it is better to tell your wife first, and the others claim it is better to let her make the discovery herself. I'm a member of the latter group and have been ever since my wife came across a jar of my hellgrammites while she was sorting through the refrigerator in search of some mayonnaise. The incident would probably have passed without any lingering ill effects had she not at the time been entertaining her church bridge club. It is difficult to describe the resulting commotion with any accuracy, but I learned later that cards from our bridge deck were found as far away as three blocks, and one of the olive-and-avocado sandwiches served at the party turned up in a ladies' restroom halfway across town. Our dog was asleep on the front sidewalk when the ladies left, and it was weeks before we could get all the dents out of him left by their heels.

I have on occasion attempted to lay in a supply of worms during the spring months while they are still near the surface and one doesn't have to dig down to the aquifer to find them. I'll stash a couple of hundred of them in a washtub filled with dirt and feed them coffee grounds. The reason I feed them coffee grounds is that numerous people have told me that is what worms like to eat. Whether they do or not, I'm not sure. In any case, I've yet to find a single worm when I dump out the tub later in the summer. I'm beginning to suspect that worms can't stand coffee grounds.

The beginning angler is often of the impression that there are only three kinds of worms: small, medium and large. Actually, the size of the worm makes little difference. Temperament and character are everything. These two characteristics seem to be determined primarily by environment. For example, I've never found a worm raised in a manure pile that could earn its keep as fishing bait. Manure-pile worms are soft and pale and accustomed to easy living. To a worm, a manure pile is a suite in the Ritz, a villa on the Riviera. A worm never has to worry about where its next meal is coming from. (If it knew, it would probably worry, but it doesn't know.) And manure-pile worms don't have any street savvy. Now, you dig up a worm out of a garden, an individual who has been through a couple of rototillings, and that worm has been around. It's going to go out and put up a good fight. Nothing builds character in a worm like a good rototilling.

Some time ago a sporting-goods company sent me a package of freeze-dried worms. Honest. At first I thought it was some kind of veiled threat, but then I found a note saying that if I soaked the worms in water they would reconstitute into fishing bait. I stuck the package in my backpack with my other freeze-dried food and a couple of nights later at a mountain lake took it out and soaked the contents in some water. It turned out to be macaroni and cheese sauce. "That's funny," my friend said. "I thought we ate the macaroni and cheese sauce last night." The freeze-dried worms never did turn up.

The most troublesome of all live bait is the grasshopper. By the time you've caught enough of them you're usually too tired to go fishing. Furthermore, grasshoppers are not content simply to sit around in a bottle waiting to be fed to some fish. Once a worm is in the can, he pretty well knows his fate is sealed and will lie back and take it easy until his number comes up. Not so with grasshoppers. They are no sooner in the bottle than they're plotting their escape. Every time the lid is lifted to insert a new inmate, half a dozen of the others will try to make a break for it. While I was still a young boy, I learned the only way to foil their escapes was to shake the bottle vigorously and then slip the new grasshopper in while the others were still dazed. What apparently happens is that the grasshoppers get high from the shaking and like it so much that after a while you can hardly chase them out of the bottle with a stick. They just lie on their backs, smiling. Of course this is confusing to the new grasshopper, who thinks he has been incarcerated with a bunch of degenerate insects who keep calling out, "C'mon, man, give us another shake!"

To my mind, the best live bait is the hellgrammite, an insect that resides on streambeds and builds little cocoons for itself out of pebbles. Fish cannot resist them, in their shells or out. They are the salted peanuts of baits. Not long ago I was fishing a stream in Idaho and hadn't had a nibble all day. Then I discovered a nice patch of hellgrammites and within a half hour had nearly filled my limit with plump cutthroat. There were a dozen or so other anglers on the stream, and they were so astonished at my success that they could not help expressing their awe by jovially threatening to slash my waders the next time I was in deep water. Finally, after I had creeled my final catch, a couple of them came over and demanded to know what I was using.

"These," I said.

"Jeez, those are ugly-looking things!" one of them said. "I almost hate to touch them."

"Trout love 'em," I said. "Here, take a couple of mine just to try them out." I figured it was the very least I could do.

As I was climbing into my car, I heard one of the other fishermen yell, "What was he using?"

"These nasty-looking things," the first fellow yelled back. "Big red, white and blue flies!"

I felt a little bad about the deception. On the other hand, you can never tell. There could be such a thing as a patriotic fish.

Patrick F. McManus

The 5th Wave

By Rich Tennant

"Someone should tell Phil he's sautéing three of my lures in that pan of onions and garlic."

7

REEL WOMEN

I could not, at any age, be content to take my place by the fireside and simply look on. Life was meant to be lived. Curiosity must be kept alive. One must never, for whatever reason, turn her back on life.

Eleanor Roosevelt

The Old Stick in the Corner

If you can give your son or daughter only one gift, let it be enthusiasm.

Bruce Barton

In the corner of my bedroom stands an old, mostly straight branch of wood, nearly four feet in length, not quite an inch in diameter. Near the bottom of the stick, adhesive bandage tape has been wrapped round and round for about six inches. Cream-colored crochet thread used to dangle from the top of the pole, but it long ago disappeared.

I keep the stick to remind me. . . .

Red-haired, freckle-faced Kirsten was five years old. She woke up one morning and said, "Mom, I want to fish." For days we talked about fishing. We sang songs about fishing. We spoke of fishing poles. We sang songs about fishing poles. Finally, it was time to give it a try.

"Shall we ask Daddy?" I asked her.

"Does Daddy know how to fish?"

Yes, I assured her. But our young family was struggling. We were starting life over, as they say. We had lived in a shelter for three weeks during a very snowy winter before we were finally able to afford a very small place of our own. By summer, we had managed to acquire some furniture and even some new clothes, but we certainly did not own a fishing pole.

Kirsten asked her father for one, but his answer was "no." No reason given, just "no."

It was a difficult time.

A few days later, Kirsten bounced into the apartment with a really big stick.

"Honey, sticks have to be played with outside," I explained.

Kirsten asked for some bandage tape, which I gave to her.

"I'm making a fishing pole!" she announced.

I watched my precious little girl carefully wrap that stick with adhesive tape and make a good handle grip.

"Come see my fishing pole, Mom! I'm ready to go!"

"Go where?" I asked her.

"Down to the park! A bunch of neighborhood kids said they were going down there today to fish."

"But, honey, did they have fishing poles?"

"Yes! Come on, Mom. I'll show you. Let's go!"

With the stick propped on her shoulder, Kirsten grabbed my hand to lead me down the street. We walked five blocks. I remember thinking how happy, how confident, how carefree my young daughter looked. I remembered when I was five years old and my father had taken me fishing for the first time with a brand-new fishing pole. How I wished I could provide the same opportunity for her.

We reached the park to find seven neighborhood children, complete with seven new poles and one tackle box. The children had been there since morning, standing on an arched bridge, casting their lines.

"Mom, we have to go home." I expected her to notice that she had a stick while the other children had real rods and reels. "Mom, I forgot about the fishing line."

We hurried home, where Kirsten found some cream-colored crochet thread. She cut a ten-foot length and asked me to help her tie it to the end of her pole.

"Mom, what can I use for a hook? Do you have a nail?"

I didn't have a nail, but we did find a safety pin, which we tied to the end of the crochet thread.

This time, Kirsten skipped joyously to the park. She was happy to find the other children were still there. A boy offered one of his worms from his bait box and carefully showed Kirsten how to bait her safety pin. She then expectantly cast her crochet thread over the side of the arched bridge.

"Mom! Mom! I've got a fish!"

I prepared to explain about moss and weeds in the water. All the other children set down their poles and ran over to watch. Kirsten pulled up the stick, and as her crochet thread lifted out of the water, I couldn't believe my eyes. A beautiful bluegill was attached to her safety pin hook. Every child cheered. It was the first catch of the day.

Kirsten and the children spent the rest of that afternoon fishing with the lucky pole and catching so many fish we had to send someone home to get another bucket. Without exception, every child caught at least one fish that day— all with that stick with the carefully wrapped adhesive-tape handle, the crochet thread and the safety pin.

Over the years, the stick has moved with us. The young fisherman is now a teenager who uses a "real" rod, reel, bait and tackle from the store.

I keep the stick to remind me of a small fisherman's dream that even in hard times, a little faith goes a long way.

Cathy Strough

Bait and Switch

Saturday morning everyone arrived at Friends Lake for their weeklong stay. Assigned to Cabin #5, my Aunt Nancy found a HUGE fish, gutted and frozen, that the campers before them had left in the freezer. As usual, the women were in the camps getting unpacked and preparing for their vacations while the men and boys had already begun their fun. Therefore, only my Aunt Nancy, Aunt Dawn and Mom knew about the frozen fish. They kept it their own little secret, waiting for the right moment to spring it on the rest of the family in some surprising way.

The men and boys spent the whole week fishing. These so-called experts returned from their early morning fishing expeditions each day with nothing more than a few small perch or an occasional rock bass. All their high-tech gadgets and experience couldn't help them land the "big one."

"The lake's gone dry," they told everyone after yet another unsuccessful early morning outing. Each day brought more excuses. The women grew tired of all their excuses and wanted to put an end to them once and for all. Finally, the girls pulled out their secret weapon—the big frozen fish they'd stashed away. They grabbed some poles and other fishing equipment and hurried down to the lake.

"We'll show you guys how to catch a fish!" they said, making a big scene as they untied a rowboat. Meanwhile, they had wrapped the fish in a beach towel and placed it with their fishing supplies. They pushed off from the docks and began rowing toward the center of the lake.

"Hurry up before anybody sees what we are doing!" Dawn said excitedly as Mom rowed them away from the throngs on the beach. Nobody suspected them of such a devious plan—everyone assumed they were just having some fun. None of the men thought they had any chance to catch a fish, never mind a big fish.

So off they went, the three of them in their aluminum rowboat, oars squeaking against the sides. They could see the men and kids on the beach snickering at their attempt at fishing. Finally, far enough out so that the casual observer couldn't see their actions from the beach, Nancy unwrapped the partially thawed fish and hooked it on to Dawn's line. They carefully dropped the fish overboard, making sure they didn't lose it.

"Will they really believe us?" they asked each other. "How long should we wait before rowing in to show our big catch?" They didn't wait long—it was too much to hold in. After about four minutes, Dawn started yelling and screaming, "Oh! We caught something!"

Dawn did a great acting job. Everyone knew that touching a fish was her biggest nightmare. The pole bent with exaggeration from the big fish, heavy with half-melted ice—at least that's how it looked from shore. All of their excitement had caught the attention of the beach-goers once again. The men watched in amazement as the ladies lifted the fish out of the water. Nancy grabbed the line above the fish, displaying their trophy for all to see. Dawn tentatively held a small green fishing net below the fish to ensure they didn't lose their catch. Mom turned the boat to face their audience on the beach.

"How did they catch such a big fish?" one of the husbands asked.

Everyone on the beach, young and old alike, ran up to the diving board to get a closer look. Mom started rowing back to shore so that they could show off their prize catch. They had to make sure the fish only faced one way, because it had already been cleaned. They couldn't let their fans see the exposed bones and flesh.

For several minutes, Mom slowly rowed the boat toward the docks, building the anticipation. The people on the beach leaned over the railing of the diving board, trying to see the huge fish for themselves. The three women were in no hurry to end this delightful joke on their fishermen husbands. The men on shore were wondering out loud what the women used for bait.

"Don't lose it," they warned, holding onto only a sliver of pride in their own fishing abilities. The looks of astonishment on the men's faces, having been one-upped in their own special skill—fishing—were priceless.

Finally, Nancy, Dawn and Mom couldn't stand it any longer. They rowed in even closer. When they were within ten feet or so of the board, somebody finally noticed that the fish wasn't exactly right.

"That fish has already been gutted," one of the men said in utter astonishment.

Silence ensued. The men were speechless, now realizing that they had been suckered into one of the greatest Friends Lake pranks in history. Nancy, Dawn and Mom were proud then and remain proud nearly two decades later. They still laugh about the day the women taught the men how to catch the "big one." However, on that day, it was the fishermen of Friends Lake who really got "caught."

Kevin Martone

"Will it help our relationship if I throw it back?"

A Half-Inch to Spare

My husband Bill and I had rented a campsite at Smith Mountain Lake. It was small, in the midst of a public campground, and our tent took up nearly all of the space. Bill had promised me that on our first weekend camping out, he would take me fishing. I told him that I went fishing as a kid, and I had been pretty good with a cane pole and a bobber; however, this was going to be my first time with rod and reel, trolling from our power boat.

Early Saturday morning we started out. He wasn't going to fish, just guide the boat ever so slowly through the shallower water in nearby coves. Deep down inside, I knew he figured we'd spend an hour or two, and then he could do some serious fishing on his own. There were few boats out, and the water was glassy, rippling only in response to a gentle wind that blew between the mountains. It was quiet except for the growling of the engine on the back of the boat. Every so often I'd reel in the Rebel lure Bill had chosen for me to use.

"I've got one!" I said when I felt something hit the line. The strike was a strong one.

Bill throttled back. "Don't jerk the rod," he said.

"I'm not." And I wasn't. But he was so convinced that I

had no idea what I was doing that he couldn't help giving instructions.

The line slackened and I started reeling frantically. Then the line tightened again and, suddenly, a beautiful fish broke the water, writhing to break free.

"It's a trout," Bill said.

Neither of us knew there were trout in the lake.

"Be careful," he said as the fish broke water again.

He had moved to the back of the boat where I was, his eyes watching the line and the spot where the fish had just disappeared. His hands were balled into fists. He wanted to take the rod from me and bring in the fish himself, and it was all he could do to keep from grabbing it.

The very moment I realized my husband's desires, the line went slack.

"He's running under the boat," Bill warned.

I could see then that the line was beginning to bend toward the boat. With a paddle, Bill awkwardly turned us. I reeled in the slack. Vibrations in the rod told me the fish had not shaken the lure. My fish was still there.

It broke the surface again, and I knew what "fishtailing" really meant.

Down it went again, and I reeled in some slack. For several minutes I pulled and reeled, bringing the trout closer to the boat. We both knew it was a big one. My heart pounded, and Bill wouldn't look at me. Every so often he gave another instruction, but he did not physically interfere.

Finally, I had the fish near the boat. Bill had the net in his hand. The gallant fish was tired. In an instant, the net swooped down, and my trout lay in the bottom of the boat.

"It's beautiful," I said.

Bill nodded in agreement.

Carefully, Bill reached down and removed the hook from the fish's mouth. Hooking a finger in the gill he held it up. "It's a big one," he said. "Let's take it to Chuck and see how long it is." Chuck was a friend camping next to us.

When we arrived, Chuck was sitting in a chair outside his camper, and he waved as we pulled up. Bill held up the trout and Chuck asked, "Who caught it?"

"She did," Bill said, and pointed at me with pride. "We need to see how long it is. Got a ruler?"

Chuck went inside, then reappeared with a ruler. The fish measured fifteen-and-a-half inches. Chuck looked at it longingly. We knew he loved fresh fish, so in silent agreement, we gave it to him.

On our way home Sunday, we stopped by my in-law's house to say hello. Bill immediately told his father, a good fisherman himself, about my phenomenal catch. His father beamed, proud to have a woman in the family who could actually catch fish.

"What'd you do with it?" he asked.

We told him we'd given it to Chuck to eat. He laughed and shook his head. "There was a fishing tournament at the lake over the weekend," he said. "I'll bet that trout of yours could've won it."

Only partially deflated by the possible loss of a trophy fish, the next day at work, I was telling everyone who would listen to my wonderful fish story.

"Yeah, I heard there was a tournament down there last weekend," one friend said. "How long was yours?"

"Fifteen-and-a-half inches," I said proudly. I was sure in my heart that it must have taken a much bigger fish to win a tournament.

He grinned at me and shook his head.

"The winning trout was only fifteen inches."

Cary Osborne

The Gypsy Angel

Let us not be too particular. It is better to have old second-hand diamonds than none at all.

Mark Twain

It was 1993, the beginning of another great summer at the lake. My fifty-five-year-old mother, Helen, who had just recovered from a partial mastectomy and many months of chemotherapy and radiation, announced that she was now the proud owner of a boat.

I smiled and shook my head because I never knew what my adventurous and free-spirited mother would be up to next. I remember one Christmas she told her family and friends that all she wanted was power tools so she could learn how to build things. When she initially told us she wanted a boat and a friend had one for sale that needed a little bit of work, I was worried. I had seen my mother drive our wave runners at a very fast speed. When she announced that it was a slow-moving pontoon boat, I was relieved—until I saw it. The conglomeration of metal made her idea of "a little bit of work" a huge understatement. I did not see how this thing was going to float, much less run. Momma insisted that with a good cleaning and a few repairs, the boat would look brand new. I, on the other hand, didn't think it would make much difference, but I didn't have the heart to tell her.

After taking the boat to a local car wash and hosing it down, we took it to a neighbor who serviced boats. With the repairs completed and the addition of a new canopy, I must admit it looked pretty good. But looking at my mother's face, you would have thought she was the owner of a millionaire's yacht.

The next step was taking it out on the lake and seeing how it would run. I was still apprehensive as we backed it down the ramp and put it in the water for the first time. We held our breath as Momma put the key into the ignition and turned it. The first three tries, nothing, but on the fourth try, it came alive with a low humming of the motor. We started venturing out of the cove and onto the open lake. Before long, we were soaring across the water with the wind softly blowing on our faces. The sound of the water slapping against the boat was like music in the air.

I was in awe of my mother, and in my eyes there wasn't anything she couldn't do. As I looked at her behind the wheel of her new boat, her hair finally growing back, I saw she was absolutely glowing, and I knew she was in her element. Later that evening, we sat under the stars, trying to pick the perfect name for her new treasure. We tossed around a few and finally decided on the *Gypsy Angel*. Momma had collected angels for many years, and we all knew that she was part gypsy, because at the drop of a hat she would be off to a new place to add another experience to her life.

Many mornings at the break of dawn, Momma would wake me and her small grandbabies and we would head out to check the limb lines that she had baited the night before. We were still in our pajamas, mind you, and were assured we would come right back before it got too light outside, which was never the case. We did eventually come back to the house, but only to eat lunch, change into our bathing suits, and of course grab more bait, and then we would head right back out on the *Gypsy*. It took us to places on the lake that we hadn't before discovered, and we would get ourselves so deep in some of the coves that we didn't know how we were going to get out. Somehow the *Gypsy Angel* never failed us.

During one incident, Momma had set out some new limb lines, and we went to check them the following morning after it had stormed all night. As we were nearing one of the limb lines, Momma noticed that the line was frantically moving. She maneuvered the *Gypsy Angel* over as close as she could, but the branches on the trees were very low, and with the water being up so high from all the rain, she couldn't quite reach the line. Momma knew she had a big one, and she wasn't about to leave it behind. I heard a big splash and looked to find Momma out in the water swimming with a knife in her teeth, which she used to cut the line. What a sight: her swimming back to the *Gypsy Angel* with a huge catfish by her side. I hurriedly grabbed the camera and took a picture of her holding that eighteen-pounder over her head, her eyes gleaming with excitement. Her grandchildren must have thought they had the craziest grandmother in the world.

As I recollect all the times we stayed overnight on the *Gypsy Angel* and shared so many magical moments among a grandmother, her children and grandchildren, it came as a shock when Momma decided she should sell it. She couldn't afford to keep up with the repairs that the old boat needed. She promised us that when the time was right, she would buy a newer one.

As that glorious summer ended, the *Gypsy Angel* was

sold. When the new buyer came to get her, we told him all the wonderful memories that had been made because of her. With our voices cracking we pleaded, "Please take good care of her." I know he must have felt somewhat guilty for having to take her away from us. As we watched from our front porch, *Gypsy* rolled down the country dirt road, out of our sight and out of our lives forever, leaving us all with broken hearts. We mourned for days. The vacant spot by the dock was too painful to look at. Little did I realize how much *Gypsy Angel* would come to mean to us. She nourished our souls and helped us establish a lifetime bond with each other.

When I look back I am so thankful that my courageous mother had the desire to become the owner of a pontoon boat. The following year Momma started feeling pain again. After many tests and a bone scan, the doctors confirmed our worst fear: the cancer was back. It had metastasized and was spreading fast. In the short months I was able to take care of her, we talked endlessly about our escapades on the *Gypsy Angel*. Her eyes would light up with each memory. On June 4, 1999, I said good-bye to the most adventurous and free-spirited soul I had ever known, my best friend, my mentor, my mother—*my* Gypsy Angel.

Lucinda Shouse

Fishing the Partridge and Orange

Bright warm days on the Gallatin River are more picturesque than productive. Fish just don't come out of their hiding places the way they do when the clouds brood and cast a gray light on the canyon walls that cup the Gallatin in its stony hands. At least that had been my experience.

On this particular day I guided Beverly, an older woman with great enthusiasm for fly-fishing. Not only did she like to fish, but she subscribed to every fishing magazine on the market, and she had an elaborate filing system for the articles she saved that were of the most interest to her. She tied her own flies and only bought samples to copy from.

Usually I scramble quickly down the steep rocky trail to the river, but Beverly's knees were arthritic and she couldn't be rushed. We had to take our time, pick our way around the larger rocks, and step carefully where the ground was flatter. To steady herself, she put both hands on the top of my shoulders, and I led her slowly down to the river's edge.

The Gallatin River sparkled on this bright, cloudless July day. On the shoreline where we stood, the river tumbled over its rocky, boulder-strewn riverbed like kids excused for recess. During the summer, this section of the river in the canyon between Bozeman and Big Sky, Montana, is cooled by the colors of summer green; in autumn, its shoreline burns hot with the reds, oranges and yellows of the changing birch and aspen. Beverly praised the beauty of the river, uttering a heartfelt *wow!*

While she stood admiring the water, the trees and the sudden appearance of an osprey, I busied myself preparing her leader and choosing a fly for her to fish with. Clipping and twisting the leader into deliberate and strong knots, my fingers flew through the motions with the experience of over twenty years of fly-fishing. It was imperative to hurry since the shadows on the water, necessary to catch fish, were quickly disappearing as the sun rose above the canyon walls.

But Beverly wanted to show me something.

"Look what I picked up at our local fly shop!" Beverly held up an insect screen that had been stitched in the shape of a glove. "See, you go like this." She donned the insect-net glove and held her hand about a foot under the water. When she pulled it up, there were small nymphs squirming in her palm. "Look, mayfly nymphs!"

I paused mid–blood knot and silently observed her discovery.

"Since there are nymphs here, do you think we could fish a soft-hackle fly?"

I had never fished a soft-hackle fly before. I felt rather ashamed that I did not know about soft hackles, what they imitated or how they were supposed to be fished. I knew that they were old patterns that had originated in England and that people wrote entire books about them. My lack of knowledge made me feel vulnerable.

"Do you have one?" I asked.

Beverly held in her hand a partridge and orange soft-hackle that she had tied herself. It was the most elegant fly I had ever seen. Orange silk thread wound around the hook shank to form the body. Partridge hackle, sparse like a whisper, flared just behind the hook eye. That was it; no lead, no gold beads, no tricks. Simplicity and beauty, centuries old.

"How do you fish it?" I asked, my curiosity helping me to forget my ignorance.

"It's supposed to sink just under the surface like an emerging nymph. But I don't know how to fish an emerger. Maybe you can show me," said Beverly.

Even though I had no experience with this pattern, I could still try. The standard instructions for emergers is to cast out a little less than ninety degrees from the bank, keeping the rod tip high so the fly sinks and is carried downstream. As the line begins to pull in the current, the fly arcs back towards the surface, at which time you lower the rod tip and follow through with the rod pointing downstream. Hits can be expected as the fly begins its swing.

At first the fly did not want to sink and floated on the surface like dryer lint.

"I have something that will fix that," said Beverly as she unzipped a vest pocket. "Look what else they sold me—Xink!" She held the bottle up like it was a lucky penny. After applying a few drops to the fly, it sank. We studied the water, looking into its depth for a response.

I didn't have hope for much success since the sun was finally high enough to cast its glare upon the water's surface, but miraculously, silvery scales flashed like little sparks as fish made several investigative dashes at our fly. On the second cast, Beverly set the hook. She caught a fourteen-inch rainbow. For over an hour, sparks of light in the late morning sun winked as rainbows chased, struck and hooked themselves on the soft-hackle fly.

I was mesmerized. The Gallatin doesn't fish well on sunny days, but what did I know! And, for once, it felt like it was all right not to be the know-it-all guide. Beverly had left herself open, and I was open with her. My not knowing about soft hackles did not upset her, just as her not knowing how to fish an emerger did not upset me. We had bridged our gaps of experience.

Jennifer Olsson

The Secret of Going Fishing

I think contentment the greatest wealth.

George Shelley

In the darkness, I rubbed my weary eyes and groaned as the clatter of a wind-up alarm clock sounded, bringing a harsh, abrupt end to my night's rest. Momentary thoughts drifted through my hazy brain: *Just go back to sleep! You can do this later; he'll never know, and you'll have kept your promise.* But the nagging guilt of being less than completely honest with my husband didn't let the thoughts linger too long. With a sigh, I swung my legs over the side of our tent-trailer bunk, stretched, then gazed at the still-sleeping form of our six-year-old daughter. *Perhaps she'll change her mind. She is so difficult to stir in the morning at normal hours. What will she be like at five o'clock on a cold June morning in the Sierra Nevada?*

"Erin," I whispered, trying not to disturb my sister, who had joined us for a week of camping at Hume Lake, California. "Erin, it's time." To my complete surprise, and perhaps dismay, she raised her tousled head energetically.

"Is it morning already?" she asked. No escape there! I

yawned and stretched again, watching my daughter bound from her sleeping bag with uncharacteristic morning enthusiasm.

"Yes, it's morning, sort of," I muttered quietly back to her. In the predawn chill and dark, we slipped into our sneakers, donned sweatshirts and padded off to the restrooms in silence. Returning to our campsite, we retrieved the fishing pole and tackle box my husband had painstakingly prepared for the trip. I could still see his hands, skillfully tying knots in the slippery fishing line, still hear his patient instructions as he briefed me on how to teach Erin to use the rod and reel. I recalled telling him that if the line broke, we would be finished . . . there was no way I could tie the hook and sinkers back on the way I'd seen him do it. He just smiled.

"You'll do fine," he told me. "I just wish I could be there to help." His smile slowly faded as he gazed off into the distance. "I really should have done this sooner," he said. "Guess you'll have to do it for me."

I gently reached out and touched his arm.

"I wish you could, too. Isn't there some way you can?" I asked, more to assure him that I understood—that I knew how badly he wanted to be with us. He slowly shook his head.

"The business is just too new for me to leave for the week. I have to take care of our customers, or I can't take care of us." Then he smiled and looked at me. "Maybe next year."

I slowly nodded in agreement.

So here I was, yawning in the dark, groping for my thermos of coffee and praying that this wouldn't be a total disaster. Erin tugged at my sleeve.

"Come on, Mommy! We have to get the fish early. Daddy said so." I took her warm little hand in mine and headed down a path in the direction of the lake, hoping I wouldn't stumble into it in the darkness, literally. As we walked, Erin kept up a stream of happy chatter.

As we neared the lake, the coffee had begun to do its job. My head started to clear, and with the clearing came other awakenings: an awareness of a sharpness in the crisp morning air chilling my nose, cheeks, ears and hands; the stillness of the woods anticipating the dawn; the sweet clarity of mountain air filling my nostrils and lungs; the utter timelessness of the moment; the overwhelming sense of well-being that comes from appreciating the awesomeness of Mother Nature.

We rounded a corner and the path abruptly ended, opening up to the shoreline. I set down the pole and tackle box and took one final gulp of coffee. Erin had fallen silent. Apparently she, too, was captivated by the glorious magic of the early morning. As I turned toward the lake, I noticed a faint silver glow had appeared, ever so delicately, hanging about the edges of the jet-black Sierra across the small lake from us. Slowly, the midnight blue-black of the sky began to take on a lighter hue, and as it did, a chorus of bird songs punctuated the morning silence.

"Mommy, look!" Erin pointed to the surface of the lake. I remember the sight today as clearly as if a motion picture were playing in my mind. From the placid, motionless surface of the water, there arose in ghostly swirls and rifts a thin veil of white. The morning mist over the lake swelled and grew until the face of the water had become a dance floor, with hundreds of cloudlike dancers gently bowing, twisting, rising and whirling to the music of the woods. There in the predawn light, Mother Nature was orchestrating a natural ballet, as wisps of fog gently flowed and meandered in the air, covering the surface of the lake in an ever-churning rhythmic motion. We stood and watched in silent awe. Recalling the camera slung around my neck for photographing the morning's "big catch," I snapped a few pictures, though I realized no picture could ever recapture the breathtaking experience we were sharing.

Years have not dimmed the clarity of how I remember that morning; Erin remembers it the same as I. Neither of us recalls much more about the details of the remainder of our fishing adventure, including whether or not any fish were caught. But mention "going fishing" to my now eighteen-year-old daughter, and this moment at Hume Lake is the first thought that comes to her mind. The predawn experience expressed my husband's love of fishing to both of us more than any fish tale ever could. We now understand why he can say it's not about where you go, your gear, your boat or even how many fish you catch. It's more about time, reverence for creation, Mother Nature, putting life on "pause" for awhile. It's about "going fishing."

Melody Plaxton

Taking the Bait

*G*ood *fishing never stops. There are only times*
when in some places it is better than others.

George Fichter

The *biggest* fish I ever caught was about 300 pounds. The *most* fish I ever caught? I have been fortunate enough to have caught more fish in one day than some folks get to net in a lifetime.

The *best* fish I ever caught? That's a good fish story. About 175 pounds, six feet long and sporting a delicious chestnut mustache.

It was my maternal grandma who taught me everything I needed to know about fishing—and about men, for that matter. "Always spit on the bait and sing this little song," she'd say. Then she'd smile and sing out, "Sue culla, sue culla-culla." (Finglish or Finnish-English for *"Here, fishy fishy"*). "Now don't set the hook until you're sure you've got a good nibble; always let a man or a fish chase the bait until you're sure you've caught 'em." She would always say this with her wise and knowing smile, and she always out-fished Grandpa.

I was living in Auke Bay, Alaska, under the small general store. It was handy. I lived downstairs, worked upstairs, and I was near the harbor.

I loved fishing. I also loved to eat fresh fish. It's something you never really get out of your blood, or out of your backpack if you don't wash it out in time.

Sometimes I would eavesdrop on the fishermen who stopped to buy supplies or gas. I always got the best tips on where to catch fish.

One sunny summer day, a particularly cute fisherman stopped in the store. He seemed rather shy, but after chatting at the counter for a while with him, he asked me if I was interested in taking a preseason flight to Burners Bay to check out moose hunting areas. I declined, since I already had plans to climb the Mendenhall Glacier trail as high as I could and get some good photos.

A few weeks later, he returned to the store and asked me out again, this time suggesting that we go fishing. Good move. I never turned down a chance to go fishing, especially since he was a professional fisherman. I figured I could learn a few new spots, and besides, he was rather cute.

Fishing together became a fairly regular event for us. Other suitors had bought me predictable gifts such as bouquets of flowers, cards or candy, but not this guy. He left vacuum-sealed smoked salmon at my door. Still, I was enjoying being single, and I did not want to be like the salmon, vigorously swimming upstream only to spawn and die. I wanted excitement.

It was three o'clock. Late for work, as usual, I bounded upstairs; suddenly, before I could reach the third step, a note and little box, attached to fishing line, were being dangled in front of my face.

Puzzled, I looked around, but I could not see the prankster. As I grabbed at the line, it rose just above my reach. I could hear the clicking of a reel being cranked.

The note and box dropped again; after several attempts to grab the bait and see the perpetrator of the insane little joke, who was laughing out loud by this time, I finally grabbed the box. I unfolded the note and read: "Need a deckhand and a tax deduction." In the box was a gold nugget band.

I'm not sure who hooked whom, but I promise, I did not spit on him or sing to him. I am still hooked on fishing and on the fisherman. We now have a small fry of our very own so my life continues to be exciting, and I still out-fish my sweetheart. I will teach our son everything he needs to know about fishing—and about fisherwomen, for that matter. And I will wear a wise and knowing smile.

Jacqueline Jean Michels

Saved by the Lady in Red

Plunge boldly into the thick of life!

Johann Wolfgang von Goethe

During a family fishing trip in the 1970s, I realized that my mother was no ordinary mom. It also became apparent that she had a profound appreciation for the environment.

We'd found a likely place to try our luck for trout, a broad stream trailing down from the Cascade Mountains in Oregon's Three Sisters area. Fallen trees lying just beneath the surface of the water proved a challenge even for my father's precise casting.

I was thirteen, and as the eldest, I was able to fish on my own; but for my twelve-year-old sister and our mom, Dad did everything but hold their rods. My younger sister and brother's job was toting the net and tackle box.

Between my father and me, we'd caught three good-sized browns and were thinking of moving upstream. Then Mom suddenly jerked up and started reeling. The line went taut when her fish swam beneath a submerged log in midstream. It appeared that the weight of the fish wouldn't allow the line to slip free. Patiently, Mom continued to yank and work the line as the fish jumped tantalizingly beyond the log. Realizing this wasn't going to work, she dipped under and over Dad's and my sister's lines to get to where she could just reel straight in. But, flipping and flailing, that dratted fish stayed hung up. Several times Dad offered to cut her line, but Mom wouldn't allow it. Instead, she became more determined.

Then as we gaped at Mother in astonishment, she started stripping off her jeans, shirt, shoes and socks until she stood there in the fanciest fire-engine red lace bra and panties I could have ever imagined a woman would wear, especially MY MOTHER!

Immediately, without even a quick toe-test, she dove straight into the icy-cold water. Submerging a moment later by the log, she freed her line and, with the line clenched between her teeth and dragging the fish, she swam quickly back to the stream bank. Dad was there with his sweatshirt to cover her as she came shivering out of the water. Though we kids knew we probably should have felt embarrassed, instead we were proud and delighted with our amazing mother.

Later, Mom explained that she'd gone into the cold water not simply to catch a fish, but because she couldn't bear to let that poor fish die.

Afterward, I never again saw my mother in quite the same way. After all, I didn't know of another mom who would go to such lengths to save a six-inch, small-fry trout from drowning.

Rosalie P. Griffin

The Native

It is only with the heart that one can see rightly.

Antoine de Saint-Exupery

"Grandpa and I are going fishing," my father called on his way out the door.

I jumped up from the cabin floor and grabbed my red plastic fishing pole. "Can I come too?"

"I'll take you tomorrow, sweetheart." He headed out the door.

I trudged to the kitchen where my mother and grandmother were washing dishes. "It's not fair. I want to go fishing."

"When Daddy takes you fishing, he has to spend all his time making sure you don't drown," my mother said. "Let him fish with Grandpa today. He'll take you tomorrow."

"I won't fall in. I'm not a baby."

"Lisa, you're only six years old."

"Why don't you catch toads?" my grandmother asked.

I scowled and said, "I already did that."

"Then go fish behind the cabin." She held out a cup of night crawlers she retrieved from the refrigerator.

The creek my father and grandfather fished, across the road from our cabin in the Allegheny National Forest, was deep and wide, more like a river. Behind our cabin, a tiny stream ran under the road and into the bigger creek.

"But I want to fish in the big creek with Daddy and Grandpa."

"It's the little creek or nothing," my grandmother said.

As I left the kitchen, my mother said in a low voice, "Mom, there aren't any fish in that creek."

"I know that," my grandmother said. "But she doesn't."

I ignored them. My grandmother didn't know everything. I'd show her.

An hour later, I wondered if my grandmother knew more than I'd thought. My first night crawler still dangled on the hook. All I'd caught were crayfish.

Just as I decided to go hunt more toads, my line jerked really hard. I yanked the pole to set the hook like my father had taught me. The hook flew out of the water, empty. Something had taken my bait, and it wasn't a crayfish.

I lost two more worms without a glimpse of what took them. I threaded another worm onto my hook and cast into the little pool in the stream.

After a long time, the line jerked again. I wrenched the pole back and cranked the reel, hands shaking. Whatever it was, it was still on the line and fighting.

I wound the reel furiously until my sinker rose from the water. Right behind came a fish, flopping and twisting at the end of my line, belly gleaming silver. Before I could swing the pole over solid ground, the fish jerked and disappeared with a splash. I'd lost it. Determined, I jabbed the hook through another piece of worm and dropped my line.

My mother called, but I didn't answer. That fish could bite again at any moment.

She crashed through the brush. "Lisa Ann, I know you heard me. Come change your clothes."

"Shhh," I whispered. "There's a big fish in here. How am I supposed to catch it with you making so much noise?"

She narrowed her eyes and whispered back, "It's time to go to Mass."

I argued, but my mother said if there was a fish in that creek, it would still be there when I got back from church.

My father and grandfather were back; they hadn't caught anything.

"I almost did," I said, "but I lost it."

My grandfather raised his eyebrows. "In that little creek? Must have been a minnow."

"Nuh-uh. A big fish. I'm going to catch it."

He laughed. "That's a fish story if I ever heard one."

All through Saturday evening Mass, I prayed to catch that fish. My mother always told me not to pray for selfish things, like a new bike. I was only supposed to ask God to do something important, like make sick people well.

My mother would think praying to catch a fish was wrong, but I was sure God understood. This wasn't just about a fish. First I'd been treated like a baby, and then I'd been laughed at. I needed to catch that fish.

When we returned to the cabin, I refused to eat supper. My mother said I had to be back by dark, and that wasn't far off. "I'll eat later," I promised, running out the door.

For the longest time, I sat on a rock next to the creek and waited for a bite. Dusk fell. Maybe the fish had swum farther down the creek. I'd never catch him, and no one would ever believe he existed.

Finally he nibbled. In my excitement, I yanked too soon, and the line came up empty. I fumbled in the dark for bait.

I felt another tug and counted to three. When I jerked the rod, the weight and force of the fish dragged against it.

I reeled and he fought, just like last time. But this time, instead of lifting him straight up out of the water, I ran up the bank of the creek, rod over my shoulder.

The fish—*my fish*—skimmed out of the water and up the bank behind me. Only when I was well away from the creek did I lift him from the ground.

I didn't know how to take a fish off a hook. My dad always did that. So I set off for the cabin with the fish still flopping on the line.

My father looked up from a magazine when I walked through the door. "Holy cow, you caught a fish."

My grandfather's mouth dropped open. "I don't believe it. That's a brook trout—a native."

I grinned. "I told you it was really big."

"We'd better make sure it's legal," my father said.

My heart sank. The fish looked huge to me. Now it might not even be big enough to keep. My accomplishment seemed to dwindle with the size of the fish.

My father got his tackle box with inch marks on the lid. I stood behind him and my grandfather, craning for a peek while they measured.

Seven inches, I prayed. *Let it be seven inches.*

"Six and three-quarters," my father said.

My grandfather bent over the tackle box. "Tail's kind of curled up. Flatten it out."

I waited in silence, barely breathing. For all my insistence about not being a baby, I felt like crying.

My grandfather turned, fish in his hands. "Seven inches," he said, with a wink. "I'll cook it for your dinner."

He did, and to this day I've never eaten a better meal.

Lisa Wood Curry

Butch

Every man is bound to leave a story better than he found it.

Mary Augusta Ward

As a young woman, I was determined one summer to learn how to fish. After purchasing fishing gear, based on the advice from a sporting goods clerk, my black lab Butch and I headed for the nearby lake.

I pulled over at what appeared to be the local fishing hot spot; several cars were already parked along the roadside. A morning mist still hovered above the water, clearing as the morning warmed. It was a wonderful day to wet my line for the first time. Fishermen were catching spawning crappie by the bucketsful, some probably destined to be buried in the garden for fertilizer rather than landing in a frying pan. Actually, I was hoping for a little more luck— I wanted to catch a bass.

I tied on a lure and added a brightly colored round bobber. I proceeded to cast my line and work my lure with what I thought was a most enticing jigging motion. When I quickly got a bite, I remembered the need to set the hook, so I pulled my pole up with gusto and sent my little fish flying in the air past my head. The poor fish hit the steep bank behind me with a smack. I repeated this several times with the fish usually falling off my hook and flipping back into the water. Butch lay well behind me, wary of my casting backswing after I'd managed to hit him with a soaring fish or two. I scrambled in pursuit of each escaping fish, stepping into the lake water—and a couple of times into underwater critter holes. I kept getting wet, first up to my knees and finally above the waist, much to the amusement of the experienced onlookers.

Apparently my knot-tying skills also needed improvement. I had soon lost all of my lures, with few fish to show for my efforts. The fisherman next to me took pity (or maybe wanted further entertainment) and offered some tie-ups so I could continue fishing. I thanked him and went back to work. His kindness and my persistence paid off. I had a hard strike! My pole bowed down, almost touching the water. My mentor was excited too, shouting, "Bet you hooked a bass! Bring him in easy now. Don't jerk too hard."

Laughing, I landed the fish without it becoming airborne. But it, too, came loose when my line broke just above the bobber, and both the bobber and my fish slipped back into the lake. As the other fishermen groaned, we watched the bright red bobber mark where the fish traveled. The fish towed the bobber round and round the cove, sometimes tantalizingly close to the bank, only for it to disappear underwater for what seemed like a long time and then pop up somewhere else. The fish grew in size, at least in our minds, the longer it stayed under. As the bobber cruised its course past other fisherman, they cast out, trying to snag it without success.

A rowboat was hailed to help. Just about the time they'd get close enough to grab it, the bobber would sink out of sight. "It's over here now!" a spotter would yell. One enterprising fellow climbed a tree, broke off a long branch and joined the rowboat's efforts. They finally gave up and went back to their own fishing.

Discouraged, wet and muddy, I prepared to leave. I called my dog and ruffled his neck. I was seeking consolation. Suddenly I got an idea—one of those lightbulb kind. As the bobber made another pass, I said, "Go get the ball, Butch!"

As everyone watched, Butch wagged his tail, spotted the ball moving across the water and happily fetched it, fish and all. We went home with a nice-sized bass.

A few days later, I returned to the same cove and set up next to another woman. She commented that more women must be taking up fishing, then told my own fish story back to me, as her fisherman husband had related to her. I nodded and giggled in all the right places. The story, being a fish story, was slightly embellished, of course.

"That's quite a fish story," I acknowledged. "I have one, too. I'm that same lady. It was my dog that fetched the fish!"

She wasn't the only one who unknowingly repeated my story to me. On a visit to replenish my lost gear, I shared my experience with the sporting goods' clerk.

"That was you and your dog?" he grinned. "A customer was just in here this morning telling me about it!"

For one fishing season, at least, Butch and I became one of the legends of the lake.

Dixie Ross

Nothing Less Than Perfect

Sometimes it's worse to win a fight than to lose.
Billie Holliday

I have the firm belief that brothers were put on this earth to torment their sisters. As the oldest child, I have three younger siblings—my brother, Cory, who is three years my junior, and two sisters. I also have a "surrogate" older sibling, my mother's youngest brother, Bruce. Although he was my uncle, Bruce was only a few years older than me, and we played together, laughed together and practically grew up together. Thus, in my mind, I have two brothers.

Our family loves camping, and we took many trips to Burney Falls Memorial State Park, just south of Mt. Shasta in Northern California. My grandparents, along with Bruce, joined us for these trips where we would spend entire days fishing Lake Britton and Hat Creek, topped off in the evenings with wonderful family fish-fries.

As the overachiever of our family, I always thought myself to be perfect at everything, including fishing. But my "brothers" set out to prove me otherwise. While fishing a hole on Hat Creek, Bruce and Cory began teasing me about everything, from my fishing ability to whether or not I stuffed socks in my bra, all within earshot of the other fishermen. Now, the fishing jabs were okay, but the bra comments crushed me because they were not true (at age thirteen, I was also an overachiever in the puberty department).

I tried my best to ignore them, but they continued the torment. Finally, to throw them off, I threw them a challenge.

"Okay," I yelled, "whoever catches the biggest fish gets to be waited on the rest of the day!"

"You're on!" said Bruce, adding, "But the loser has to clean *all* the fish!"

My heart dropped to my stomach. The only thing I had not accomplished in my many years of fishing was controlling my nose; the smell of a fish being sliced and gutted always made me nauseated. I would usually release a fish so I didn't have to clean it, or I would sweet-talk my father or grandfather into cleaning my catch.

"Well, you game?" chided Cory.

At a loss for words, and with all the other fishermen hanging on my bated breath, I nodded in agreement. The competition was on!

From that point everything was a blur. I was so nervous about the possibility of having to clean a fish—a skill that every great fisherman possessed, except me—that I couldn't concentrate on my fishing. All the while, Bruce and Cory were in cahoots as they worked the hole; they usually released their catch, but they were now loading up their stringers with as many fish as possible! Ugh! More fish to clean! It appeared that Bruce's counter-challenge was going to haunt me forever.

Lost in my own *Twilight Zone* episode, my line jerked me to reality. Fish on!

I worked the fish, finally landing my prized catch. A fisherman came over and helped me pick it up—the fish was huge! I can't remember the exact size, but it was bigger than anything my two nemeses caught. I had won the challenge, and my secret was safe.

Bruce and Cory were crushed at first. Then, after an impromptu but very loud conversation, they agreed to clean my fish plus all the fish they had caught. Not trusting their snickering, I stuck around for the cleaning, but at a safe, nonsmelling distance.

They cleaned their entire catch first, without too much fanfare; then it was time to clean my prize. Bruce was on his haunches with his back to me, and Cory was looking over his shoulder. Suddenly, Cory jumped back and with horror in his voice, yelled, "OH MY GOD!" Bruce groaned and fell backward on his butt.

I was terrified that Bruce had hurt himself with the knife, or worse, had sliced his finger off. I ran to help, but when I got there, Bruce flung the fish into my face and squished fish guts on me.

"Gross!" I screamed, madly trying to wipe the blood and innards off me. I thought I was going to be sick. Laughing so hard they were in tears, Bruce and Cory finished cleaning the fish, talking loudly about how yummy everything looked and throwing more guts at me. It was then I realized they knew my secret—I wasn't perfect after all. It was one of the best lessons my brothers ever taught me.

Dahlynn McKowen

8

FISHING LESSONS

Little by little, we human beings are con-fronted with situations that give us more and more clues that we aren't perfect.

Fred Rogers

The Kindness of Strangers

As a result of the terrorist attacks on the United States on September 11, my much-anticipated annual fishing trek to the Pacific Northwest had been delayed. But I finally got a flight out of Tampa, a woman traveling alone and still afflicted with the numbing depression that seemed to settle like a shroud over the entire nation in the weeks following the tragedy. I drove to Montana's Bitteroot Valley, hoping it would bring me the peace it always had in the past. Once settled, I headed for my friend Bill Bean's fly shop in Hamilton in search of a fishing license, a few flies, some advice and, most of all, a reason to smile.

There they were, three fellow travelers from the East Coast, getting ready for the final float trip of their weeklong vacation. We struck up a conversation, as people inevitably do in cozy, small-town fly shops like Bill's. Their trip, an annual event cherished as much as my own, also had been delayed. We talked about how we had almost not made the journey at all. First, it was a question of whether we *could* go, given the state of airline travel at the time. Then, it was a question of whether we *should* go. How could we blithely trot away on vacation while our nation was suffering the most horrific nightmare we had ever known?

But, in the end, we agreed. We were right where we needed to be and very grateful to be there.

We wished each other luck, and they left. "Nice guys," I told Bill.

He agreed, noting they had been coming there for years.

A few minutes later, the one called Creature walked back into the shop and came up to me.

"We talked about it amongst ourselves," he said. "And we've got an extra space on our float trip today. Why don't you come with us?"

I just gaped, speechless for possibly the first time in my life. Creature obviously mistook my stunned silence as reluctance or apprehension.

"We're pretty good guys," he said hastily. "We aren't perverts or anything. Just thought you might want to fill up that empty seat on the raft."

For one fleeting instant, thoughts of my mother intruded. She worries about me, constantly getting into boats with strange men, or at least men *she* considers strange. To me, they're just typical fly fishermen—a little offbeat, but generally harmless.

"That isn't it at all," I stammered, still trying to decide if this was some sort of joke while mentally running down my equipment checklist. "I just happen to have my rod and waders in the car. Are you really serious?"

"We'll wait for you outside, and you can follow us to the launch," Creature said.

I asked Bill how much he thought my share of the trip would be. The last, and only, time I had hired a guide on the Bitteroot, it was close to four hundred dollars for the day. I had quickly determined guided trips were a luxury I could not often afford.

"They don't want you to pay, Nanette," Bill said slowly,

as if speaking to the village idiot. "They want you to be their guest. Just go, have a great time and let me know how you do."

And go I did, with tears in my eyes, completely overwhelmed by the incredible, unexpected generosity of these three strangers.

What followed was one of those all-time, top-ten days—the kind you never want to end and never will forget. The fishing was slow, with few fish rising and even fewer biting, but no one seemed to care. I know I didn't.

I was paired with Creature, a charter fishing guide out of Hatteras, North Carolina, whose nickname refers to his boat, *Sea Creature*. He specializes in fly-fishing for the Big Boys—bluefin tuna and white marlin. The two other fishermen were both named Mike. They were longtime friends from Maryland. They had all become buddies and now made the trek to Montana yearly.

I cast to risers and missed strikes twice. Creature, batting clean-up in the rear of the raft, nailed them. I told Creature I appeared to be his lucky charm. He smiled and admitted that might be true.

We waded awhile, spreading out in companionable solitude along the river. A bald eagle flew overhead. The river's gentle lullaby gradually took the place of the CNN static still rattling around in my brain from days of nonstop news watching. As it always has, the rhythm of fly-fishing worked its mental massage on me and also on the three strangers scattered nearby.

Back in the raft, I hooked a huge rainbow, the biggest of the day, then promptly lost it. Not long ago, I would have cursed my stupidity, letting that lost fish gnaw at me like an ulcer and spoil my entire day. But instead, I laughed about it and laughed some more.

In fact, I caught no fish that day, despite my best efforts. But I felt immense joy in seeing Creature, a man who makes a living battling the behemoths of the sea, take unabashed delight in landing a fourteen-inch rainbow trout. I watched the two Mikes teasing and joking, in that easy way of old friends who have no need to take each other seriously anymore. Picnicking on a gravel bar along the river's edge, we dined on grilled salmon, homemade cheesecake with berries and ice-cold beer, talking about our families, friends and the rivers we loved, about America and what had happened to her, the uncertain future we now faced and our suddenly real fears.

Heading for shore in the twilight, the sky a deepening sapphire blue, we heard coyotes howling in the distance. I looked up to find Sirius, the Dippers Big and Little, and Orion blinking on for their nightly show.

This unforgettable day, this remarkable gift was bestowed on me by three men I had never met before and probably will never see again. *This is what fly-fishing is about*, I thought, *a community of kindred spirits who find a way to connect across the miles, even across the madness.* From the bottom of my heart, the thoughtfulness of two Mikes and Creature restored my faith in the goodness of humanity.

Nanette Holland

On the Road

It was a warm Saturday morning in Montpelier, Idaho. I had worked all week and was thinking about passing on my much-needed yard work for a day of fishing. I'd never been to this particular reservoir before, but had always thought about going there. Some of my customers at the feed store had told me how to get there, but it wasn't what most people would consider an easy trip.

Working around the yard that morning, it wasn't until 2 P.M. that I finally convinced myself I needed to stop and head for the reservoir. I called my brother-in-law, Ron, and invited him to join me. I didn't bother to tell him our destination until I picked him up. He agreed to my unexpected offer, so I threw my equipment into my old blue Jeep and headed over to Ron's place.

"It's way too late to try and find it," he said when I finally announced where we were headed. But he still went along anyway.

Driving without benefit of a map or exact directions, we drove down the highway until we came to a dirt road, where I turned off. After another ten miles we finally came to a fork in the road—I simply turned without any hesitation.

"How'd you know which way to turn?" Ron asked.

"I'm not sure," I replied.

That probably reinforced Ron's reluctance as he kept insisting that it was getting way too late to even try and get some fishing in. Another five miles passed, another fork in the road came, and yet another unhesitant turn didn't help Ron's confidence in me. He was convinced we were going to get lost.

Finally, at sunset, we crested a small hill and were greeted by the sight of a beautiful reservoir. With the exception of one little, topless Jeep parked near the water, there was no one else around for miles. We would have the entire lake to ourselves.

When we approached the other Jeep, a young man happily greeted us. He was there with his wife and their newborn baby, and their car battery was dead. They had no matches to build a fire, no coats, and there was only one thin blanket for the baby. He had been very worried, knowing that his wife and baby wouldn't make it through the night if he had walked out the many miles for help. And since it was getting dark, he might even have gotten lost.

The young man told us he had just had the Jeep overhauled and was out with his family for the day. After the battery died, he had decided to stay with his family and simply hope that someone would come along.

Ron and I got out our battery cables and gave his Jeep a jump-start. He profusely thanked us, and they left for home.

As we watched them drive off, Ron turned to me. "You still want to fish?"

"No" was all I said. We got back in our own Jeep and followed them out to make sure they got home safely.

That was over thirty years ago. I have never returned to that reservoir, and I am not even sure if it's still there. But there is one thing I am sure about: the Lord answered a father's prayers through my love for fishing.

Doyle Portela

Fishing Patriots

It's no fun being old if you haven't enjoyed being young.

Jim Collins

It was a gorgeous day to go fishing. There is nothing like September in Oregon when the sun is shining. The temperature was perfect, and the sky was a brilliant blue. The group going fishing at the Sandy Trout Farm was from the Avamere Assisted Living Facility. There were a few folks from the Alzheimer's unit of the facility, including my mom. This was the most well-groomed, spacious fishing farm I had ever seen. The paths were easy for our people to navigate, and the ponds were accessible and well-stocked, all perfect ingredients for a perfect day.

As a volunteer, my job was to help put worms on hooks, cast if necessary and assist when needed in landing fish. One of the things that is so amazing about the old folks is that they remember how to do things they had once enjoyed. Even from wheelchairs, some were able to get their lines in the water. The smiles on their faces were as bright as the sun overhead. But one lady started crying.

When I asked her what was wrong, she said holding a pole made her think of her father and how much he had loved to fish. There was no comforting her as she was lost in her recollection. Some shook their heads and said they didn't want to fish, but their eyes told another story. And when I handed them poles, not one refused. Others, like my mom, who had fished a lot in their lifetimes, became quite excited when they saw fish coming out of the water.

Each person got to catch two rainbow trout, and they were beauties. Our activity director laughed, saying, "Oh dear. I think I've gone way over my spending limit in fish for today." Of course that brought on talk about "limits" and "firsts" and "biggest" fish. Were these the same people who had gotten off the bus looking old and tired? I wasn't so sure. They had forgotten about the aches and pains of life and remembered the right fishing lingo and the competition of the sport. It was fun to watch the transformation.

As the fish were being cleaned, we moved the group to an eating area and began to set up the food for our picnic. When the fish were delivered, we added a little butter, salt and pepper and wrapped each one in foil for the grills. One woman stepped up and asked if she could help. She said she and her husband had run a small restaurant locally and she missed the work. She was a great resource and enjoyed every minute of it. Others helped set tables. It took awhile to get the fish done, but every person was willing to wait and each had their fill.

After a wonderful dessert of chocolate cake, we began to clean off the tables and get things packed for the trip home. As I picked up paper plates, I said to Mom, "Isn't this a wonderful place to be today?" As if cued in an onstage musical, she started singing "God Bless America." I was caught off guard at first but soon joined her song. While I had been thinking only about the small space of the trout farm as being wonderful, this marvelous lady was thinking of America as a wonderful place to be. One by one the whole group joined in, some putting their hands over their hearts. The realization came to me that we were losing this generation of incredibly loyal Americans who sacrificed more than many young people will ever understand. Even though Alzheimer's and age have taken so much from these folks, they still remembered their patriotism.

Then came the topper. It was a comment from one of the fellows as we headed for the bus. He said, "Boy, we sure know how to have fun, don't we?"

Bonnie Nester

Play It Again, Sam

Memories tug at my emotions as I hear it. The words come to me through the low, moisture-laden clouds that nourish the river where I'm standing. Then the words are echoed by the soft symphony of the river's currents.

I pray my father knows how deeply flows the current of the heritage he passed on to me. My heart is filled with memories of childhood days I spent with him; days when I played among the huge boulders of Oregon's Sandy River while he fished for the beautiful migratory steelhead.

I remember the powerful sound of the river as he held me precariously on his still young and strong shoulders. I felt my feet sometimes dipping in the turbid water as we crossed from bank to bank.

I felt him search for footholds as he carried his rod in one hand, his other arm wrapped tightly around my dangling legs. I could feel the tension and the excitement, the necessity of getting to the other side of the river where the fish held.

We sat in hog lines on the mighty Willamette River. I heard the slosh of the water, the pull of the current against our anchor, the sounds of the rushing Oregon City Falls nearby. I have learned the sloppy sound of the tide coming in on the Columbia, the rush of the water as it is going out to sea.

I remember catching trout at Diamond Lake, one after the other, giggling, while he would say to me, "Play it again, Sam!"

I was born with Marfan Syndrome, a connective tissue disorder that affects many systems, but primarily my eyes and my heart. The lenses in my eyes are dislocated, hanging by broken muscles; my aorta is prone to dissection with increased blood flow.

"What shouldn't I do?" I ask the cardiologist.

"You should not play big game fish, nor should you have children."

I play big game fish, and I have two wonderful children. Not because I am defiant, but because it is deeply engraved in my soul. I have to fish, I have to be on the river, and I have to pass this on to my children.

Until my diagnosis, I grew up knowing touch and sound more keenly than sighted people. I have for years, sometimes without realizing it, listened more intensely than others. I know that my love for music is due to my challenged vision. We naturally do what is easy, and it is easier for me to listen than to see.

At age three, my parents were still not aware that I could not see well. I would sit at the piano for hours, listening, playing, picking out tunes. In my baby book it is recorded that I would pick out tunes on the piano such as "Puff the Magic Dragon" and others, as early as four years old. Gifted? I don't know. I think I was just doing what came naturally to me. Listening was easy, and all children mimic what they hear!

People talk of some magical, mystical heightened ability to use one sense if another sense is decreased or absent.

Nonsense. It is not magical, it is necessary. It is developed.

Thus, it is true that when I fish, I listen. Sometimes I feel left out and unhappy when people point out fish to me and I can't see them. In *A River Never Sleeps* by Roderick L. Haig-Brown, I read how often he sees fish before he casts to them. My first reaction to this is self-pity. I don't see those shadows of great fish very often.

This leaves me at a serious disadvantage, although I truly believe that listening while you fish makes up for it in many ways.

I have learned how to cast by listening. I get a thrill out of hearing my line peel out as I cast eight ounces of weight from the Oregon beaches of the Columbia. An uneven, strong whir caught by the wind tells me before it hits that perhaps I should have purchased a Washington license, which lies directly across the water, but is deceivingly far away. Sure enough, the screaming reel sounds long enough for it to hit somewhere near the opposite bank. Well, not quite, but I can dream.

I met my fiancé, Bill, two years ago while rafting the whitewater of the North Fork Nehalem. I have spent many hours admiring the sounds of his cast. I hear how gracefully it lands, thus not tearing the bait to bits. I learned how to mimic that by the sound of his reel, his line and the final landing of his lure.

"I must have a G. Loomis rod and a Calcutta reel just like yours," I told him. "I must, so that I can totally mimic what I hear when you so artfully cast."

Bill's cast is a beautiful symphony of the spool's release of line. An elegant lob that sends monofilament gracefully arcing across the width of the river with a constant and steady melodious tone.

I was born with perfect pitch, the capacity of a person to identify a musical sound immediately by name, without reference to any previously sounded pitch. I believe his cast to start with a low A, below middle C. It then rises to a D sharp before it descends in tone again. It lands with a gentle breaking of water. The tricky part is to make it smooth, legato, an interrupted phrase. The goal is to not disturb what lies beneath.

I close my eyes as my feet adjust to the feel of the rocks on the riverbank, and shut out any visual input. I practice those tones as I hold that piece of cold-gold, metal Calcutta in my hand and rehearse.

"Listen while you fish" repeats through my head to the tune of "Whistle While You Work."

"Shoot one out there," I hear Bill say. That would be a staccato, quick cast. I know the sound of a quick cast, and I have practiced listening to it. I know how to produce that sound by feel. My rod, my reel and my line are my orchestra, my hand the conductor and my river the audience.

My fish, therefore, the applause.

Locate the fish, play your rod and reel like an orchestra, and wait—wait for the sounds of the applause, the applause that echoes water breaking against the canyon walls of the river. Hear the sounds of that silver-sided, tail-dancing steelhead as it draws you back onto the stage for a standing ovation.

Then play it again, Sam.

The river plays music to me, and I will not stop fishing even if it kills me. If I cannot play it again, who will play it for me? If I cannot hear the sounds of the river, or know the feel of a fish on the end of my line, the pull of the current against my lure, that surely will kill me.

I have genetically passed along the special ability to listen and feel to my son, Andrew. He also has Marfan Syndrome and was born legally blind. I am terribly sorry he will need to live with the threat of a shortened life span and endure challenges beyond what a healthy body would require.

My other son, David, is unaffected. I can't help but

think that he too will pick up the special listening and feeling skills that he sees Andrew and I practice.

I hope that in living along the banks of Oregon's Kilchis River, where they can hear the rush of the flood and the trickle of low waters, they will hear the music. It will imprint on them my love for fishing and they will know their heritage.

Should the eighty-pound salmon I will one day hook prove too much for the weak connective tissues of my heart, it will be my time to go. There could be no better way. If and when it happens, I know what my prayer will be.

I will ask God that my beloved sons will hear it from me as I now hear it from my father—*Play it again, Sam!*

Jennie Logsdon Martin

Just another day in fishing paradise for Jennie.

Photo courtesy of Bill Hedlund.

Heaven

If you want the rainbow you have to put up with the rain.

Dolly Parton

The disappointment within me grew with the accumulating thunderhead that Dad and I watched from our backyard. I realized that the storm was coming toward us, and no matter how hard I wished it would go away, it was still coming. I couldn't stop it.

"Think it'll miss us?" I asked hopefully. I saw Dad's brow furrow as he studied the movement of the clouds. Then he put his big hand on my shoulder.

"No. It's coming. Sorry, son. We'll have to wait until next weekend."

He squeezed my shoulder and walked into the house. I stood alone in the backyard that suddenly seemed as big as the universe. My seven-year-old heart was broken. Not only was I helpless against the approaching storm, Dad was telling me that he couldn't stop it either. How was that possible? I always thought Dad was Superman in a baseball cap, and there was nothing he couldn't do. He had even apologized to me for not being able to stop the rain from coming. That realization was more shocking than the first cold drop of rain on my face. Dad wasn't invincible. Another drop of rain landed with a splat on top of my bare foot.

It was Saturday, and every Saturday for as long as I could remember, Dad would wake me at the crack of dawn, we would eat breakfast, get in the truck and drive to heaven. At least it was heaven to me. Dad took me fishing.

During the week and after my chores were finished, I fished for bluegills in the creek that ran in front of our house, but I lived for the weekend trip with Dad. We drove to my uncle's farm pond and fished for largemouth bass. It was the majestic fish that graced the cover of Dad's copy of *Outdoor Life* magazine and was the subject of numerous articles. I tried to read the articles, but mostly I was fascinated with the color pictures of leaping bass.

As I watched the clouds, a gust of wind blew tiny particles of dust into my watery eyes, and I prayed that God would stop the storm. I could smell the rain now, and more big drops fell on the ground around me. Dad opened the door and called me in. He was smiling, and I was glad that the rain concealed my already-wet cheeks. I ran to him; he lifted me up, the smile never leaving his face.

"Next weekend will be here before you know it. Those old bass can't go anywhere, right?" I could only smile back and nod my head as I tried to swallow the lump in my throat.

I fish competitively today in as many tournaments as I can, and on those days when I carry an empty sack to the weigh-in stand, I remember that stormy day when Dad taught me that there would always be disappointments in life no matter how hard we wish they would go away. Because of Dad, I know they will pass just like a summer storm, and the sun will shine again. And on those bright sunny days when I'm not fishing a tournament, my son and I get up early, eat breakfast and drive to heaven.

Ronald Niswonger

Hook Them with Love

Eventually, all things merge into one, and a river runs through it.

Norman Maclean

There was a time in my life when I couldn't sleep the night before a fishing trip. Instead, I'd spend most of "Fishing Eve" checking my tackle, tying flies, practicing my cast in the driveway and packing the car.

And yet, despite these memories, I don't know why it happened, why I fell out of love with fishing. The only reason I can think of is that I had instead fallen in love with my second wife, LaRena. And, in the heat of that love, I didn't realize just how much I missed fishing.

During my first marriage I thought nothing of driving off for a weekend of fishing, leaving my wife behind. I never asked her if she wanted to come with me. And she never asked to go. Our marriage didn't end because I hadn't taken her with me, but I'm sure our time together would have been better if we had shared the joy and excitement of fishing.

So when a friend invited me to the Eel River to fish for

steelhead, the first thing I did was ask LaRena, my new wife, to come along. I wanted to share time with her on one of California's most beautiful rivers. It would be the honeymoon we never had. She didn't hesitate to say yes.

LaRena had taken on the difficult role of stepmother to my three children. Many nights she lay in my arms crying from the pain of not feeling she was loved despite her best efforts to be a good mother. She needed, and deserved, some time away from that role. And we both needed time to be together, without the children.

So, leaving the kids with a babysitter, we took our first fishing trip to Richardson's Grove State Park. We stayed in a rustic, one-room redwood cabin with two single beds, a propane stove, a small wood-burning stove for heat, a tiny table and a refrigerator. A lonely lightbulb dangled from the ceiling. It was the most beautiful place we had ever seen—and we were alone.

The next morning we drove over to my friend's house. I had never fished for steelhead, always having been a light-tackle, mountain stream fisherman. He told me where he thought the fish would be, gave me some fresh roe for bait and delivered a quick lesson on how to catch steelhead.

"You'll hardly know you have one on the line. They kind of suck in the bait, so you have to set the hook even if you just *think* you feel something," my friend instructed.

LaRena and I headed for the Eel River. Near a huge rock towering at least one hundred feet above the water I readied my light spinning rod with its four-pound test line. The trick with light-tackle fishing is to set the drag strong enough to control the fish without the line breaking. It sounds good in theory, and works on smaller fish, but as I was to find out with my first cast, theory doesn't mean much to a mighty steelhead.

I made my first cast upstream and let the bait drift slowly and naturally into the deep, green hole where the fish had schooled. Within seconds I felt just the slightest nibble on my line and set the hook on a monster. The reel sang the "fish-on-line" song that every fisherman loves to hear. Ten minutes into the fight the giant was at least fifty yards away and heading downstream when he suddenly turned and swam straight back toward me at light speed. I couldn't reel fast enough, and the line slacked. Like a magician slipping out of knots tied by a sailor, the fish effortlessly slipped my line and was gone.

LaRena was sitting nearby on a rock reading. She didn't fish. She loved to read, and she loved the towering redwoods. I didn't think she had watched the battle. But I drew comfort from knowing she was there. With my arms aching, I prepared for my next cast, setting the drag a little tighter.

LeRena waved and said, "You'll get him this time."

Again I felt the something-like-a-nibble on my line. I set the hook, and *bam!* We were off to the races again, this time with an even larger fish. I kept good pressure on it while the fish made its initial run as I gently pulled at my light rod to nudge it around instead of trying to force it to turn. I was prepared this time when the fish made a run straight toward me. I lost track of time. My only measure for what seemed like an eternity was the growing ache in my arms, which were quickly approaching the dropping-off point.

Then, just when I thought I had that monster landed, it took off for another run around the river's bend, disappearing into the fog as my line went limp. I dropped to my knees, exhausted, cursing the light tackle, cursing the fish, all with an empty yet somehow satisfied feeling inside. Losing a fight is no fun, but there is redemption in losing a good fight.

I repeated this same scenario three more times, never landing a single fish. Finally, LaRena came down off of her rock perch and stood beside me.

"Why don't you give it one more try?" she suggested.

"Do you know how much my arms are aching right now?" I whined.

"No," she answered sheepishly.

But I knew that if anyone understood about not giving up even under the most difficult circumstances, LaRena did. She had never given up on her stepchildren, our marriage or me. So I tried again.

I made my cast as before and immediately hooked another steelhead. It was smaller this time, and my tackle easily landed it within a few minutes. My catch was a yearling, having been to sea only once, but a good-sized one. LaRena was there with her camera the moment I held up the fish. I was ecstatic.

Later, back at our cabin, LaRena and I roasted the fish in the little propane oven. And, as we sat at the small table enjoying it, LaRena said, "I have something to tell you."

"What is it?" I asked, with a sinking feeling inside. No one ever likes to hear that phrase.

"Before we were married you used to fish all of the time," she began. "When you stopped, I was afraid you would resent me for coming between you and your fishing. I assumed you had stopped because I don't like to fish. But being here with you this weekend has taken away that fear. I now know you love fishing *and* me. And I learned something else," she added.

"What?" I asked quietly.

"That life, like fishing, while a battle, is also fun. From now on, when I'm dealing with the children, I'll remember those battles you had with the steelhead. You were despondent at losing those first fish, yet you enjoyed the fight because you loved fishing. I really do love the children, and one day I will hook them with love."

I didn't know what to say, so I said nothing. We hugged across the table.

I fished for two more days and didn't hook another steelhead. But at night LaRena and I sat in our fog-shrouded cabin, dreamed about our future and talked until sunrise, the venerable redwoods towering above in their perpetual strength and silence.

The children are grown now. And LaRena long ago hooked and landed them with her patient and persistent love. Now they hardly talk to me when they call home or visit. They want to talk to their "mother."

Donald W. Murphy

The Rite of Passage

From father to son, so it goes.

Ashanti Proverb

At 6:15 A.M., I drove up to the rented cabin where my daughter Kristin, her husband Gary and my grand-children, nine-year-old Shannon and six-year-old Tyler, were staying. They came up to the Adirondacks every summer to visit me, their "Pop-Pop," for a week. I made a left turn into the driveway. The cabin was dark inside, my family asleep.

I start fly-fishing and camping with my grandchildren when they reach six years of age. Shannon and I have been fly-fishing for three years already. The previous night Shannon and I went down to the Indian River where the zebra caddis hatch occurred. The hatch did not disappoint me. When Shannon and I got on the river, the caddis were so thick they were landing and crawling all over us. You can't imagine how thrilled I was when Shannon turned to me and said, "Pop-Pop, what do I do? The caddis are tickling me!"

I grinned from ear to ear. "I told you fly-fishing is a dangerous sport!"

She laughed as my heart burst with pride.

Shannon's casting left a lot to be desired, but at age nine, she tried really hard. She really didn't cast the fly line; it was more like she beat the water with the line, but during the evening she did have a few rises.

"Pop-Pop, I got one! Pop-Pop, I got one!" she yelled with excitement. I ran over with the fishing net and helped her land it. When it finally got dark, we made our way out of the river and up to the car.

As we were driving back, I turned to Shannon and said, "You know, with that great caddis hatch tonight, there should be a great caddis spinner fall in the morning. How would you like to come down with me at sunrise?"

"Can I, Pop-Pop, can I?" Shannon asked exuberantly.

"Yes, little one, of course you can," I said.

When we arrived at the cabin, I decided that we didn't have to take our rods apart.

"Since we'll be back so early in the morning," I said. "We'll just put them in the back of the car." I popped open the glass top of the rear door and slid our two rods in. Our nine-foot rods passed through the car, their tips resting on the dashboard. Back to the cabin we went.

After parking my car, I entered the darkened house and went to Shannon's bedroom, gently touched her shoulder and shook her awake. She bolted upright in bed. "Pop-Pop, are we going fly-fishing like you said?" she asked excitedly.

"Yes, little one, we're going back to see if there's a spinnerfall," I replied as her proud grandfather. She got dressed in a few furious seconds, and out the door we went.

When I parked my SUV, we both got out. Shannon, in her excitement, slammed her door shut and met me at the rear door. I opened the back glass window, reached in and took out the rod I was using and leaned it against the car. When I reached for my best rod that I was letting Shannon use, it was stuck up in front. After three gentle but unsuccessful tugs to free it, I set it down, thinking that the rod tip was stuck on the visor or the dashboard. When I went around to Shannon's side of the car, I saw the broken tip of my favorite rod dangling outside the door jamb. *My expensive Orvis Trident!*

Now, some men might have gone ballistic, but I have my own personal life story related to this very moment. What happened next has happened to us all. An old home movie ran through my head:

In 1952, I was a string-bean nine-year-old boy. My dad and I were just returning from fishing; he had taken me down the same Indian River for my first day of fly-fishing. As my dad was taking the bamboo fly rods out of the back seat of his '52 Buick cruiser, I slammed the door shut before his best rod was all the way out.

My dad froze, his mouth dropped and silence stopped the world from turning. I suddenly realized what had just happened, and my lower jaw landed somewhere around Tierra del Fuego. I'll remember his next words for the rest of my life.

He calmly, very calmly, said in an even, soft tone, "You know, son, I wish you hadn't done that."

THAT WAS IT! *"You know, son, I wish you hadn't done that."* Nothing else. I found out later that my dad took his "new" three-piece bamboo fly rod back to a little store in New York City on Forty-Fifth Street and Madison Avenue for repair. I didn't know until many years later that the store was called Abercrombie and Fitch.

Now, fast forward to the quandary there in front of me: the dangling tip. Shannon had followed me and saw what had happened.

"Pop-Pop, did I do that?" she asked, her voice upset and tears welling up.

I stood frozen, just like my dad a half century earlier. I slowly turned to her and said without emotion, "It's okay, little one, it's really okay." I started to grin, first from my heart, then all the way to my face.

I reached out and gave her a hug. A hug of love. With tears welling up in my eyes, I told her the story about my dad. At the end of the story, she too smiled and gave me a hug, a hug of love.

My next thoughts were deeply personal. I thought of my dad and the life lesson he had taught me fifty years earlier. And with tears still in my eyes, I mentally said, *Thanks, Dad. Boy, do I miss you today.*

It had happened—*the rite of passage.*

Patrick Sisti

Reprinted by permission of Tim Peckham.

At the Grave of
the Unknown Fisherman

I was in one of the fly shops down in Boulder picking up some fly floatant and some fresh tippet material. It was shaping up to be a good year. I'd already burned through a bottle of Gehrke's Gink and two spools each of 4x and 5x tippet, and the season wasn't half over yet.

It was just a quick stop, but for some reason it struck me how much fly shops have changed in the last few decades. For one thing, there are a lot more of them now (in some big fishing towns they're on almost every corner, like gas stations), and I seem to recall a time when you couldn't buy clothing in a fly shop. Now some of them are more like T-shirt boutiques that sell some expensive tackle on the side. I've been told this is the only way to "make your nut" these days. The shops also open much later in the day. Once upon a time, fishing stores catered to people who were out at dawn.

They've also become weirdly similar, like chain restaurants. You'll often find the same flies by the same overseas industrial tiers and the same graphite rods by a handful of manufacturers. Even the slogans on the T-shirts are the same: THE WAY TO A MAN'S HEART IS THROUGH HIS FLY, KISS MY BASS and so on.

My sister once told me a story about a husband and wife who drove across the country with their three-year-old son. They figured the kid would get bored, but he loved McDonald's so every night they stopped to eat at one because they thought that would give him something to look forward to. It went well enough until the third night when the kid said, "Dad, how come we drive all day and still end up in the same place?"

Don't get me wrong; I love fly shops, I'm glad they're there, and I go into them often to happily spend money on things I really need, but I sometimes feel the same way when I go into a new one. How come I drove all this way and ended up at the same place?

But the biggest change in fly shops is in how beginning fly fishers are treated, which is better now than it used to be.

When I took up the sport, you simply went down to the local hardware or sporting goods store and bought the cheapest rod, reel and line they had. You only got a few flies because they were expensive—as much as fifty cents each—and you stayed away from the small ones because they didn't seem like much for the money, and they looked like they'd only catch little fish anyway.

Fly patterns were a toss-up. There weren't as many then, but there were still too many to choose from, and the guy behind the counter knew more about duck hunting than he did about fly-fishing. I remember buying Royal Coachmen and McGintys because they were pretty. They worked, too, but it turned out that other patterns sometimes worked better. Then you'd go out and flail around on your own until you got the hang of it.

There were a few instructional books around and they weren't bad, but they never seemed to start right at the beginning, and when *you* were right at the beginning, they could be incomprehensible. After a season or two of fishing, you'd go back and read the book again, and this time it would make a little more sense.

There may not have been an actual fly shop nearby, but if there was you'd eventually find it, and it would be tantalizing and mysterious, like the first real bar you ever walked into. There were odd gizmos displayed in glass cases, strange animal parts hanging on the walls and a distinctive odor you finally identified as mothballs. Everyone but you seemed to know what they were doing.

Some of the people there would be helpful in a vague sort of way, but there was always the air of a private club about the place, and no one knew quite what to do with a rank beginner except to smile wisely, remembering themselves back in the day. You'd feel like the inevitable tenderfoot in a John Wayne movie, with most of the frontier philosophy going right over your head.

One way or another, you learned how to fly-fish anyway.

I was in a fly shop once when a guy walked up to me and asked how long it took to get really good at this. (He may have thought I worked there, or I may just have looked like an old fisherman who'd know something like that.) I said, "Ten years, if you fish three or four times a week." His face fell. He was thinking a couple of weeks, tops. The face of the clerk who was signing him up for a few courses fell a little too. I tried to save it. I said, "Well, that's how long it took me, but I didn't have much help."

That was true, I really *didn't* have much help, but learning how to fly-fish on your own wasn't all bad, either. You spent a lot of time on the water—maybe not catching fish, but nonetheless out on the water where it all happens, seeing the hatches and spinner falls you'd only read about, spooking trout, thinking *What the hell were they doing there?* and just generally wandering around and getting a feel for the places fish live. With any luck you were young and footloose, unaware that your time was worth anything more than what you happened to be doing with it at the moment.

There were things you reasoned out for yourself, some that came from books and snatches of free advice, and others you learned through a process of elimination, by doing it every possible wrong way first. And there were the things you picked up quickly—wading safety, poison ivy identification, the peculiar habits of rattlesnakes.

There was also something unforgettable about being young and dumb, in the middle of the worst day of fishing you'd had so far and, at that precise moment, running into the kindly stranger who says, "Excuse me, son. Do you mind if I make a suggestion?" Years later it occurs to you that you are now supposed to be that helpful stranger. Not because you've become so wise, but because you've finally learned how to offer advice without being condescending.

A friend of mine said recently, "I don't know what some of these young fly-fishers are doing, but they can sure catch the hell out of trout." Actually, they're doing pretty much what we're doing, albeit with unfamiliar flies and funny-looking tackle. It's just that some of them are doing it better.

Most days I'm a perfectly happy fisherman—it's my mission in life—but now and then I do catch myself making old-guy noises about how it is now as opposed to how it once was. I used to worry about that because I dreaded turning into a geezer, but then I thought, *What the hell, you might as well embrace what comes next because what else can you do?*

Once I told a young fly-fishing guitar player I know that I thought fly-fishing was getting to be like rock and roll: more about glitz than substance. I was proud of the succinctness of the phrase. When most fly-fishers complain, they go on and on.

He told me I was wrong about both music and fishing: That in fact plenty of rockers were playing for free or for drinks and tips, or kicking it out in basements and garages, annoying the neighbors for the sheer joy of it— just like they've always done.

And the same goes for fly-fishers. Young and old, quietly fishing on unfashionable waters and doing it very well with a handful of flies and perfectly good, but cheap, tackle from Cabela's and Kmart. You don't notice them, he said, because they don't show up on the covers of magazines and they don't write books about it.

Then he suggested we go look at this little mountain lake I'd been telling him about, the one I thought was just as good now as it had been back in the old days.

This is why you should always have some young friends.

John Gierach

Witness to Glory

A man who gives his children habits of industry provides for them better than by giving them a fortune.

Richard Whately

My first steelhead trip was wet, rainy and Pacific Northwest–cold. I was with my friend Paul, a diehard winter steelheader. When I got my first glimpse of the bank of the Nestucca River, anglers were shoulder to shoulder as far as I could see. We squeezed onto a parcel of mud, where I faithfully worked my postage-stamp-size allotment of water as the hours passed and the rain fell. As the morning wore on, the streamside crowd thinned until, by noon, there were only a few of us left.

I had been watching the anglers around me, and a father and son had caught my eye. They silently worked their own water. The father had released two fish that would have reduced me to tears of joy. The son, decked in neoprene waders, had seen a couple of battles, but had lost each. Suddenly the boy, perhaps fourteen years old, was nearly jerked from his feet as his rod tip lunged for deep water, line screaming off his reel.

The first time the fish jumped, my jaw dropped. "He's got a chinook, and a big one," Paul whispered. "Happens every once in a while."

The boy stayed calm, but between the current and the huge salmon, he was slowly edging toward a deep shelf that cut across the river in front of a wide series of rapids. We knew that if the Chinook hit those rapids, it was all over. The boy's father had set his own rod aside, but never so much as shouted a word of encouragement. He just stood there, watching intently.

The boy reeled the fish in three times, and each time it blasted off downstream again, fighting its way toward the whitewater. After fifteen minutes, the fight was obviously taking its toll on the boy. Even from a distance, I could see his arms shaking as he clung to the rod. The icy river had inched up to his ribs and was beginning to lap toward the top of his waders. The chinook had gone deep, fighting for all it was worth. The rod continued to twist and jerk—and then the boy was gone.

He emerged a second later, shaking his head to clear the water from his eyes, his bluish fingers still clutching the rod. Paul grabbed our net and jumped in.

"No!"

I spun toward the verbal warning and saw the boy's father pointing toward Paul.

"No," he repeated. "When he wants help, he'll ask for it."

Paul nodded and stood at the bank of the river, net in hand.

Then the fish cut hard for the bank and slipped into the thick branches of a partially submerged tree. We all waited for the rifle shot sound of the snapping line. Instead, the boy lunged forward, driving himself into the mass of tangled limbs.

Everything grew still. The man called to his son, but his response was lost in the noise of the river. Paul waded closer and called back that the boy had the fish, but couldn't get both himself and the salmon out of the branches. Paul began pulling back the dead limbs as the boy backed out of the brush, fighting to keep both his balance and his fish. Shivering with cold and exhaustion, he emerged clutching a thirty-one-pound Chinook salmon to his chest with both arms. He waded a few feet, paused to get his balance and continued, slowly working his way back across the river.

His father handed him a short length of rope to secure the fish, then reached down and helped him up onto the bank. The boy lay on his back in the mud, gasping for breath, his eyes never leaving the huge fish beside him. Paul had a portable scale with him and asked the father if he could weigh the salmon. He looked at Paul and said softly, "You'll have to ask my son. It's his fish."

As we drove home that evening, I realized that in the pride in the man's voice, in the look of victory on his son's exhausted face, I had witnessed a rite of passage. The father had allowed the boy to take the glory and the right to tell his own children about *his* first big fish—and how he had taken it like a man.

Perry P. Perkins

The Last Big Catch

We can do no great things; only small things with great love.

Mother Teresa

When I think of all the fishing trips, the one that stands out is the trip that took place on November 27, 1997. Grandpa was lying in a hospital bed that was set up in Grandma's dining room. Dad had spent the night with him. Around 1 A.M., one of my aunts came in to wake up Dad. Grandpa was having delusions, thinking he was trapped in the hay barn, even though he was still in bed.

"Dad, why don't we sit on a bale of hay and take a breather," my father suggested.

Grandpa was out of breath and panicky. When Dad finally talked Grandpa out of the "barn," he suggested they go sit under the maple tree in the front yard. Grandpa agreed, and he sat up in bed. All was quiet as he looked at the imaginary land and water before him.

"Did you see that?" Grandpa asked Dad.

"See what?"

"That fish jump. There's another one," Grandpa said, as he cast out his line.

"Dad, what are you doing?" my father asked, curiously.

"Shhh," Grandpa said, "can't you see I'm fishing?"

"Mind if I join you?" Dad asked, deciding to join in on the fun. Being careful not to disturb the fish, Dad moved closer to Grandpa's bed and cast out his line.

Together, they fished from the hospital bed as if they were floating in a boat on a clear summer's day. After some time had passed, Grandpa finally got a bite. "I've got one!" he exclaimed, as he excitedly brought in his line. After much effort, Grandpa landed "the big one."

My aunt came over to the bed and asked Grandpa if he wanted her to cook his fish for supper. Grandpa was pleased with the offer and gladly handed over his "catch."

She went to the kitchen, took some haddock out of the freezer and prepared it just the way Grandpa liked it. With a flourish of grandeur, she presented the cooked fish to Grandpa. Grandpa insisted that Dad had to eat with him, so they shared the meal. Later, Grandpa told Grandma that he didn't know what that woman did with the fish, but the one he ate came from the freezer.

After dinner, my grandfather and father continued to fish until my dad had to leave for work. By then, it was early Thanksgiving morning, Grandpa's favorite holiday. All the relatives came to Grandma and Grandpa's house, but it wasn't to celebrate the traditional holiday. It was to say good-bye.

Only hours after his fishing had ended, Grandpa passed away. He had spent the last morning he had, with his son, doing what they loved to do best.

Sonia Hernandez

Fishing in Sierra Leone

I find that there is no worthy pursuit but the idea of doing some good to the world.

John Keats

A trail of dust settled ahead of our rickety Toyota taxi as we chased a pickup truck down a dirt road through the bush of central Sierra Leone, Africa. The elephant grass gave way to rice paddies, and we drove slowly through a village as the taxi driver navigated between the chickens. I waved to a mother feeding her baby by one of the huts. She waved back with an enthusiastic smile that helped to assuage my apprehension about what we might find in Masongbo. We were on an assessment trip for the international organization Search for Common Ground, hoping to set up a reconciliation program in Sierra Leone. This Sunday morning trip was my opportunity to fulfill every former Peace Corps volunteer's dream: I was returning to one of the two villages where I had lived between 1985 and 1989. The Catholic bishop of the area had assured us it was safe and volunteered to take us to Sunday mass in Masongbo, but even he could not dispel my nervousness.

I made many close friends in Sierra Leone, especially the Conteh family who lived in Masongbo village. Soon after I left, the country erupted into a bloody and chaotic civil war, and I had no way of communicating with the Contehs. During the war, the rebels and the government army both turned against the civilian population, leaving villagers to fend for themselves while they waited for international intervention. The war was marked by horrific atrocities committed against women, children and elderly alike. For years, I trembled at each news story about the war. Filled with anger and concern, I worried about my friends.

I first fished on the Rokel River during my second year as a volunteer. That was also the first time I met Pa Conteh and his sons. The Contehs are Limbas, a tribe known for their palm wine, farming and humility. Even though they were subsistence farmers, they were gracious hosts and very accommodating of my enthusiasm for fishing. Having come from a family of ten children in rural Indiana, I had developed a love for fishing at a young age and spent many days with my brothers at farm ponds, catching bluegills, catfish and an occasional largemouth bass. The idea of fishing in Africa was exotic, and the first day out changed my life.

After several hours of getting tangled in nets and on rocks, elderly, soft-spoken Pa Conteh encouraged me to try casting one last time as the sun sank behind the palm trees. Wham! A huge fish struck the lure, and after a twenty-minute battle, I realized with joy and amazement that I had landed a twenty-five-pound Nile perch!

That fish—believe it or not—convinced me to sign up for a third and then fourth year of Peace Corps service. I moved to Masongbo to live with the Contehs and started fishing nearly every evening during the dry season. The Conteh brothers—Moses, Sanpha and Bokarie—quickly became my close friends. We spent hours telling stories, laughing and eating together. We got a kick out of sending fishing photos to my family in Indiana, who I knew would gawk at the huge basslike fish.

More importantly, fishing had taken on new meaning as I was helping to supplement the diet of more than thirty people, including the Contehs and their friends, with much-needed protein. But fishing became an ethical quandary when I started losing lures to large fish and jagged stones. I could not afford to buy expensive imported lures with my Peace Corps stipend, nor could the Contehs. Each lure cost as much as a teacher was paid in a month.

For months I pondered the problem: How could I justify sharing my passion for fishing while introducing a technology that was not sustainable by my friends? The answer was to make the lures myself. I tried to carve wooden, fishlike lures, but the Contehs quickly took the sticks from me, afraid I would hurt myself. They carved all their own hand tools and knew the qualities of every tree in the bush. They were willing to help me, but were strangely unenthusiastic. It took me a long time to figure out their uncharacteristic reticence; they were embarrassed by trying to make a "white man's gadget," at which they felt they would surely fail.

I made sure that whatever materials we used were locally available. The only place I yielded was letting Sanpha use some of my shoulder-length hair to make paintbrushes. After all, I was easier to catch than a goat. With a lot of back and forth, we eventually made lures that dove and danced in the water, just like the expensive "English baits" or Rapala lures. And we caught fish. Before long, the Contehs had a small business making and selling lures and giving workshops to other Peace Corps volunteers and Sierra Leoneans. One day Sanpha caught four Nile perch, weighing over one hundred pounds in total, all with lures and a reel he had made himself.

Now, as our taxi pulled into the village of thirty houses, we could hear the small church rocking with drums, singing and clapping. I remembered the night I danced under a full moon with the entire village, celebrating Pa Conteh's funeral. The music and dance reflected the rhythms, the movements of daily life—farming, cooking and lovemaking—and its joys and sorrows.

After so many years away, my heart pounded. I began to sweat in the heat of the crowded church. I was worried about my friends—were they able to survive the trauma of the rebellion? Then I spotted Sanpha, clapping and singing. We looked at each other in amazement. His face turned into an ecstatic smile as he threw his arms around me. He pinched me to see if I was real. Then someone tapped me from behind. It was Moses! And Bokarie! All the Conteh brothers were there. In celebration, we sang the same hymns I had sung in church as a kid in Indiana, but now in an African dialect.

After the church service, men, women and children crowded around to greet me: "Mr. Bob, Mr. Bob, you done come back." Children in tattered clothes handed me mangos, coconuts or whatever they could offer. And I was surprised when the village chief handed me kola nuts, the symbolic offering of respect. "He who gives kola gives life."

The Contehs then took me to the water well to show me that it was still in use a decade after we'd built it. They also showed me their oil-palm plantation, which they had doubled from 250 to over 500 trees. I was thrilled to see that the work we had done together had continued, a true testament to their work ethic and self-confidence.

The tone shifted, though, as the Conteh brothers showed me around, talking about the Revolutionary

United Front (RUF) rebels' occupation of the village. A sixteen-year-old boy who called himself "Lt. Colonel Rambo" and his group had held the village captive. They took whatever food they wanted and left little for anyone else to eat. Sanpha said the family nearly starved, surviving only by hiding in the bush for months on end.

The Contehs were greatly relieved to have the RUF out of their village and were ready to get back to their lives as subsistence farmers, a life that was hard enough in itself. Sanpha then took me to the side to show me something. With a big smile, he pulled out a small piece of wood, painted red and white with shiny hooks hanging from it. Looking closer, I saw it was a fishing lure. "I made this," he said.

I was stunned. Looking into Sanpha's eyes, I listened as he said, "The RUF made me fish for them, but I always went to where there were no fish. They got bored and quit. When they were not looking, I went fishing on my own. With the fish I caught, I fed my family who hid in the bush."

There were no words to be said. You *can* go home again.

Phil Bob Hellmich

My First Trout Goes To . . .

About five years ago, I stopped in to visit Uncle Leroy and Aunt Margaret. Aunt Margaret was in her late eighties, and her brother, Uncle Leroy, was in his early eighties. They lived together in the small town of Indian Lake, New York. They're not my blood relatives, but in an Italian family, the titles of "uncle" and "aunt" are given out like the queen of England gives out knighthoods. It's a privilege earned through love and respect.

During my visit, I told Aunt Margaret that I was going fly-fishing at the nearby Indian River later that night to catch some browns. She casually mentioned that it had been awhile since she had eaten a trout, since Uncle Leroy didn't go fishing anymore. Although Uncle Leroy had slowed down in his later years, he still got around pretty well. Uncle Leroy had taught me about the woods. He taught me how to hunt, how to fish and how to trap. He taught me about beavers, red squirrels, chipmunks, hawks, deer, foxes and all the other animals that live in the woods.

But of all the sports Uncle Leroy taught me, fly-fishing became my addiction. When Aunt Margaret mentioned she hadn't eaten trout in a long time, my first thought was an old saying, "Give a man a fish, and he'll eat for a day. Teach a man to fish, and he'll eat for a lifetime." Well, it was now pay-back time for all those lessons Uncle Leroy had given me.

That night I went down to the Indian and caught and kept two brown trout. One was fourteen inches, and the other was sixteen. I cleaned the fish and took them to Aunt Margaret, who was thrilled. All she said was "Goody, goody, goody!" And I got a huge hug to boot.

That simple gift started a ritual that lasted for three more years. Aunt Margaret always got my first trout and Uncle Leroy got my second one. After a few months, Uncle Leroy casually mentioned that the larger trout were too much fish for him and Aunt Margaret to eat for dinner, and he thought that the small ones, between eight and ten inches, were even tastier. It was easy enough for me to fix that problem, and so my "New Rules of Catch and Release" were to keep only browns between eight and ten inches; I returned everything else to the river.

I then thought of other elderly people in town who probably hadn't eaten fresh trout in years, so I caught a few extra fish during one of my evening trips. In the morning, I visited three of my family's old friends, all of whom were widows who had known my parents. I asked each of them if they would like trout for dinner. Each of the ladies, all eighty-something, thanked me profusely. They each shared that they hadn't had a trout since their husbands had passed away years before. And so the ritual expanded; I now had six girlfriends in town, all thirty years older than me.

A sad day came three years later when Aunt Margaret got sick and left us. Her family asked me to give the eulogy at the church service. I was never prouder than to have the honor of saying good-bye to a lady as grand as Aunt Margaret.

Even with my aunt's passing, the fish ritual continues, but now Uncle Leroy gets my first trout. This last July, I returned to an Adirondack pond to camp overnight and fish for brook trout. I caught three brook trout and took them with me when I went to see Uncle Leroy on a Sunday. His eighty-sixth birthday was the next day, and I wanted to surprise him with three fish instead of his usual one.

Uncle Leroy wasn't home when I got there, so I put the fish in his refrigerator and left. I didn't need to leave a note—I knew he'd find them, and he'd know who put them there. In Indian Lake, you never lock your door because you never know when someone is going to sneak into your house and put trout in your refrigerator.

Monday morning before going to work, I stopped uptown to wish Uncle Leroy a happy birthday.

"Are you going to your nephew's house for a birthday dinner tonight?" I asked.

"No, he didn't call so I'll probably eat at home tonight," Uncle Leroy said in a dejected voice. I felt badly that I couldn't have dinner with him on his birthday, but I had other commitments that night.

"So you have nothing special to do tonight?" I asked.

Uncle Leroy put his head down for a moment and thought. Slowly his head rose, and he had a big smile on his face.

"Yep! I got something special for tonight. I got me three brook trout in my refrigerator for supper. That's special, ain't it!" he beamed.

I felt good, for I was able to give back to my aging uncle everything he had given to me over the years. Now my old adage has become: "Teach a man to fish, and he'll give you trout for the rest of your life."

Patrick Sisti

The Old Man by the Bridge

I fish the stony, rain-fed rivers of the north of England, which are fast and rise quickly with the water that falls on the surrounding moorland. The trout are small, but feisty and the golden flash in the rivers' peaty depths never fails to leave a lump in the throat of any fisherman. In this part of the country, the annual "Duffers Fortnight" of the mayfly hatch doesn't happen. The beginner has what might be termed a more difficult apprenticeship than someone lucky enough to learn his or her craft on a southern chalk stream.

Several years ago, when I was a novice, I ventured out on a trip to my local club water. Like most beginners, I put my faith in equipment and bristled with the latest tackle, my fly box full of the fashionable patterns. The stretch of the river was two miles, fishing both banks, at the southern end of the Yorkshire Dales National Park. Other anglers had previously told me that fishing the first three hundred yards was a waste of time, this section being barren, so I was surprised when I saw someone casting close to the access bridge.

As I approached, I could see that my fellow fisherman was old and that he walked very slowly. I later found out that he had fished this poor stretch of the river from necessity, a longer walk being impossible for him. His rod was an ancient cane model warped from age, and wound on his old reel was a greased sash cord, the price of a modern fly line being beyond his meager means. Yet the style of his casting was faultless. His graceful actions could have been set the music, his fly landing on the water like gossamer. As I watching his mastery, he suddenly struck, and within a minute landed a half-pound fish, holding it steady in the flow as he released it. I congratulated him and asked him what fly he was using.

"Same as always," he said, "snipe and purple. It's all I ever use." Seeing my bewildered expression he continued. "Think about it: If you were hungry and someone offered you turkey you wouldn't say no because it wasn't Christmas, would you? If you make it look right, they'll eat it."

Armed with his advice, I went on my way, thinking about the old gentleman's words. I had about twenty patterns in my fly box; he had one. With my next cast, I tried to copy his style. I practiced for hours. I then pared down my number of fly patterns and my catch rate increased.

As the seasons passed, my knowledge of the river became more comprehensive. I caught fish along the full stretch, but still the fish of one particular pool defied my efforts. The bull pool, as it was known, defeated me every time, and to catch a fish there became my goal. Every season I'd see the old gentleman, and with each passing year I noticed it became harder for him to walk. He fished closer and closer to the bridge where the fishing rights began and he always made a catch. We joked about my failure at the bull pool and I quipped that I could carry him up there so he could show me how it was done.

One day I came across him fishing so close to the bridge that he was in its shadow. We talked about the bull pool as usual and he said, "Fish an upstream snipe and purple good busy one, gather it in with a slow retrieve. Work the hackles in the flow; make them look like an insect's legs and see what happens."

When I reached the bull pool I did as I was bid, and after half an hour crouched low over the water, I was rewarded with a beautifully marked three-quarter-pounder. I gleefully went to tell my friend but he had already gone.

I never saw the old gentleman again, but to this day the first and last fly I use every season is a snipe and purple.

Philip Edward Carter

Who Is Jack Canfield?

Jack Canfield is one of America's leading experts in the development of human potential and personal effectiveness. He is both a dynamic, entertaining speaker and a highly sought-after trainer. Jack has a wonderful ability to inform and inspire audiences toward increased levels of self-esteem and peak performance.

He is the author and narrator of several bestselling audio- and videocassette programs, including *The Success Principles, Self-Esteem and Peak Performance, Maximum Confidence, Self-Esteem in the Classroom* and *Chicken Soup for the Soul—Live*. He is regularly seen on television shows such as *Good Morning America, 20/20* and *NBC Nightly News*. Jack has coauthored numerous books, including the *Chicken Soup for the Soul* series, *Dare to Win* and *The Aladdin Factor* (all with Mark Victor Hansen), *100 Ways to Build Self-Concept in the Classroom* (with Harold C. Wells), *Heart at Work* (with Jacqueline Miller) and *The Power of Focus* (with Les Hewitt and Mark Victor Hansen).

Jack is a regularly featured speaker for professional associations, school districts, government agencies, churches, hospitals, sales organizations and corporations. His clients have included the American Dental Association, the American Management Association, AT&T, Campbell's Soup, Clairol, Domino's Pizza, GE, ITT, Hartford Insurance, Johnson & Johnson, the Million Dollar Roundtable, NCR, New England Telephone, Re/Max, Scott Paper, TRW and Virgin Records. Jack has taught on the faculty of Income Builders International, a school for entrepreneurs.

Jack conducts an annual seven-day Living Your Highest Vision Training. It attracts entrepreneurs, educators, counselors, parenting trainers, corporate trainers, professional speakers, ministers and others interested in creating the life of their dreams—both personally and professionally.

For further information about Jack's books, tapes and training programs, or to schedule him for a presentation, please contact:

The Canfield Training Group
P.O. Box 30880
Santa Barbara, CA 93130
phone: 805-563-2935 • fax: 805-563-2945
Web site: *www.jackcanfield.com*

Who Is Mark Victor Hansen?

In the area of human potential, no one is more respected than Mark Victor Hansen. For more than thirty years, Mark has focused solely on helping people from all walks of life reshape their personal vision of what's possible. His powerful messages of possibility, opportunity and action have created powerful change in thousands of organizations and millions of individuals worldwide.

He is a sought-after keynote speaker, bestselling author and marketing maven. Mark's credentials include a lifetime of entrepreneurial success and an extensive academic background. He is a prolific writer with many bestselling books such as *The One Minute Millionaire, The Power of Focus, The Aladdin Factor* and *Dare to Win,* in addition to the *Chicken Soup for the Soul* series. Mark has made a profound influence through his library of audios, videos and articles in the areas of big thinking, sales achievement, wealth building, publishing success, and personal and professional development.

Mark is the founder of the MEGA Seminar Series. MEGA Book Marketing University and Building Your MEGA Speaking Empire are annual conferences where Mark coaches and teaches new and aspiring authors, speakers and experts on building lucrative publishing and speaking careers. Other MEGA events include MEGA Marketing Magic and My MEGA Life.

He has apeared on television (*Oprah,* CNN and *The Today Show*), in print (*Time, U.S. News & World Report, USA Today, New York Times* and *Entrepreneur*) and on countless radio interviews, assuring our planet's people that "You can easily create the life you deserve."

As a philanthropist and humanitarian, Mark works tirelessly for organizations such as Habitat for Humanity, American Red Cross, March of Dimes, Childhelp USA and many others. He is the recipient of numerous awards that honor his entrepreneurial spirit, philanthropic heart and business acumen. He is a lifetime member of the Horatio Alger Association of Distinguished Americans, an organization that honored Mark with the prestigious Horatio Alger Award for his extraordinary life achievements.

Mark Victor Hansen is an enthusiastic crusader of what's possible and is driven to make the world a better place.

Mark Victor Hansen & Associates, Inc.
P.O. Box 7665
Newport Beach, CA 92658
phone: 949-764-2640
fax: 949-722-6912
Visit Mark online at: *www.markvictorhansen.com*

Who Is Ken McKowen?

Ken McKowen recently married coauthor Dahlynn McKowen, gaining two stepchildren, in addition to his adult son Jason. He has spent more than twenty-seven years with California State Parks as a park ranger, a planner and a writer. He currently manages the state parks' statewide trails program, which includes the distribution of several million dollars in grant funding annually.

Ken is also a freelance writer, having sold his first article to the travel section of a major newspaper in 1977, the same year Jason was born. Since then, his writing career has included several years as the head writer for the California State Parks marketing and public relations office; writing feature articles for magazines and newspapers, brochure text, speeches, and advertising copy; writing state park general plans; and as a freelancer selling outdoor and travel-related articles to magazines and newspapers. Ken has had two books published, the last of which was the highly acclaimed *The Longstreet Highroad Guide to the California Coast*. He has had hundreds of his photos published, and he has edited books and articles for other writers.

Ken's very successful efforts over the years in writing grant proposals, and in reviewing grant applications in his present job, has led to him teaching the art of successful grant writing in numerous seminars, and occasionally penning grants for nonprofit organizations. He also works with Dahlynn to turn out freelance articles and the photos that accompany them.

With a new family that includes Dahlynn's twelve-year-old daughter Lahre and seven-year-old son Shawn, Ken spends many enjoyable evenings and weekends fishing, bicycling, kayaking, hiking and helping with homework. He still finds time to improve his piano playing, learn to play the clarinet, tie a few fishing flies, build furniture and wooden kayaks, travel, write screenplays and novels—and really enjoy life.

Ken can be reached at:

Ken McKowen
Two Writers' Ink
P.O. Box 607
Orangevale, CA 95662
info@fishsoul.com

Who Is Dahlynn McKowen?

Dahlynn McKowen is the mother of two great kids, Shawn, age seven, and Lahre, age twelve. She married Ken in 2002, and became stepmother to Jason, Ken's adult son.

A freelance writer since 1987, Dahlynn stopped counting the number of articles published after passing the two-thousand mark. Her focus has been on people and destination pieces, writing everything from business and travel stories to music and bed-and-breakfast reviews. Many years ago, Bud Gardner, coauthor of *Chicken Soup for the Writer's Soul*, was responsible for nurturing, encouraging and inspiring Dahlynn's writing career.

Dahlynn is the primary owner, along with her husband Ken, of Two Writers' Ink (TWI), a business they started many years prior to their marriage. TWI provides writing, editing, and publicist and author representation services, as well as screen- and ghostwriting.

In a past life, Dahlynn worked for the state of California's office of tourism, helping to create travel guides. She also served as a speech-writer and publicist for the director of California State Parks and as the media and public relations director for the start-up of the California sesquicentennial commemoration.

Dahlynn, an accomplished musician, is helping teach her daughter Lahre and husband Ken to play both clarinet and piano, with Lahre being the better student. In return, Lahre, a talented and aspiring young artist, helped Dahlynn and Ken with *Chicken Soup for the Fisherman's Soul* by drawing a cartoon for the book. Shawn has done his part also; that's him on the book's cover, wearing the green vest, catching his first trout on a fly rod while in Colorado!

Dahlynn's family has played a key role in her success as a mother and a writer, from grandmother DeEtta Anderson's constant phone calls of encouragement and love, to her parents Cliff and Scharre Johnson, who taught her to be true to herself and never give up on her dreams. They have taught her well.

You can reach Dahlynn at:

Dahlynn McKowen
Two Writers' Ink
P.O. Box 607
Orangevale, CA 95662
info@fishsoul.com

Contributors

Darryl Allen has a love of fishing passed down through many generations. He attended Ohio State University and is the proud father of two sons and one daughter.

Luke Altomare received his bachelor of science degree at Western Michigan University in 1977. Since then, he has enjoyed a career in automotive sales. He is the father of three and considers his wife, Terry, his best friend. He loves fishing, hunting and woodworking and makes giant fishing lures called "Titanic Tackle." E-mail: *lunkerluke@sbcglobal.net.*

DeEtta Woffinden Anderson is the wife of a military man whose assignments introduced her to many and daily changes of culture, ideas and challenges. She feels she grew in understanding with each one. Optimism has served her well. She can be reached at *DeEtta@fishsoul.com.*

Peter Balsino is a freelance writer and attorney living in Tucson, Arizona, with his wife and three young children. He writes and speaks about lifestyle and simplification issues, and continues to strive to find the perfect balance between work and family life. Reach him for writing and/or speaking at *pmb@aronaz.com.*

Banjo Bandolas lives in Eugene, Oregon. His ability to weave a story has been passed down through the family and reflects the best of Southern storytelling tradition. Banjo is currently working on a compilation of his many new and already published outdoor stories. Please contact him at *Banjo@realbeer.com.*

Chuck "C.L." Bray attended the University of Puget Sound, served in the U.S. Army stationed at Camp Century, Greenland, and then worked for an aluminum company until his retirement in 2001. He has written and is seeking publication of a historical fantasy novel and can be reached at *versevender1@ yahoo.com.*

Tanya Breed lives in Arizona. Her writing focuses on relationships and the importance of developing spiritual growth and maturity, hoping to inspire others in their daily struggles. She has been published in several magazines, including *Science of Mind, The Secret Place* and *Beautiful Gardens.* Contact Tanya at *tbreed@quick.com.*

Anne Carter, a native New Yorker, resides on Long Island, near the water. A freelance writer, her inspirational stories have appeared in major publications. Anne dedicates this story to her husband, Dick Carter, "A True Fisherman of the Soul." Contact Anne at *carteracdc@webtv.net.*

Philip Edward Carter is an electrician who lives in the United Kingdom. He has been married to his wife, Isabel, since 1999. Phil loves to travel with his wife, walk with his dogs, fly-fish and write.

Ann I. Clizer lives in the mountains of northern Idaho, where she operates a contracting business with her husband. She enjoys kayaking, hiking and playing at the lake with her grandchildren. Ann is at work on a book-length memoir entitled *On Higher Ground*.

Lisa Wood Curry grew up in Chicora, Pennsylvania, graduated from Indiana University of Pennsylvania, and now lives near Pittsburgh with her husband, two sons and two dachshunds. A freelance catalog copywriter and aspiring fiction author, she is a contributor to *Chicken Soup for the Working Woman's Soul*. E-mail: *lisawc@brads.net*.

Dan DeVries received his bachelor of science degree in electronic engineering technology from the DeVry Institute of Technology in 1984 and is currently an engineering manager for the Boeing Company in Seattle, Washington. Dan enjoys fishing, camping and spending time with his wife and five children. Dan can be reached at *sheiladhh@aol.com*.

Vic Dollar graduated from Brigham Young University in 1979 with a bachelor of science degree, and from the University of Utah School of Physical Therapy in 1982. Vic works in the field of geriatric home health care in Provo, Utah.

Mike Duby, from Seatac, Washington, spends his summers fishing in Alaska on his boat *Huntress*. Mike is the author of two books, *The War King,* a biblical story about the life and history of King David, and *The Tale of the Assassin,* a fantasy adventure thriller. Mike will continue to fish and write for as long as he enjoys it, making the most of the blessings and talents God has given him. Web site: *www.alaskafishhunter.com*.

Kenny Duncan Sr. is an Apache native of Arizona. With the guidance of his grandparents, he was immersed in the traditions of his people and is an accomplished storyteller, lecturer, flute player and craftsman. He graduated from the Institute of American Indian Arts and is a distinguished Native American cultural consultant. Web site: *www.yellowbirdindiandancers.com*.

Terri Duncan, a retired teacher with a bachelor of arts in early childhood education, is a certified paralegal. An avid writer, she is also a published lyricist and author of children's stories. She enjoys spending time with her family, going camping and, of course, fishing.

Curtis Foreman works as a writer and editor in Vancouver, British Columbia. He and his wife Janna spend as much time as possible at their cabin on South Pender Island, where the fishing is good and the deck chairs are comfortable. You can reach him at *curtis@foreword.ca*.

Brett Foster is Shelly's husband and Mallory and Brooke's dad. He makes his living as a lawyer but aspires to write fiction and tend bar at a little place on a Caribbean island. He thanks his mom and his high-school English teachers—Janie Brewer and Margaret Hall—for teaching him to love reading and writing.

Jenny J. Foster is a native Arizonan whose work is strongly influenced by the rich colors and distinct imagery of the Southwest. She feels her artwork is a celebration of colors, creatures and the spirit of life. Visit her Web site:

www.jfosterstudio.com.

Ryan French is a family chiropractor practicing in the town of Bolton, Ontario, Canada. Ryan enjoys spending time with his family, playing hockey, fishing, golfing and working with children. Please email him at *ryan.french@rogers.com.*

Rosalie P. Griffin has lived in seven states and attended as many colleges. She is a survivor of many cancers, and her doctor calls her the "miracle woman." She began writing at eleven years old and continues to keep her brain young. She retired from twenty-five years of marriage and work in government, but not life.

Christopher Gudgeon is an award-winning screenwriter and author who's also the worst fisherman on God's green earth. He and his wife, writer Barbara Stewart, divide their time between Los Angeles and Victoria, Canada. Chris loves hanging out with his three favorite tax deductions, Charlie, Tavish and Keating. E-mail: *bighair@coastnet.com.*

Patrick Hardin lives in his hometown of Flint, Michigan. His work appears in a variety of books and publications, both in the United States and abroad. He may be reached at *phardin357@aol.com.*

Jonny Hawkins has been cartooning professionally since 1986. His work has appeared in *Barron's, Saturday Evening Post, Field and Stream* and over 250 other publications. His recent books with Bob Phillips, *The Awesome Book of Heavenly Humor* and *A Tackle Box of Fishing Funnies,* are available at bookstores or by contacting him at P.O. Box 188, Sherwood, MI 49089, or by e-mail at *jonny hawkins2nz@yahoo.com.*

Phil Bob Hellmich grew up fishing Indiana farm ponds with his nine siblings. He joined the Peace Corps in 1985 after graduating from DePauw University. Currently, he works for Search for Common Ground, an international organization working to transform how the world deals with conflict. He loves gardening and kriya yoga. E-mail him at *phellmich@sfcg.org.*

Sonia Hernandez has taken several writing courses and has an associate's degree in photography. She works with the developmentally disabled in upstate New York. In her free time, Sonia enjoys gardening, quilting, photography and writing.

Joseph Hines is the director of patient and environmental safety at Norwalk Hospital in Norwalk, Connecticut. Joe grew up on the north shore of Long Island and is the youngest of nine children. He is married and enjoys raising two children of his own. Please reach him at *Joseph.Hines@norwalkhealth.org.*

Nanette Holland received a journalism degree from the University of Florida. She was a reporter for several Florida newspapers and now works for the Tampa Bay Estuary Program. Her passion is fly-fishing, and she is president of the Tampa Bay Fly Fishing Club. Contact her at *nanetteholland@aol.com.*

Pamela Jenkins lives in Oklahoma with her husband Stanley and their four children. She is the office manager for a veterinary clinic and enjoys writing in her spare time. She is also a contributing author to *Chicken Soup for the Grandparent's Soul* and *Chocolate for a Woman's Dreams*.

Cliff Johnson graduated from Cal Poly Pomona in 1972. He spent thirty years in prison—in uniform and administration—and was finally released (retired) in 1995. He enjoys golf, distance running, biking, gardening, metal sculpture and above all else, his wife Scharre. They live in Crescent City, California, the most beautiful place on earth.

Stan R. Kid is an avid fisherman who lives on Long Island with his wife and three children. He pens a regular monthly column for *The Rockville Centre Herald*. He tries to get away to fish as often as possible . . . but never again with snakes!

Richard Knott is a fisherman, leaving tomorrow for a three-week hike down the John Muir Trail to fly-fish for golden trout. He also teaches at an alternative high school in Northern California. Needless to say, he enjoys life to the fullest.

Kathleen Kovach spent twenty-three years traveling with her husband, Jim, courtesy of the Air Force. They now live in Colorado, where she enjoys singing in church and, of course, camping and fishing. She is a mommy of two grown sons and a grandmommy. She plans to write inspirational romance.

Joseph T. Lair enjoys hiking, biking and walking with his wife and three children throughout southwest Montana. Joseph also enjoys writing and public speaking. E-mail him at *JosephLair@montanaspeakers.com*.

Gregory Lamping received his bachelor of science in English and journalism from Southwest Missouri State University. He lives in St. Louis and enjoys fishing in clear-water streams for any fish big enough to bite on his worm. E-mail him at *glamping@charter.net*.

Gaynor E. Lawson (née Pettitt) has always been a storyteller. Today she is a freelance writer and editor of her own publication, *The Quill*, in the beautiful Midlands area of KwaZulu-Natal in South Africa. She has always been entranced by the sea, which inspires her.

Julie Long is a freelance writer and coauthor of the humor book, *BABY: An Owner's Manual* (Broadway Books, 2003). She recently completed a childhood memoir about the year her father died. Julie lives with her husband on a farm outside of Pittsburgh. Contact her at *jlongwrites@mac.com* or visit *www.Baby AnOwnersManual.com*.

Keith Long went to be with the Lord in October 2003. Until his death, he served as a professor of creative writing at Southwestern Oklahoma State University. His published devotional book, *Room to Grow*, is a collection of his ordinary life experiences, which teach deep spiritual insight. He lived to serve men and honor God.

Gary B. Luerding is a retired army sergeant living in southern Oregon who worked for the local school district for two decades years prior to retirement. Married for forty years, with three children and eight grandchildren, Gary enjoys fishing, gardening, playing the piano and struggling with a computer. E-mail: *garluer@cavenet.com*.

Pat MacIver retired from an extensive career in aviation, having chased the wily brown and rainbow in all corners of the world. And he's still at it!

Jennie Logsdon Martin is an accomplished classical and jazz pianist with an extreme fascination, love and appreciation for the outdoors, and especially for angling. Jennie owns and operates *www.ifish.net*, where she communicates with anglers throughout the Pacific Northwest on one of the nation's largest fishing discussion boards.

Kevin Martone is an aspiring author searching for publishers for three completed books: a coauthored book about how to take advantage of the period of unemployment, a fictional account of a fantasy sports league titled *Ship of Fools* and a novel titled *Livin' the Ninth Life Now*. E-mail: *kmartone@yahoo.com*.

Allison McWood holds an honors degree in English literature from York University in Toronto, where she specialized in Renaissance drama. She also received a diploma from the Institute of Children's Literature. Allison is a full-time playwright, lyricist and children's author. E-mail Allison at *amcwood@rogers.com*.

Jacqueline Jean Michels is a wife, mother and avid outdoorswoman. She lives in Soldotna, Alaska. Currently, she is writing *Off the Beaten Path*, a memoir, love story, fishing/trapping/hunting/airplane flying/crazy adventure about a homesteading family in Chinitna Bay, Alaska. E-mail: *jjoila@hotmail.com*.

Carla Mistic has a master's degree in social work and has worked as a medical social worker for the past eleven years. She recently opened an adult foster care home in her hometown of Bemidji, Minnesota. She looks forward to fishing with Dave and writing more stories. E-mails welcome: *carlamistic @hotmail.com*.

Raymond Morehead, Esq., FSA, Scot writer and poet of Scottish descent, believes in God, family, freedom, loyalty, honor, remembering the men and women from whence he came so that they may live on, and that "Can't never did anything, you have only to try and try again."

Gaylord Moulds recently retired from the State of California, where he worked for more than thirty-four years in purchasing, the last fifteen years in management capacity. He received his bachelor degree in economics from the University of Oregon. Gaylord plans on spending more time traveling and enjoying his family.

Donald W. Murphy received his bachelor of arts degree in molecular biology from the University of California, San Diego. He is the deputy director of the National Park Service and the author of *Love Vignettes*, a collection of seventy-five sonnets.

Carol Nelson succumbed to metastatic breast cancer on July 24, 2003, having enjoyed a useful and productive life more than ten years after her initial treatment. A California state park ranger for twenty-eight years, Carol was the first black female park superintendent. Carol was admired for her soft-spoken, thoughtful insights and advice.

Bonnie Nester recently retired to help care for her mother, who suffers from Alzheimer's disease. She is in the process of writing a book about finding hope and humor in that terrible confusion. In her spare time, she volunteers for the Alzheimer's Association and enjoys horseback riding, gardening and crafts.

Ron Niswonger lives in Jackson, Missouri, with his wife and two children. A freelance writer and bass tournament angler, Ron is a Prostaff member and contributing writer for *Midwest Bass Tournaments Magazine* and their Web site, *www.MWBT.com.* You may contact Ron at *rniswonger@hotmail.com.*

Jennifer Olsson, a former Montana fly-fishing guide, is also the author of *Fly Fishing the River of Second Chances: Life, Love and a River in Sweden,* and *Cast Again: Tales of a Fly Fishing Guide.* She divides her time between Bozeman, Montana, and Gimdalen, Sweden. Contact Jennifer at *www.scandiwestflyfishing.com.*

Cary Osborne received her bachelor of arts (summa cum laude) from Mary Baldwin College in Staunton, Virginia. She is currently seeking an agent for her most recent works of fiction. You can e-mail her at *iroshi@cox.net.*

Nelson O. Ottenhausen, a retired army officer and native of Northwest Illinois, earned a bachelor's and MBA, both from Western Illinois University in Macomb, Illinois. A nationally published poet residing in Gulf Breeze, Florida, Nelson enjoys fishing, and writing poetry and novels. Please e-mail him at *nottenhaus@earthlink.net.*

Tim Peckham grew up in Newfoundland, an island on Canada's east coast that's completely surrounded by fish. He's all grown up now and living in Toronto, Ontario, with his wife, Natalie. Once a year she lets him go fishing with his friends from *The Toronto Sun* newspaper, where he works as an artist and graphic designer. To invite him along on your next fishing trip, drop him a line at *tim@nofixedaddress.com.*

Perry P. Perkins and his wife Victoria live in the Pacific Northwest. His work appears regularly in Christian magazines, script collections and outdoor sports periodicals. Perry is currently finishing his second mystery novel. The first, *Just Past Oysterville,* will be released early in 2004.

Robert Pierpont graduated from the University of Redlands in 1947. He started his career as a broadcaster for the Swedish Broadcasting Company from 1948 to 1951, then worked for CBS as a correspondent during the Korean War. In the early 1950s, he was the CBS Far East Bureau Chief, Tokyo, then became the CBS White House Correspondent, a position he held from 1957 to 1975, covering six presidents. He retired from CBS in 1990 to fish and play tennis.

Melody Plaxton received her bachelor of arts in English with highest honors from the University of California, Sacramento, where she is completing her master's degree and teaching composition. She enjoys skiing, camping, gardening, music and, mostly, her family. She plans to continue writing short stories. Contact her at *mjplaxton@juno.com*.

Doyle Portela was born in Afton, Wyoming, where he learned to fish with his father and brothers. The seventh of eight children, Doyle moved to Montpelier, Idaho, married his high school sweetheart and raised five children. He worked and managed the Walton Feed, Inc. for forty-three years. Doyle loves to fish!

Robert Bruce Riefstahl, in the situation of being "downsized" after thirty-one years in engineering, has found an opportunity to start writing. He is currently working on a novel based on his parents' experiences during World War II. He enjoys spending time with his wife, three children and especially his six granddaughters.

Dixie Ross is a retired, nature-loving grandmother of nine, embracing the Northwest rural lifestyle with writing, photography, gardening and crafts. An equal rights trailblazer and single-parent feminist of the 1970s, Dixie is a self-motivated entrepreneur in sales and advertising and is publisher of a multi-state dairy farming magazine.

Leigh Rubin is the creator of the popular syndicated cartoon *Rubes,* distributed by Creators Syndicate to more than four hundred newspapers worldwide. He is the author of twelve books, including *The Wild Life of Cows* and *The Wild Life of Dogs.* You may contact him at *rubes2@earthlink.net.* To see Rubes, visit *www.creators.com.*

Robby Russell is a freelance copywriter. He received a bachelor of arts degree from Auburn University and is also a graduate of The Portfolio Centers copywriting program. An avid trout fisherman, terrible golfer and passable handyman, Robby lives in Atlanta with his wife, Krista, and twin sons, Graham and Anders.

Rod Scott is an army intelligence officer with a master's degree in homeland security and criminal justice. He is also a licensed private investigator. Rod likes to play volleyball and softball and scuba dive, and he also loves to fish with his Fish Master father, Jack. He has a beautiful chocolate Lab, Shena. E-mail: *investg8r@aol.com.*

Lahre Shiflet is the twelve-year-old daughter of coauthor Dahlynn McKowen. She is an aspiring pianist, actress, singer and artist. She especially enjoys drawing cartoons, including animals, her favorite being dogs. She is a cartoonist for her local newspaper. Contact her at *lahre@fishsoul.com.*

Lucinda Shouse loves reading, gardening and being with her family, whether they're fishing or playing cards. She is passionate about her two children, Skye and Cheyenne, and considers her life blessed for having such an incredible mother, who taught her to embrace life and its mysteries. E-mail: *Ibelieveinyou444@aol.com.*

Patrick Sisti, having earned his living as a printing salesman for forty-two years, has begun a second career in writing. An avid fly fisherman who lives in the Adirondacks in Indian Lake, New York, Patrick portrays Father Christmas during the holidays and is madly in love with life because of his nine grandchildren.

Christian Snyder started his cartooning career in 1994. His cartoons have appeared in *The Saturday Evening Post, Aquarium Fish Magazine, Bioscience, Physics Today, Nature Genetics, Pipe & Tobaccos, Smokeshop* and *Medical Economics*. He has also had his cartoons published in two other *Chicken Soup for the Soul* books.

Robert Spencer received his bachelor of arts degree in anthropology and geography from the University of Miami in 1996. He is currently a massage therapist in Denver, Colorado. Robert enjoys hiking, mountain biking and snowboarding. Every year he returns to his native Ohio to continue his search for "killer catfish."

Cathy Strough is a business consultant who specializes in research, technical writing and training. An avid historian, she can often be found researching local history and writing about it back at the campsite, while her daughters are fishing. Please e-mail her at *cstrough@fmtc.com.*

Rich Tennant produces the popular computer cartoon panel, *The 5th Wave*. He is syndicated by Universal Press Syndicate and is resident cartoonist for the . . . *for Dummies* book series. His cartoon panel now covers hundreds of subjects. Special use and licensing: *www.the5thwave.com.*

Steven Treanor is a 1972 University of California, Berkeley, forestry graduate. He served thirty years as a California state park ranger and retired as Southern California division chief in 2002. Steve loves wilderness backpacking, canoeing, outdoor volunteer work and teaching at the California State Park's Ranger Academy.

John Troy has been a cartoonist for forty-eight years and has authored eleven cartoon books. He is the creator of Ben, the hunting retriever, and is looking for a publisher for his sixth, and final, Ben book. He can be reached at 35 Stillwater Road, Hardwick, N.J., 07825, 908/362-6624, fax 908/362-6234.

Tanith Nicole Tyler is an aspiring writer who lives in Richmond, California, with her husband, Donnell Gordon, their three dogs and Oliver the cockatoo. When not writing, Tanith enjoys delivering Meals on Wheels, remodeling, reading and hiking with her pets. E-mail Tanith at *tanithtyler@yahoo.com.*

Gary Usery enjoys spending time with his family, canoeing and catching smallmouth bass in the beautiful mountain rivers and streams of Arkansas. He received a bachelor of science in chemical engineering from the University of Arkansas in 1986. Gary can be contacted at *garyalan@ipa.net.*

Emily VanLaeys is a writer whose essays have appeared in numerous publications, including the *Chicago Tribune* and *Unity Magazine*. Emily's book, *Dream*

Weaving: Using Dream Guidance to Create Life's Tapestry, from A.R.E. Press, contains more stories about her life and adventures with husband, Mark, and children, Vera and Peter.

Mark VanLaeys is a physician's assistant and home improvement contractor. He has done mission work in Ethiopia and in several Central American countries. Mark is a hang glider pilot, a lay preacher and a songwriter/guitarist. In his spare time, he enjoys canoeing, kayaking, biking, target shooting and being with his family.

Karri J. Watson recently completed her bachelor's degree in English and is now pursuing her master's degree. She writes articles, short stories, book reviews and poetry. Karri enjoys weight training, yoga, reading and spoiling her cat, T.C. She plans to branch out into business writing. Please e-mail her at *wtsn1@comcast.net.*

Becky Lee Weyrich is a retired romance novelist now living, golfing and fishing on a lake in Florida.

Janet Hall Wigler grew up in a remote wilderness in British Columbia, spending many hours on the riverbank with her father, who inspired her to reach for the biggest and best catches life has to offer. She is a playwright, loves to travel and is currently working on her first novel.

Jeff Wise grew up in Fair Oaks, California, and now lives in Lincoln, California, with his family. He is a building inspector for the City of Roseville and enjoys golfing, boating and, of course, fishing. Logan is now a seventh-grader and loves camping, fishing, basketball, baseball and playing the drums.

Harmony Zieman was born and raised in Whittier, California, where she has spent the first eighteen years of her life. She plans to attend college, pursue a personally gratifying career and continue writing. Her hobbies include reading, playing the piano, singing, writing, fishing and photography.

Donald Zimmermann retired from twenty-three years as a programmer/analyst, is now pursuing a writing career, freelancing magazine articles and currently working on two books. A husband, father and grandfather, Don continues to believe that a disability can be a valuable asset. E-mail him at *wheelsdz@yahoo.com.*

Permissions

We would like to acknowledge the many publishers and individuals who granted us permission to reprint the cited material. (Note: The stories that were penned anonymously, that are in the public domain or that were written by Jack Canfield, Mark Victor Hansen, Ken McKowen or Dahlynn McKowen are not included in this listing.)

Fear of Flying. Reprinted by permission of Christopher J. Gudgeon. ©2000 Christopher J. Gudgeon.

One for the Books. Reprinted by permission of Becky Lee Weyrich. ©1998 Becky Lee Weyrich.

Hooked Forever. Reprinted by permission of Charles L. Bray. ©2002 Charles L. Bray.

Becoming True Fishermen. Reprinted by permission of General H. Norman Schwarzkopf. ©General H. Norman Schwarzkopf.

Old Grumpa, A Special Place and *A Day to Remember.* Reprinted by permission of Michael Patrick Duby. ©2002 Michael Patrick Duby.

A Fish Story. Reprinted by permission of Nelson O. Ottenhausen. ©2001 Nelson O. Ottenhausen.

Dog Days. By Joel Vance. Copyright 2003 Time 4 Media, Inc. Reprinted with permission from FIELD & STREAM magazine. All rights reserved. Reproduction in any medium is strictly prohibited without permission from Time 4 Media, Inc. Such permission may be requested from FIELD & STREAM magazine.

Gone Fishin'. Reprinted by permission of Pamela Sue Jenkins. ©2002 Pamela Sue Jenkins.

To Honor, Cherish and Collect Bait. By Alan Liere. Copyright 2003 Time 4 Media, Inc. Reprinted with permission from FIELD & STREAM magazine. All rights reserved. Reproduction in any medium is strictly prohibited without permission from Time 4 Media, Inc. Such permission may be requested from FIELD & STREAM magazine.

The Empty Hook. Reprinted by permission of Anne Elizabeth Carter. ©2001 Anne Elizabeth Carter.

The Fisherman and His Femme Fatale. Reprinted by permission of Janet Hall Wigler and Angela Hall. ©2003 Janet Hall Wigler.

A Simple Plan. Reprinted by permission of Kenneth Duncan Sr. ©2003 Kenneth Duncan Sr.

Hezekiah. Reprinted by permission of Robert Bruce Riefstahl. ©2002 Robert Bruce Riefstahl.

The Kindness of Strangers. Reprinted by permission of Nanette Ellen Holland. ©2002 Nanette Ellen Holland.

On the Road. Reprinted by permission of Doyle Portela. ©2001 Doyle Portela.

Fishing Patriots. Reprinted by permission of Bonnie Rae Nester. © 2002 Bonnie Rae Nester.

Play It Again, Sam. Reprinted by permission of Jennie Logsdon Martin. ©2002 Jennie Logsdon Martin.

Heaven. Reprinted by permission of Ronald Niswonger. ©2001 Ronald Niswonger.

Hook Them with Love. Reprinted by permission of Donald W. Murphy. ©1999 Donald W. Murphy.

The Rite of Passage and *My First Trout Goes to* . . . Reprinted by permission of G. Patrick Sisti. ©2003 G. Patrick Sisti.

Letting Them Go. Reprinted by permission of Gary A. Usery. ©2002 Gary A. Usery.

At the Grave of the Unknown Fisherman. Reprinted with the permission of Simon & Schuster Adult Publishing Group, from AT THE GRAVE OF THE UNKNOWN FISHERMAN by John Gierach. Copyright © 2003 by John Gierach. All rights reserved.

Witness to Glory. Reprinted by permission of Perry Phillip Perkins. ©1996 Perry Phillip Perkins.

The Last Big Catch. Reprinted by permission of Sonia Lynn Hernandez. ©1998 Sonia Lynn Hernandez.

Fishing in Sierra Leone. Reprinted by permission of Philip Monroe Hellmich. ©2003 Philip Monroe Hellmich.

The Old Man by the Bridge. Reprinted by permission of Philip Edward Carter. ©2001 Philip Edward Carter.